HOW TO GET THINGS CHANGED

HOW TO
GET THINGS
CHANGED

A Handbook for
Tackling Community Problems

BERT STRAUSS and MARY E. STOWE

DOUBLEDAY & COMPANY, INC.
Garden City, N.Y.
1974

Library of Congress Cataloging in Publication Data

Strauss, Bertram W
How to get things changed.

1. Community organization—Handbooks, manuals, etc.
2. Community life—Handbooks, manuals, etc. 3. Commu-
nity leadership—Handbooks, manuals, etc. 4. Social
participation. I. Stowe, Mary E., joint author.
II. Title.
HM131.S827   309.2′6
ISBN 0-385-06457-8
Library of Congress Catalog Card Number 73-15369

CONTENTS

86346

PART FOUR—APPENDIX

INTRODUCTION

Probably never before in history have we Americans been so aware of so many situations that we think should be changed. We constantly identify them on every level—national, state and local.

Some of these problems are relatively new (the dangerous population growth, for instance; the energy crisis, the upswing in drug abuse, student and race dissatisfaction). Some only seem new because of new awareness. (Concern in recent years for the disadvantaged is an example. So is concern about air and water pollution, the whole gamut of problems covered by quality of environment.)

All too many other problems have been with us and thoroughly recognized for a long, long while. With most of these chronic problems there has been considerable effort to "do something." But the efforts have rarely succeeded. The solutions offered were ineffective —or they were implemented in an ineffective way. Nothing has yet seemed to produce more than fragmentary results. The problems are still here—and staying.

How can this welter of problems be solved? We have written this book in the belief that the answer lies in making better use of the vast storehouse of intelligence, creativity and energy that reaches across the nation in our concerned, and our not yet concerned, citizenry.

As a nation we have become adept at identifying problems, but we have a lot to learn about the other vital steps. From finger-pointing and protest to solving a problem is a long and usually complex route, as truly effective leaders have long recognized. With the magnitude of difficulties facing us today, we cannot afford too many dead ends, detours and self-created obstacle courses. We cannot

afford to indulge in deeply ingrained but ineffective approaches that
have handicapped our former efforts to reach solutions. Wherever
we are, in whatever arena, we cannot afford to let ego domination
by the few waste the valuable resources of the many. We cannot
afford the squandering of energy in futile hostility. We must discard
old methods that only bog us down and use instead the best of modern techniques designed to pull people together rather than apart.
These techniques help communication within and among groups.
They enable people to make better use of their time and abilities
and to achieve greater skill in obtaining the understanding and support that can make solutions workable.

How? By starting where we are. In this book, emphasis is on the
local effort. The local arena is the one in which most of us are most
likely to be able to make significant contributions. Besides, those
working in larger arenas will find that the same techniques and skills
can be applied to make our state, regional and national efforts more
effective.

This book deals above all with meetings and conferences, for,
maligned though they are, it is in getting the right people together in
a right way at meetings and conferences that we can initiate successful
action.

Part One tells the stories of recent efforts to help achieve needed
solutions. We made most of these efforts in the Northern Virginia
area where we have worked recently.* However, the problems tackled are the problems that exist anywhere in the country, and the lessons learned can have universal application.

This part relates how the participants went about their efforts and
offers evaluation of why they succeeded when they did succeed or
why their efforts fell short. We give these case histories in the belief
that, through study of such experiences, techniques of problem solving can be made more flexible, more foolproof and surer of success.
We have learned, through actual workability, which methods to keep
and which to discard or improve.

* In 1966, Bert Strauss and two other men created a project to carry
out in Northern Virginia the provisions of Title I of the Higher Education
Act of 1965. These provisions aim at helping communities solve problems
with the aid of resources provided by universities and colleges. Mary E.
Stowe joined the project a year later. When that project ended in 1968, it
was replaced by the Community Education Program of George Mason
College, then the Northern Virginia branch of the University of Virginia,
now, by act of the Virginia General Assembly, George Mason University.

Part One also introduces the hero of every effort described, from huge conference to basement gathering of six—the facilitator, a new kind of small group leader who can pull the maximum good from any sort of group he or she serves.

Part Two explains why the facilitating approach works. It summarizes briefly the findings of forty years of research in the social and behavioral sciences which underlie the techniques we use.

Part Three tells how we do our job. It explains the steps we have found necessary to stimulate interest, activity and support. Appendices supplement the other sections. Included is an evaluation form to help us. We've never seen such a form in a book but your reactions are important to us.

We hope the book will help thousands of worthy efforts to be undertaken with greater skill and greater chance of success. We intend it to show that citizen and official apathy is usually a delusion, a result of not knowing what to do or how to go about it, or of people being mishandled or ignored instead of being recognized and used in a creative way.

We want the book to help our nation take fuller advantage of its human resources—the time, ideas and potential effort of its citizens and officials everywhere—converting what may seem apathy into interest, concern and constructive action.

Mary E. Stowe   Bert Strauss
Round Hill, Virginia   *Falls Church, Virginia*

Part One

WHAT WE DO

1

THE ORGANIZATION
EVERY COMMUNITY NEEDS

This is the story of an experiment in one community, Loudoun County, Virginia, the story of an organization that only a few people wanted at first. Now, however, its rolls are filled with enthusiastic members and you hear such opinions as:

"This is the one meeting I try never to miss."

"The county used to seem so fragmented. Here I can see a unity developing that I used to think impossible."

"This organization really gives you a countywide picture. And you don't just learn what's actually going on; you begin to think about what should be going on."

It's called the Committee of 55 for Loudoun County, a name chosen because, in the beginning, fifty-five people were asked to join. Its name isn't important, however. What matters is what it accomplishes.

Every two months, a heterogeneous group convenes. The place might be a newly remodeled church social hall, still smelling of paint and freshly cut lumber, a Negro community center, the Board of Supervisors' meeting room, the dance hall above a local firehouse or a plush country club.

Some of the people present, conferring with mutual respect, are representatives of segments who once went out of their way to avoid association. Now they look forward to it.

People of influence in all geographical areas of the 516-square-mile county belong to this unique organization. Not all of them are always present but "turn-out" figures are exceptionally high.

Where but in a group like this* can one expect to meet both blacks and whites, Republicans and Democrats, liberals, conservatives and moderates, farm leaders and industrialists, merchants, lawyers, educators, artists, press, officers of the League of Women Voters and the DAR, of the Lions, NAACP, PTAs, garden clubs, Kiwanis, the health and welfare organizations, not to mention so many town and county officials and department heads?

Where else, with all these locally influential people, can you listen to informed panelists discuss what is being done and should be done about some issue of concern to all of you: land use, for example, or the environment, or industrial development, or the financing of needed services? Where else can you discuss these issues in small groups and then question the experts and hear so many viewpoints of what the community should do, viewpoints that you discover aren't really so divergent as you once would have expected?

Kinks there have been, setbacks, discouragements. But the organization has never lost faith in either its purposes or its chosen methods for achieving them. The need for the organization was and is there. The plan, clearly stating how the organization would meet the need, was well laid. Some initial confusion about what the organization was and was not was quickly dispelled. Its founders and a gradually growing rank of converts knew they had the ingredients for success—a need to be met, a way to meet that need, and a determination to remove each stumbling block as it arose.

But let's begin at the beginning.

Loudoun County's experience can be illuminating both as to possible problems and rewards. It sets an example that could be followed in any community.

Introducing the Idea

The beginning was an October day in 1966 when our three-man team went to Leesburg, the Loudoun County seat, to conduct two conferences, both of which had been prearranged with the executive secretary of the county Board of Supervisors.

One conference was in the morning with the executive secretary and other county officials: the superintendent of schools, the planning

* Or like Arlington County's Committee of 100, an equally influential group which served as a model for the Committee of 55.

director, the director of economic and industrial development and the sanitation engineer. The other was in the afternoon with three community leaders. Six had been invited by the Board of Supervisors, one for each magisterial district, but, apparently only three thought the meeting important enough to crowd into already crowded schedules!

With both groups, we demonstrated two basic tenets of successful group process:

1. We brought together people who were or should be interested in the purpose of the meeting (which in this case was to identify the problems of Loudoun County).

2. Except for explaining why the participants had been brought together and helping them carry forward their discussion in an orderly way (serving as facilitators),† we did not run the meetings. As a result, the participants in both meetings could be sure that the ideas that came forth were *their* ideas, not our Program's.

By the end of that October day in Loudoun, both the group of officials and the three community leaders had agreed on the county's principal problems. Above all, and affecting all others, came problems developing from its present and future growth. The county, so long rural, predominantly conservative and stable in population, was on the outer fringes of the Washington, D.C., Virginia suburbs and beginning to experience population explosion. Its time for expansion had come, just as Arlington and Fairfax counties' times had come previously. So for Loudoun County in late 1966, it could be written on the facilitator's flip chart:

Loudoun County: Major problem: How best to meet the many problems created by vastly accelerated growth.

Several problems of growth were suggested that day—providing quality education, getting the industry that would be needed to help pay for the services that would be required, keeping the county beautiful and preserving its historic landmarks, providing adequate law enforcement . . .

† Reminder: Facilitators are the new kind of small group leaders mentioned in the introduction, persons who do not dictate but who help make the meeting a success by encouraging discussion of all viewpoints, keeping the discussion focused and forward-moving, making sure there is general agreement on major decisions, etc. For how to train and use them, see Chapter 14.

But meeting time ran out. Neither Rome nor the Committee of 55 could be built in a day. Our three-man team made a date with the three community leaders for another meeting.

Exploring the Problem

This second meeting started where the other had ended. The group looked back on the problems listed, added several, then agreed there should be some systematic method for people of the county to consider these problems in a thorough and widely represented way, a way in which all the significant viewpoints could be heard.

In order to do this, discussion disclosed, two related needs would first have to be met:

1. Need for sufficient communication and understanding among the various segments of the county—the more than 100 citizen organizations, the seven incorporated towns and the county government, the two races, the still rural west and the already urbanizing east, the people wishing to encourage development and those resisting all change.

2. Need for a co-ordinated focus on problems of concern to all the county, for a way to disseminate important in-depth information on a countywide basis and encourage an informed exchange of views among the various segments.

The second meeting ended with the decision to bring representatives of all the diverse elements of the county into the discussion. But the three community leaders agreed that in order to be sure of good representation of all the county's segments they should first confer with several other leaders whose contacts and knowledge reached into areas other than their own. The initial three leaders agreed to invite three others with differing areas of influence to the third meeting.

At the third meeting, these six community leaders listed fifty-five persons (including themselves) to represent the county. They selected people to represent geographical areas (towns, rural areas, magisterial districts), political parties, principal religions, both races, organizations concerned with civic matters, business, industry, agriculture, the professions, officialdom. The six participants then divided the names in order to extend personal invitations for a meeting on county problems.

The Kickoff

Of course, not all the fifty-five agreed to come. About thirty, however, realized that here was something new and exciting, a meeting of people from *all* segments of the county to talk about problems of concern to *all* the county.

In makeup and in mood, the meeting of Loudoun leaders in Leesburg in January 1967 was a forecast of the organization that was to come. The people were diverse, curious about one another's interests and viewpoints, anxious to communicate, anxious to "do something" about county problems.

No one told them what the county problems were, let alone what should be done about them. Once again, serving only as facilitators, we turned the thinking, the discussion and the decisions over to the participants.

We used special methods and techniques, however, to help the participants make their decisions in a way that was both orderly and most likely to assure every participant the chance of being heard. The participants divided themselves into around-the-table discussion groups of five or six persons. Each group was asked to list the several community problems that most concerned it. Each group was asked, also, to choose one person to report to all the groups when time was called in twenty minutes.

Thirty-four different problems were listed at the various tables in Loudoun that night. As each was given at report-back time, we wrote the problem in magic marker on a flip chart for all to see.

"Now, let's see if some of these can be co-ordinated under general headings," we suggested. "There seems to be a lot of concern here, for instance, about preserving Loudoun County's natural beauty without losing economic opportunity. Let's start with that and see if some of these other concerns will fall into line under it."

Others would, indeed, fall into line. The participants eagerly went to work deciding that seven specific difficulties were part of this first major problem. So it went. As other general categories were suggested the participants identified the concerns that they could list under each.

A flip chart sheet is usually about twenty-five inches wide and thirty-eight inches long. We reproduce one here to show how they look. As each is finished the facilitator tears it from the pad and, with a short strip of masking tape, fixes it to a nearby window or wall space so the participants can consult it as the discussion continues. This technique, by focusing the group members' attention on both the content and progress of their discussion, helps to keep it on the track and move it along. We discuss this tool in more detail in Chapter 13, "What We Do with a Request for Help."

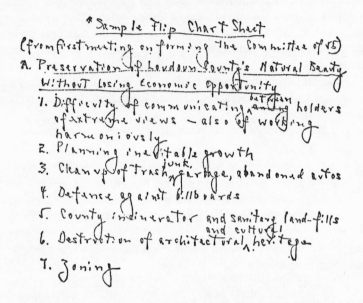

*Sample Flip Chart Sheet
(from first meeting on forming the Committee of 45)
A. Preservation of Loudoun County's Natural Beauty Without losing Economic Opportunity
1. Difficulty of communicating between holders of extreme views — also of working harmoniously
2. Planning inevitable growth
3. Clean up of trash, junk, garbage, abandoned autos
4. Defense against billboards
5. County incinerator and sanitary land-fills
6. Destruction of architectural and cultural heritage
7. Zoning

As usual in untrained groups, the participants listed any number of goals as problems. Planning inevitable growth, for instance, is not a problem. We did not risk confusing the participants or dampening their zeal by any insistence on wording their problems as problems should be worded: *Lack* of adequate planning for inevitable growth, for instance. Or *lack* of a good system to provide for trash, junk, garbage, abandoned autos. Nor did we state stuffily that such an item as zoning was neither a problem nor a goal, merely an area that needed attention. Instead, we conveniently overlooked our training in terminology for the moment and, with no more than a blink, lumped all the suggestions under the umbrella of "situations of concern." After all, the participants knew what the problems were even though in so many instances they hadn't stated them correctly, and nit-picking very easily could have turned them off at this vital point.

Instead, they obviously were enthusiastically turned on, eager to set another date for another meeting to decide what to do about their list of "problems."

* Items 1, 3 and 6 show changes facilitator made to reflect group's intentions more accurately than what he first wrote.

Getting Organized

In spite of threatened snow, they met with us again in February 1967. This time the around-the-table discussion groups began with the question: What would we like to do about the concerns we listed at the last meeting—and others that may confront the county in the future?

From all tables, the answer came back: We could do nothing without some sort of organization. This led logically to two further questions:

1. What purpose or purposes do we want our organization to serve?

2. What kind of organization can best serve this purpose or these purposes?—a forum? a study group? an action group? a combination of these?

Table discussion was animated, and at several tables argumentative for the first time, as several participants tried to persuade others to join them in organizing for action on specific problems, while people with opposing views on these problems let it be known that if so-and-so's stand were endorsed, they wanted out.

The Committee of 55 nearly died aborning that night. If it had, a small action group might have emerged. More likely, however, this meeting merely would have been the last, leaving the county more fragmented than ever, its dissident groups more than ever suspicious of one another.

Fortunately, the majority of participants realized that in these planning sessions, they already had begun the sort of organization the county needed. Moreover, they had enjoyed unprecedented communication among people whose various views represented all the views of the county, and they didn't want it to end.

"Now, wait a minute," said the president of the Farm Bureau. "If we take a stand, I don't care what it is, any stand on anything, we're sure to antagonize some of our members and all the people they represent. Then we lose not just these members but all the people behind them. And so, with every stand, we lose more and more of this wonderful business of being something really countywide. That's what's been different so far. That's what really excites me."

"And me," said the president of the League of Women Voters, whose organization was often at odds with the Farm Bureau. "Any number of organizations take stands. Let's make this one so thor-

10 WHAT WE DO

oughly non-partisan that the whole county will trust the information
about county problems coming out of our meetings."

The head of the county's largest industry agreed. So did the head
of the Community Action Program, the developer of a planned community in the eastern section, the Boy Scout leader, the head of the
Ministerial Association, the school board chairman, etc., etc., and
etc.—a resounding majority, in fact.

After more discussion, onto the flip chart went the two purposes
of the new organization:

1. *Communication.* Providing a regular meeting of all the diverse elements of the county.

2. *Education.* An informed, non-partisan focusing together by all these elements on matters of
concern to all.

A committee was selected to draw up by-laws for review at the
next meeting. Suggestions were made for a name for the organization, and the name Committee of 55 for Loudoun County was chosen.
A temporary chairman, vice-chairman, secretary, and treasurer were
selected.

In March, the Committee of 55's by-laws committee handed out
copies of the suggested "Rules Governing the Affairs of the Committee of 55 for Loudoun County." These were studied in the small
discussion groups which by now had been accepted as the best way
for all to be heard. Reporting-back time brought several suggestions
for changes. Everyone discussed these suggestions; a few changes
actually were made; other suggestions were withdrawn. The entire
evening was devoted to by-laws, but there was little grumbling about
time being wasted. All realized that these by-laws were as important
to their organization as the Constitution was to their country. By
the end of the meeting, everyone was satisfied with the result, satisfied in no little part because he, personally, had been given a whack
at every word.

Finishing the Planning

In April, at the final planning session, the group divided itself
according to members' preferences into committees on program,
membership and nominating, each committee going to work only
after receiving suggestions from the others. Members of each committee were reminded of the purposes of the organization and asked
to base their decisions on these purposes.

The program committee decided that the first meeting should be in May, a dinner meeting with wives, husbands, friends. The subject would be one of concern to all the founders: "Problems of Local Education in a Period of Growth." A format was agreed upon. A panel of three speakers (the chairman of the county school board, the superintendent of schools and the assistant superintendent) would each speak for ten minutes. To assure that the panelists understood the new organization and its purposes and would bring the sort of in-depth information needed, there would be a warm-up session for them and the program committee. For this and every program meeting, announcements would be mailed to all Committee of 55 members. At the meeting, after the panelists had finished speaking, the persons at each of the tables would be given ten minutes to discuss what they had just heard, decide what question they most wanted to ask and appoint one of their group to ask it. The moderator (program chairman or committee chairman) would call for the questions at the end of the discussion period, taking each table in order. When all group questions had been answered, individuals would be given an opportunity to question the panelists during the remaining time.

Meanwhile, the membership committee decided upon a number of new persons to be asked to join the organization before the first meeting, people who either represented significant segments of the county previously overlooked or who could represent the same areas of influence as the few who had dropped out for one reason or another (including dissatisfaction with the no-action stand in the bylaws).

Meanwhile, also, the nominating committee was busy. With a determination to make the Board reflect the widely representative nature of the organization, it chose a slate consisting of an Episcopal minister for chairman, a woman realtor who was also a private school teacher and clubwoman for vice-chairman, a well-known lawyer as secretary and a black leader as treasurer. The Board members included the president of the conservative Farm Bureau, a county official, the president of the League of Women Voters, a commuter-to-Washington active in civic affairs and a Presbyterian minister who was also chairman of the county Council of PTAs. This slate was as widely representative geographically as it was in its concerns. (Several other Board members were appointed later as committee heads.)

Before the meeting ended, each committee reported to the entire group, dues were collected by the temporary treasurer to pay for mailings, and one of the founders, a reporter for the local newspaper, agreed to prepare a news release for her paper and for the local radio station explaining the new organization and announcing its first meeting.

Growing Pains

So the Committee of 55 was launched—an organization so widely based, so uncontroversial in its goals and methods and yet so unquestionably needed that it *should* have been hailed enthusiastically by the community it sought to serve. Instead, even before the first meeting, rumors spread that it was a new *subversive* organization!

The publicity explaining the organization was read over the local radio station and printed in the county newspaper, but not everyone heard or saw it and even many who did were confused. From this confusion came suspicion, especially among those who also were fed the rumors of subversion. No one is sure why the rumors began. Perhaps the name of the organization suggested something sinister to some people fearful of anything new and unknown. Perhaps the lack of publicity during the planning stages was equated with secrecy and secrecy with danger. Or, maybe, the founders had erred in not making public who they were and what they were doing and why at every stage of their planning. In any event, the rumors were so disturbing that several of the founders (the sort so cautious about their "image" that they do not associate their names with anything but the thoroughly proven and unquestionably accepted) did not even attend the first meeting.

Even so, first meeting attendance was very good. The temporary chairman acknowledged the rumors and re-explained the purposes of the Committee to members and guests—but the media were absent and no one was made responsible for follow-up publicity, unquestionably a major goof.

Moreover, the then program chairman forgot that the meeting's format called only for questioning the speakers, not lecturing them. From his position of power, he orated about his pet peeves, and, after the meeting, the school board chairman, feeling both betrayed and misused, resigned from the new organization. Several other members never appeared again.

So the Committee of 55 was indeed launched—upon rather stormy seas.

These seas grew calmer, however, as the new organization applied the lessons it had learned—to provide both "before" and "after" publicity, both kinds always stressing the organization's purposes and its non-partisanship. This and significant programs gradually created the right "image."

Each monthly Board meeting became an evaluation as well as a planning session, and several innovative methods were used to strengthen the organization.

Strengthening the Organization

To help fulfill the Committee's educational purpose, the Board early in the first year began to issue special invitations to a list of people, different for each meeting, who would or should be interested in the chosen subject. For instance, invitations to a meeting on industrial development were mailed to bankers, merchants, farm leaders, town and county officials.

Because the executive committee did so much planning it began to fear the general membership would feel left out and devised a "10 P.M. Thoughts" sheet to give the general member a part in evaluation and planning. (See Appendix, Chapter 1, for a copy of the sheet.)

After several dinner meetings, the Board learned that while many members greatly enjoyed the dinners and the "happy hour" which preceded them, a few members could not easily get away from jobs or family responsibilities in time for dinner meetings. A few others found the monthly expense a hardship, especially if they brought their wives or husbands. Some did not approve of "happy hours." Compromising, the executive committee decided to have only two dinner meetings a year. All other meetings would be at 7:30 P.M. The assumption that even those who preferred only evening meetings would be able, somehow, to get to, pay for or endure the social hour of only two dinner meetings a year proved sound. So did the assumption that even those who preferred dinner meetings would be interested enough in the subject to come at 7:30 P.M.

Off and Running

Thanks to adherence to the organization's purposes, consistent publicity, evaluation by the Board and the members, good attendance and programs on a wide range of county issues, the organization ended its first year with a commendation from the county Board of Supervisors.

This commendation proved a valuable aid in bolstering membership during a drive in January 1969, to fill the gaps in representation that inevitably had appeared by that time. A membership committee selected for its wide representation sent copies of the commendation with a carefully prepared letter of invitation to a selected list of potential members, each chosen for the representation he or she could give. Again in 1971, 1972 and 1973, similar letters mailed to other carefully chosen people restored full membership and consistent countywide representation.

At the same time, the Committee decided it did not want to be an exclusive organization. Membership drives to assure full representation, yes. But the chance to benefit from the communication and information provided at meetings should be given to any interested citizen. By 1971, advance publicity was making this clear, emphasizing that anyone who wished to belong was welcome and even those who did not want to be members could attend at any time.

Inevitably, as time has passed, certain other changes also have been made. In 1972, for instance, the membership voted to return to dinner meetings—for those who wanted to come in time for dinner. Those who didn't could come for the program only at seven-thirty or eight. A simple and effective solution to the old controversy. Then, to overcome the fact that some members liked the socializing at dinners but not the cost, the Committee in 1972 and 1973 introduced a series of well-attended potluck meals (fifty to sixty people) followed by even better-attended programs as anywhere from fifteen to sixty additional people arrived in time to hear and question the panelists.

And certainly contributing to the fact that attendance has been so consistently high has been the subject matter chosen, the variety of issues of countywide concern: law enforcement, drug abuse, youth problems, race relations, planning and development, education, environment control, to name but a few.

Assessing the Results

What has the Committee of 55 accomplished? What has it *done?* Potential members used to action groups sometimes ask the question.

Certainly the Committee can point to no boycotts, marches, sit-ins, presentations of petitions, campaigns, crusades, public endorsements or damnings of any kind.

It cannot even say that it has sent so many kids to camp or provided so many Christmas baskets or raised money for a new hospital wing or research on some disease.

It can, however, be sure that it has been a major source of the citizen and official understanding necessary to many important changes in the county. Things happen as a result of meetings. People have learned something. Some use it for direct action. Others merely spread the word that brings acceptance. Both action and support for action are essential for change.

The Committee of 55 gave a program on drug abuse. Those at the meeting were alarmed by the facts disclosed. Soon other organizations were sponsoring such programs. Before long, the schools of the county adopted a drug policy to educate students about drugs and to protect them from pushers.

When the advantages of attracting industry to the county were little understood, the Committee devoted a meeting to pros and cons of industrial development. Another meeting followed a year later, then another. Now, with great citizen support, the county can seek desirable industry.

Many of the new sources of revenue which, again with wide citizen support, the county is tapping or seeking to tap were first explained, discussed, modified and accepted in Committee of 55 meetings.

Problems of adequate planning—and the very need for it—first received widespread public attention through Committee of 55 meetings. Committee of 55 programs did much to allay initial suspicion that Loudoun's joining the Northern Virginia Planning District Commission would bring loss of local control. The citizenry now is overwhelmingly in favor of the county's membership.

On and on. The Committee never can claim entire credit for bringing about any change. Yet always it can be sure it helped—and forcefully.

Above all, it can point to continuous success in meeting its two original goals of education and communication. These goals are met at every meeting.

Members have learned to expect brightness, innovative thinking and candor both from panelists and discussion groups. In a forum that prides itself on giving voice to all pertinent viewpoints, disagreements are inevitable but usually expressed with good humor. In this atmosphere, rancor seems to vanish. Members and panelists both expect to have a good time—to laugh, to learn, to change a little for the better.

At a meeting on race relations, for example, the spokesman for one buzz group that happened to be all white posed this question: "We want to ask you black—or should we say 'Negro'?—panelists what you would like to be called. We used to think we were showing respect when we said 'Negro.' Now some people say you want to be called 'black.' Which is it?"

One black panelist answered: "Black is the word, man."

Another panelist turned on him with a grin. "Now, wait a minute. What's all this black stuff? Just because some young city punks dreamed it up, now we're all supposed to be black. Nuts. I'll admit I'm brown. I'm even a good dark brown. But I'm not black." He looked at the buzz group spokesman. "What I want to be called is 'mister.' Now, if you know me awfully well, then, of course, it's all right to use my first name. But if you know me that well, then I know you that well and it's all right for me to use *your* first name, too." He laughed good-naturedly. "Just don't ever call me 'boy.' Not that I wouldn't like to be a boy again, but I haven't been a boy for many long years."

Panelists and members alike smiled appreciatively, and the disagreement was over, but the frankness continued.

A woman panelist added her bit:

And I'm not some white woman's "girl" either, just because the only way I can support my family is to clean her bathrooms. Of course, she doesn't intend to be unkind. She's really a sweet person. She just doesn't understand how it hurts my pride to hear her telling her friends over the phone that her "girl" is there today —as if I didn't even have a name—that and being given her hand-me-downs. We'd rather have a decent wage so that we can buy our own clothes. They won't be from Garfinckel's, but they will be our own, not somebody's Lady Bountiful charity.

Several white women exchanged sheepish glances as the point reached its mark. And a white civic leader, known to be old guard, shook hands with the "dark brown" panelist after adjournment. "Good going, Emmett."

The panelist smiled. Here was that first name use again. "Thanks, Jim."

The old guard leader was only momentarily jolted. Then he smiled, too. "Right on."

Not that all exchanges at Committee of 55 meetings begin good-humoredly. They just usually end that way.

One night the subject was low income housing. A social worker in one buzz group listened to a member of the group, a farmer, argue with passion against such housing: "It will just bring in a lot of people who will have a lot of kids. Now, on low income property these people won't be paying enough taxes to pay for the education of even one of these kids, let alone a house full of them. So who will pay? The rest of us. Higher and higher and higher property taxes for the rest of us."

"Listen to that fat cat!" the social worker whispered to a friend.

The farmer heard. "What did you call me?"

She blushed but said fearlessly, "A fat cat. Now do you want to call me a bleeding heart because I'm for low income housing?"

"I'm not a fat cat," he said. "I probably have less income after taxes than you do."

"But you have all that land."

"I'll have to sell it if my taxes get any higher."

Another buzz group member spoke up. There's always such a member, long with the Committee of 55 and used to seeing through to the real problem. "I don't think your argument is against low income housing per se. But you worry about how we're going to pay for the increased school costs."

"That's right," the farmer conceded. "Hell, I'm just as anxious as anybody for low income people to have a decent place to live. So maybe a brass tacks question to ask the panel would be: How can we support the higher education budget that low income housing would bring without taxing farmers out of business?"

"I don't want to put you out of business," the social worker admitted. "And, of course, we all want to keep our open spaces. They're what make our county so beautiful, why all of us live here. So—okay. Let's ask your question."

We are proud of the Committee of 55 and our part in creating it. An organization which provides both communication among diverse segments of a community and information needed by all these segments is an extremely useful one. We wish similar organizations could stretch from coast to coast, breaking down barriers and bringing the facts, ideas and understanding we need for wise decisions about today's problems.

2

APPROACHES TO PROBLEMS OF YOUTH

Worry about youth. It has always been present, of course, but in the past decade it has become agonizing. Among millions of parents, it is the number one concern, shared by officials, educators, religious leaders, all thoughtful citizens . . . increasing drug abuse, delinquency, a turn to revolutionary methods, alienation from traditional standards and, always and apparently growing wider and deeper, the generation gap.

Worries of youth . . . war, materialism, the hypocrisy of society (parents especially), economic need, the difficulty of communicating with "the establishment" (parents especially).

Small wonder that problems of youth led the field when in October 1966 our Community Education team asked various officials and civic leaders of the Northern Virginia region where to begin with our assignment of helping the communities of the area solve some of the problems most troubling them.

Northern Virginia, consisting of four counties (Arlington, Fairfax, Prince William and Loudoun), three cities (Alexandria, Fairfax and Falls Church) and numerous towns and communities, is considered part of Metropolitan Washington. Primarily urban and suburban, it extends into still rural countryside where pockets of both black and white poverty exist alongside comfortable villages and farms and rich estates. Its urban and suburban areas contain patches of ghetto as well as modest to wealthy residential areas.

What were the major problems of youth in this diversified region? Did the problems overrun jurisdictional lines?

A Meeting of Adults on Youth Problems

To assess the overall situation, to find out whether the problems of youth could be approached on a regional basis in this particular region, the team invited a representative group of officials, educators and citizens working with young people to an exploratory discussion.

The concept of receiving help in community problem solving from institutions of higher education was a new one in the region. New, too, to most people of the region, were the advanced techniques of problem solving that our team would be using. We first had to explain our purposes and our potential usefulness to the "right people": those with the knowledge, the influence and the ability to affect necessary change. Then, in order to introduce our new and more effective methods, we had to demonstrate their value. At the same time, we had to show that these methods were not static or sacrosanct, that as we brought them to bear on specific problems, we wished to test and improve them.

Thus each planned event had four purposes:

1. To spread the word of the Program's existence and its potential value to the region.
2. To teach participants the new techniques of problem solving which they then could use with other people to tackle different community problems more effectively.
3. To test techniques and learn how to improve them at future events.
4. And primarily, of course, to help solve the problem at hand.

The Community Education Program was new. The people invited were busy people. The sixteen who came, however, were strategically divided among the jurisdictions, so the hoped-for interjurisdictional meeting was still possible.

Interestingly, the discussion at that meeting in just this one region of one state brought forth many of the points that since have been expounded over and over again across the nation—in the media, from the platform, on the streets, in Congress, by special commissions, etc., etc.

The depth of thinking was possible because of the techniques used to bring it out—no speeches, and introductions and explanations as

brief and to the point as possible. We did not lead in the usual sense;
we facilitated, standing with magic marker before a flip chart on a
large easel, helping the group to do its best thinking in an orderly
way. We allowed no one to dominate; all found it easy to take part.
The discussion was both relaxed and concentrated, bringing out the
best that particular group had to give at that particular time.

That best holds up well even today after so many millions of
words have been written and spoken on the subject. Participants
discussed the difficulties faced by the adult community in coming to
grips with the problems of youth, the generation gap and the reasons
for it, the ambiguous and conflicting value systems in our society,
the pressures exerted on youth.

The group met again the following month, centering discussion
now on possible solutions. Here are the transcribed flip chart records:

1. Discuss with parents and youth.
2. Expose all parents and youths possible to similar small group
    discussions
    —possibly through PTAs, film strips (*Values for Teenagers*),
    churches and their groups, recreational associations, high
    school service clubs, mass media (TV geared to discussion
    groups and arrangements for feedback and newspaper pub-
    licity).
3. Try to find ways to create awareness among citizenry in gen-
    eral about the scope of the problem.

Suggested activities:

1. Teen canteen sponsored by service clubs
2. Teen council in high schools
3. Television group discussions

Big question: How to get the kids to take it?

1. A value school, a la traffic school for traffic offenders?
2. Sunday Schools?
3. Point to consequences.
4. Show reasons for ethical principles.
5. Take juveniles through a jail.

Then there was a lot of thinking to name the sort of people who
should be involved in any interjurisdictional attack on problems of
youth. The list covered three flip chart pages.

So we had made a beginning. But the participants were not members of an organization that could implement them. Nor were they
about to create such an organization. They were all busy. They were

from assorted jurisdictions. They tentatively planned a large conference involving all the people they had listed on their flip chart record, but we of the Project team had learned a valuable lesson. To be sure, the subject had been intriguing enough to draw a small group, but the group had no organizational structure to move forward with its decisions. A larger group would face the same overwhelming handicap. It would only find itself, as this group now found itself, in midair. A lot of good thinking but no way to move forward with actions.

Tackling the problems of youth by individual jurisdictions promised to be more productive. There we could involve local organizations and governing bodies in planning for specific action geared to the specific area. Organizational structure for implementing solutions already existed or could be built more easily.

These jurisdictional conferences never materialized although our team continued to consider them and make tentative plans for them for several months. We found our schedule becoming so crowded with other efforts that we did not have enough time to sell the idea. Too bad. Such jurisdictional conferences, properly planned and conducted, could have been of great benefit to this region, or any region for that matter. (See Part Three for suggestions on planning and conducting such a conference.)

Letting Kids Talk About Their Gripes

Meanwhile, we decided it was important for us to hear the other side. Adults were worrying—and complaining—about youth. What did youth have to say about adults?

We arranged with the assistant superintendent of schools of Arlington County to meet with three groups of seniors at Wakefield High School. With each class of twenty-five to thirty, the teacher gave us a government period to confer with them on the subject: "What don't you like about adults?"

The first group, all white, were average students scholastically. When we met with them in January 1967, they took to the day's subject with enthusiasm. Divided into five subgroups, each composed of six students, they began with a vengeance to list all manner of complaints. Quickly we learned that when these high school seniors spoke of adults, they meant their own parents or the parents of close friends. And there was no holding back. The kids, in fact, were having such

a good time, we regretted having to stop them to hear their reports
and record them on the flip chart, eliminating duplications.

Here it is, from the records:

Teen-agers' Gripes About Adults

1. Too nosy.
2. Don't believe we have good judgment.
3. Don't agree with our form of music.
4. Think we don't respect them enough.
5. "When I was your age . . ."
6. Make time schedule for homework.
7. Worry too much about us.
8. Want us to make straight As or Bs.
9. Don't listen.
10. Don't like our fads.
11. Look down on us.
12. Think we are all alike and look only at the bad points.
13. Think we shouldn't drink, smoke, cuss . . .
14. Think we don't spend enough time with them.
15. Some don't care what we do—some don't agree with our morals
    (but some trust us).
16. "You do what you want as long as we [Parents] like it."
17. Want us to go to a name college so they can brag about it.
18. Play favorites among their children.
19. Money.
20. Disapprove places we go.
21. Police look too closely at teen-age drivers, particularly those
    in sports cars.
22. Complain about the time we spend on the phone.
23. Can't get car when we need it.
24. Complain about extracurricular activities.
25. Push off chores on us.
26. Want us to get jobs to make money—not jobs we like.
27. Girls must be in too early.

On February 2 came a class of high-level students. These, too,
were all white. Again the class brightened when they heard the day's
subject and attacked it with relish when we divided them into four
groups for the discussion and listing of complaints. This class repeated many of the gripes given by the middle learners and added
these:

28. Comparing unequal teens.

29. Care too much about what others may think.
30. Parents do not provide correct atmosphere for doing home-work.
31. Parents do not trust us.
32. Parents require an active social life but condemn us when we come in late.
33. Parents will not allow us to hold or develop our own opinions.
34. Parents think all teen-agers are the world's worst drivers.
35. Parents must approve of the people we date.
36. Parents are prejudiced against dating people of other races.
37. Parents won't give enough independence.
38. Parents state, "Do as I say, not as I do."

Next, on February 10, we met with a class of slow learners, half white and half black. The pattern was repeated—excitement at the chance to air dissatisfactions with parents, animated discussion in groups of five with a record kept, then reporting to the whole group with consolidation on the flip chart. Although there was some repe-tition of the points made by the first two groups, this class showed major concern about the following:

1. They like to fuss too much.
2. They are too old-fashioned (not modern).
3. They are too domineering (bossy).
4. They like to have the last word.
5. They pin things on teen-agers when something goes wrong.
6. They don't have faith in teen-agers.
7. They try to get into our business too much (run our lives).
8. As a whole, they don't understand our need for conformism (dress, hair and alcoholic beverages).
9. They don't know what the world is all about.
10. They try to be too strict.
11. They don't make curfew late enough.
12. They don't try to understand.
13. They don't remember when they were teen-agers.
14. They believe other adults' stories about our friends and tell us to stop seeing them.
15. They want to bring us up the way they were brought up.
16. Teens are informed too late about the ways of life (six mem-bers).
17. Teens learn too early about the ways of life (one member).
18. Voting age should be eighteen (as it now is).
19. Teen-agers that have to fight wars should be able to drink.

Then the three special class periods were over. The kids had had a whee of a time, had cast a great deal of light on why, from their viewpoint, the generation gap was so great. Their teachers talked with us about how useful it might be if parents could hear teen-agers speaking as freely as they had in these school discussions.

Youth-Parent Conferences

So we evolved a plan for a meeting with parents. These teachers asked for a volunteer from each of these three classes. To be sure there was nothing unique about the viewpoints of Wakefield High students, we arranged with another Arlington County high school, Yorktown, for four more student volunteers. Parents? We feared the students might not talk freely to their own parents or even the parents of their classmates, so we asked the PTA of still another Arlington high school, Washington-Lee, to send six parents to an adult-youth discussion to be held at Wakefield on March 7, 1967.

On that night, we divided our group of thirteen into two subgroups, each with three adults. One group, of course, had three teen-agers, and the other four.

We asked each group to take the same subject—"Parents Should Be Consistent In Their Decisions"—and to follow the same discussion pattern:

1. Exploring the problem.
2. Deciding the goal (or goals).
3. Listing the difficulties, the obstacles to be overcome in reaching the goal (or goals).
4. Developing solutions.

The flip chart records and individual comments from both group discussions that night point to the inconsistency of parents, the barrier of self-pride on both sides, the unwillingness to try to understand the other.

Certainly, the meeting had proved the interest in discussions of youth-parent relationships. Again, the teen-agers had approached their subject with a zest that revealed their frustrations. The parents, too, seemed just to have been waiting for an opportunity to talk and to listen. In the animated milling about afterwards, both teen-agers and adults had one comment in common. While the teen-agers were saying they wished their own parents could have been there, parents were saying it was too bad they couldn't have heard from their own kids.

How could this be arranged without both teen-agers and parents either clamming up and accomplishing nothing or, worse yet, so offending each other that the rifts between them would grow wider instead of narrower?

We had heard, meanwhile, of a youth-parent discussion pattern used by Father Malloy of St. Leo's Church in Fairfax, following an example set by a priest in Hartford, Connecticut.

When we went to see Father Malloy in April 1967, he explained the stages:

After a brief discussion, participants divided into subgroups, each including only teen-agers or adults. During the first discussion period of fifteen minutes, the kids named what they liked about adults, and the adults named what they liked about teen-agers. Then the adult subgroups gave brief reports to the whole conference. Next the teen-agers' subgroups reported.

This constructive listing made both sides feel good and opened the way for acceptance of reports from the second discussion period. This was the one that really got down to business. The teen-agers answered the question: "What bugs you about parents?" The parents tackled: "What do you *not* like about teen-agers?" This time the kids reported first with the parents following. Then, after the reports, there was discussion back and forth about the points raised.

The pattern allowed each side to hear what the other thought without creating conflict between individual teen-agers and their parents. Father Malloy reported family members talking amiably about their new views as they started home.

We thought the pattern a good one and wanted to try it. An Arlington high school teacher tried to arrange it but couldn't. Then Bob Russell, then principal of Lanier Intermediate School in Fairfax City, who knew that some of his students were engaged in activities their parents should know about,* offered to arrange an evening in the school cafeteria with a number of families participating.

Following Father Malloy's instructions, we had three separate tables of students in a row in one part of the room and corresponding tables of parents in a row opposite but out of earshot.

The conference was not the success we wanted. Some of the kids apparently had been commanded to come instead of volunteering as the older group had done. Moreover, they were mostly seventh graders, too young to assume a co-equal standing with their parents for

* Stealing clothing from stores at a nearby shopping center, for instance, keeping it in their school lockers, wearing it and trading it at school.

the purposes of discussion. In the whole room discussions, involving both parents and children, both sides only reinforced their prejudices. The parents dominated, and the kids just had to take it. They resented the fact, as can be noted in these comments from typical evaluation sheets they filled out at the evening's end:

This evening has been a waste of time because we didn't laugh at their reasons, but they laughed at ours! They still don't understand us, and we don't think they got anything out of it. They laughed at us. It would be better if we went half and you went half. They still think their ways are the best no matter what we say.

The evening has been worthwhile because at least we were able to express our views even though they didn't listen.

The parents of those students about whom the principal was so concerned were not present, nor, alas, were their misbehaving kids, as one of the adults' evaluation sheets observed:

The evening has been a waste of time in many ways because the people that really have serious problems won't come and their teenagers are not here and would NOT attend.

On the other hand, about half the comments from the kids praised the evening, albeit not excessively. For example:

The evening has been worthwhile because now we have a better understanding of our parents. And we hope they now understand us a little more. We can improve our relationship because we know each other's gripes.

And this segment of youth, just entering their teens, produced a long list of gripes of their own age group. These ranged from complaints about parental unreasonableness and inconsistency to expressed resentment over favoritism.

Of considerable worth, too, were these parental concerns recognized in discussion that night:

—Value systems not as clear or generally accepted as ten years ago.
—Sanctions not applied to same extent as fifteen years ago.
—Too many parents make early choice of property over children.
—What values do you teach, and how do you teach values?
  1. By instruction, understanding?
  2. By indoctrination, direction?

The evening was not entirely a failure, we tried to tell ourselves. As some of the evaluation sheets had pointed out, the kids, at least, had had a chance to express their resentments. So had the parents. Healthy on both counts. Probably a little of what each had said had been heard by the other. Also, the parents had taken time to examine their values, express some of their concerns. Healthy again.

We felt anything but triumphant, however, as we zipped our easels into their vinyl covers, rolled our filled flip sheets and headed home. We kept thinking how much better the Hartford priest's techniques would have worked if we could have used upper teens. Thousands of such intimate and searching evenings across the nation could go a long way toward bridging our nationwide generation gap. It would be better, though, to follow one evening of listing complaints with another evening or two of deciding what to do about them. That system could chart some really practical roads to reconciliation.

So we thought then and so we still think.

Meanwhile, we have discovered that our despondency over the evening at Lanier was ill founded. We thought our effort had failed when, in fact, it had succeeded with the person whose follow-through counted most. In our work we always hope there is someone watching, learning, someone in the position to carry on after learning how. This time Bob Russell, the Lanier principal, was such a man. He had wanted ways to increase communication among students, parents, faculty and administration. Also, he wanted answers to certain questions. How did the community feel about the school? Were a few people creating trends? How much attention were parents paying to his seventh and eighth grade students? Did parents care but feel they had no way to communicate? He began a whole cycle of innovations at Lanier.

Most important of these was organizing the students into four communities, each with its own activities and PTA. This change produced groups of a size which enabled people to know each other and work together successfully.

When we checked with him in early 1972, he told us of eight parent coffees in the past two weeks, of students planning with teachers and improved faculty-student relationships, of the testing of students' physiological needs that led to the discovery of why so many were sometimes apathetic or irritable. About 45 per cent of these twelve- and thirteen-year-olds registered an improper blood sugar level. He began to give each student a personal assessment card. Students using these cards could experiment with varying amounts of sleep and different types of breakfast until they learned with what regimen they felt most relaxed and comfortable.

Early in 1969, under pressure of imminent student rebellions, another Fairfax educator, Bob Tabor, then principal of Fairfax City High School, began holding conferences there with students, faculty and parents as participants. These conferences were so successful that they soon became an institution. The school had six or seven conferences a year. Two were for seniors; two for juniors; one or two for sophomores; and one for freshmen. Each conference lasted through a school morning.

Class leaders, the student government and teachers selected students to invite. Although a few refused to participate, many others volunteered and the vast majority readily accepted their selection. Student government leaders arranged the groups of ten to fifteen, trying to get a range of students in each and an equal share of the participating teachers and parents, three or four to a group. Responsible parents were the ones who attended. "The ones who should come, didn't"—as usual.

At first, teachers monitored the discussions, then student leaders. Later no one monitored, and the discussions were freer. Each group, however, had a discussion leader and a reporter. After the discussions, these reporters gave group summaries to the whole conference. Tape recorders provided a complete account and the flavor and feeling of the discussions.

Results were many, according to Tabor:

1. More concern by students, faculty and parents for the problems of the others.
2. During the 1968–69 trouble period for students, particularly in October and November of 1969 when some groups were pushing for a war moratorium, the conferences made it possible for the school to avoid major trouble.
3. Conferences made it possible to change the school dress code without heavy resistance from parents and faculty.
4. The program helped former non-speakers learn to express themselves.
5. Some teachers began to have periods of open discussion in their regular classes.
6. Students who once resented the presence of teachers in the conferences asked them to participate.
7. The administration had learned to place more trust in the

students and became willing to let them make their own choices about running the program.

8. The principal's communication with the students was much better: he sat down with small groups of them informally, to explain why he or they couldn't do certain things and got their understanding.

9. Vandalism "was cut to a minimum."

10. Student morale was boosted by the granting of certain specific requests made in the conferences. For instance, they asked for and received a smoking room for students and a variety of table shapes in the cafeteria of the new school building into which they moved in January 1972.

One rainy morning only a few weeks after the move, we hurried under our umbrellas from the parking lot of the new school on our way to observe the first class conference to be held there. The sophomore class's turn had come.

It was only eight-thirty, but in the large cafeteria with its brightly colored walls, plastic chairs and tables of various shapes (see point 10 above) over 100 participants had gathered—student government conference officials, discussion leaders, reporters, teachers, parents and sophomore discussants. All were wearing name tags and delivering or receiving instructions over milk and doughnuts.

The student government conference chairman assigned people to groups. Although the groups were to be free to discuss any subjects of interest to them, the assistant principal made some suggestions: methods of teaching—amount and quality of learning; open campus —kids coming and going as they please; dances; the grading system; the smoking lounge; year-round school; attitudes toward the new building; community use of the new building.

A final instruction was given: "Try not to dominate your group."

Then most of the groups hurried off down the corridors to their assigned discussion rooms while a few stayed behind to gather around cafeteria tables for their talks.

A midmorning break followed. Then, after a second discussion period, came a full conference session in the school auditorium for the group summaries. Students listened attentively if not raptly as the nine chosen reporters, five girls and four boys, were introduced, crossed the large stage to the lectern in turn and adjusted the microphone to speak briefly.

Some groups had stuck to the assistant principal's suggested subjects. Others had virtually ignored them and chosen others: Should parents visit classes? Should marijuana be legalized? Pros and cons of legalized abortion. God, Jesus and the Pentecostal movement. Black problems. Coeducational gym. Personal typing versus business typing. Eight-week courses so students could change teachers in cases of incompatibility. Student evaluation of teachers. Communication with parents. Advantages and disadvantages of a pass-fail system. Drug problems. Altogether a hodgepodge.

We went away impressed with the potentialities of such conferences and the mechanics of this one. People had known where to go but had they known what to do once they got there? We were disturbed by the random, almost impulsive way groups had chosen their subjects and the general superficiality of the discussions. An opinion or two on this issue and then on to another. Nothing seemed to have been considered in any real depth. Most groups seemed to be without focus and, in those we visited, the discussion leaders seemed incapable of giving it, permitting domination by a few, many time-consuming irrelevant remarks and a general aimlessness. We wished there could have been fewer subjects and these carefully selected for their interest and importance by a widely representative planning group. We also wished that each group could have had a trained facilitator to help it keep on course and accomplish more.

Even so, we could congratulate Mr. Tabor with enthusiasm and sincerity. While the youth conferences at Fairfax City High School could be improved, they were nonetheless extremely valuable in spite of their imperfections. Certainly they were succeeding in increasing communication and understanding. They were informing parents and teachers of student viewpoints, giving students a chance to let off steam in a constructive way and introducing them to the processes and skills needed for orderly democracy.

We spoke to Mr. Tabor later and he asked us to help plan improvements for future conferences and develop a cadre of junior class members and teachers who would know how to conduct more productive meetings for the 1972–73 school year.

We proposed a series of three facilitator training sessions in May and set dates for them a week or so apart at the end of the school day. He recruited a group of thirty students and teachers for our "class," and we met with them first on May 5.

The session was a honey. No absences. Physical facilities ideal in a large room off the school library with a U-shaped table where each person could see everyone else when we all met together and folding vinyl partitions to draw for the privacy of discussion groups.

Also heartening was the fact the kids and teachers seemed intrigued by our way (new to most of them) of doing things.

We explained the purpose of the facilitator, the flip chart record and the small group, gave them the form "How Good a Discussant Are You?" (see Chapter 14) and conducted a demonstration of small group discussion with six volunteers, half students and half teachers.

This group listed subjects they thought would be interesting for the first day's small group practice discussions to follow:

1. Absenteeism, both teachers and students.
2. Bomb scares.
3. J. Edgar Hoover lying in state. (Although this was so offbeat it brought titters, we wanted to prove that the facilitator makes no judgments; we listed it.)
4. Why exams?
5. Grades versus pass/fail.
6. Legalized open campus.
7. Should Fairfax City have its own school system?
8. High-rise buildings in Fairfax City? (A proposal arousing much public interest at the time)

The whole group then narrowed the list to the four subjects they would most like to discuss: absenteeism, legalized open campus, a Fairfax City school system and high-rise buildings. Each stated his/her preferred topic, and on this basis, we formed four groups, each about half students, half teachers.

We drew the vinyl partitions for privacy. Group members formed their topic groups to sit in a semicircle of chairs facing the empty flip chart sheets. Then the discussions began with the various group members taking their turns as facilitator, observer or discussant. While little of any lasting value appeared on the flip chart sheets during the rest of the session, it was obvious the "class" was catching on fast to the techniques.

A week later we returned to the large room confident the "class," which had seemed so apt, would now be ready to make its practice discussions really fruitful. Our plan was to use the day starting the groups on discussions of ways to make the next year's youth conferences more productive, an exploration that we felt sure would require not only this session but the final one as well.

Unfortunately, the plan went kaput. Only one student and five teachers appeared!

It was a mix-up on dates, not our fault or the group's. The school office had announced the session for two days earlier. Everyone had been there then—except us.

As always, we tried to salvage the situation. Those of us present had a fine discussion about ways to use our methods in the school, and we left consoling ourselves that all was not lost. While the session hadn't produced what we had planned, it *had* been useful, and if everyone would only show for the last session, they still would have a chance for both good small group practice and good thinking about next year's conferences.

Almost everyone did show for the last session on May 24. They not only showed, they produced, helping us condense two sessions of combining training with problem solving into one. (In this we were very much helped by the little group with whom we'd talked during the salvage operation of session number two.) Fulfilling all our hopes, the various students and teachers, taking turns as facilitators, group members and observers, were able to get all this on their flip chart records:

Goal: To make student, teacher, parent conferences so valuable that many students, teachers and parents will want to participate.

Barriers:
1. Human nature—natural resistance to group work.
2. Finding good, realistic topics for discussion.
3. Adequate accommodations for different rooms.
4. Time—groups too large?
5. Refreshments?
6. Frustrations or lack of results of previous conferences.

Recommendations:
1. Determine real problems.
2. Plan ahead for time, accommodations and refreshments.
3. Make sure we follow through with each conference.
   a. Outline what was said.
   b. Follow up recommendations with action.
4. Limit size of group.
   Prepare an agenda—time allotted.

How to overcome barriers:
Make it attractive by
1. sending topics to all participants prior to meeting.
2. topics suggested by students, parents and teachers.
3. publicity in local papers—write-up and photo.
4. limit time for sessions—one coffee break.

5. specific number of recommendations.
6. leader keep written record.
7. limit groups to six to eight.
8. limit total to ten groups.
9. work on makeup of groups.

Action plan:
Planning group.
1. Planning group of Youth Conference:
   —seek volunteers and select students for representation.
   —confer with grade level counselor.
   —confer with co-ordinator of activities.
   —confer with backers to get students to help plan.
2. Planning group meets—division of responsibility:
   —select topics.
   —assemble groups.
   —plan agenda.
   —plan for accommodations.
   —plan for publicity.
   —plan for refreshments.

Evaluation plan:
1. Evaluation sheets from participants to group leader.
2. Conference planners make summary.
3. Report highlights to principal.

Follow-up:
1. Recommendations go to principal.
2. Conference planners meet with principal to discuss recommendations.
3. Report edited results to participants and press.
4. Principal implement edited results.

Unfortunately for our experiment, Mr. Tabor was given a special assignment for the 1972–73 school year, and his temporary successor did not pick up these valuable suggestions.

An Organization Hears from Youth

All these activities underline the fact that youth wants to be heard. In April 1970, when a panel of high school honor students spoke to Loudoun County's Committee of 55, the participating students again stressed this. All six expressed gratitude for the chance given them that evening to tell the hundred adults present how youth felt about a number of topics concerning the county—the generation gap, quality of education, race relations in the high schools, jobs for youth.

The format the Committee of 55 used provided an informative evening and was a first step toward bridging the gap between the participating youth and the adult audience. It was a format that any organization wanting to get a little closer to youth could follow.

Several weeks before the meeting, the Committee asked the principals of each of the county's three high schools to recruit two seniors able to speak for their peers. These six seniors met for several hours with a small program committee of Committee of 55 members to discuss what subjects each student would cover and, in general, with what emphasis. This warm-up session proved invaluable in weeding out repetition and trivial matter. It also put group thinking to work on all the subjects to produce a greater depth and range than one person was likely to achieve.

The students responded enthusiastically to both invitations—for warm-up session and actual meeting. Not only was the Committee of 55 recognizing them as having views that community leaders wanted to hear but it was giving them an opportunity to create better understanding for their whole age group.

The night came, warm with spring, as Committee of 55 members, forgetting topcoats, drove from all parts of the county toward the centrally located attractive stone building of the communications plant where the meeting was to be held. Singly and in pairs and groups, they strolled inside to greet as friends many to whom they once never spoke, claim their name tags and move on, past the courtyard pool, to the auditorium.

On the low platform at the far end of the auditorium, the girl and boy honor students, already in their assigned chairs facing the audience, waited politely for the room to fill.

Then the Committee chairman called the meeting to order. Chatter stopped. Faces turned to the platform with interest and expectation. Many were smiling their desire to be friendly and understanding.

The moderator introduced all the kids and then called on them one by one. Each had ten minutes to speak on his assigned subject.

Speak they did—in brief:

The "generation gap" was a phrase that didn't help the problem. Both sides should try to be with the other more often, really listen to the other. More meetings like this would help.

Education should be more relevant. Seminar groups and parallel reading programs would help. So would study of consumer problems, management, drug abuse, conservation, pollution. Grammar courses in high school should be abolished and more time spent on literature and composition. Vocational programs should be improved.

Many students need employment, especially in the summer, and county employers should place more trust in the teen-age group.

Lack of community swimming pools and public parks and of activity buses contribute to juvenile delinquency. It becomes "something to do" to fill a vacuum.

There would be no problems of race if the kids were not fed prejudice at home.

Ecology is a major concern of youth. Every possible step should be taken to improve the environment.

The moderator divided the audience into buzz groups of about six persons each to discuss what they had heard and formulate a group question for one or several of the panelists. Then, after ten minutes, the moderator called on the buzz groups one at a time, and the spokesman in each group asked its question. When all the group questions had been answered, individuals asked questions.

"How bad is the drug problem in our high schools?"

"Plenty bad," said one panelist. "Marijuana especially."

"Drugs are easy to get," said another panelist.

"Some do. Some don't," said another. "It depends on the group you're in and how you feel about your life. I feel good about my life. I want to make it count, and drugs don't help."

"Neither do cigarettes and liquor," said another, looking hard at the audience.

Several cigarettes were snuffed out.

"Yeah," said another panelist. "I mean, here are somebody's mother and father sitting there, a cigarette in one hand and a highball in the other, saying, 'Promise us you won't have anything to do with drugs.' It doesn't make sense and the kid knows it."

Audience interest was great. Individuals were still popping to their feet when the meeting time was over, and the moderator had to call a halt.

A splendid evening, both kids and adults agreed. There was a great deal of animated talk in small groups afterward. Too bad there couldn't be more such meetings. Too bad the students' *own* parents hadn't been there—and youth as well as adults in the audience, too. Too bad there couldn't be a series of informal meetings during which youth and adults might counsel with each other. We of the Community Education Program felt our usual consultants' frustration—if only our team could move in and organize such meetings, not just try to induce the people with the problem to do it.

Fortunately, the Committee of 55 thoroughly appreciated the value of their 1970 meeting with youth and planned another for the spring of 1971—this time with parents of the student participants urged to attend and also all interested students and *their* parents.

The approach was more inclusive, too. Student committees, not the principals, of the three high schools selected the panelists and deliberately sought a wider representation of student viewpoint.

The result was an even livelier Committee of 55 session. In appearance, the students were a study in contrasts. One boy had long golden hair, another a crew cut, another, a black, a modified Afro. (The fourth boy, somewhere between, with moderate-length dark hair and a dark tie, like a young lawyer, turned out to be the most radical in viewpoint.) The two girls also differed greatly—the red-headed vivacious girl-next-door type and the quiet-spoken, sleek-haired world traveler with great dark eyes.

These student panelists politely but firmly disagreed with one another again and again, expressing opinions that ranged from surprisingly conservative through middle ground to decidedly left. In fact, about the only thing all had in common was great likability and sincerity.

"It was refreshing," as one member put it, "to find the kids *don't* all think alike."

And another said approvingly, "That was the real Committee of 55 approach, getting all viewpoints."

"We must have this every year," said another.

And another.

So the Committee of 55 made plans to make the youth meeting an annual one, and we are glad. We wish such meetings would be held at least once a year in every community across the land. Any organization with members willing to listen could sponsor them. We recommend that such an organization hold a warm-up session, open the meeting to the public, encourage youth as well as adults to attend, and divide the audience into buzz groups for group questions, letting individual questions follow.

An Effort That Failed in One Way (But Succeeded in Another)

We include the following account of working with youth because it illustrates the fact that even when unexpected hurdles keep a group from reaching its announced goal, that group may look back and see that moving out of apathy was worthwhile even though it failed in its original intent.

We never did establish contact (except perhaps very indirectly) with the kids who were causing the trouble in the Syphax apartments back in the fall of 1966 when the Syphaxes asked for our help. We accomplished a few other things, however.

Near Bailey's Cross Roads, outside Washington, D.C., is a small black community settled long ago when the surrounding area was still rural. Large trees and old, inexpensive single family houses on attractive narrow lots line the blacktopped streets. In the mid-1960s, suburban growth began to close in on the settlement, and the Syphaxes, who are black, built several small three-story walk-up apartments close enough to its heart to dominate it.

The apartments were occupied by blacks. Many of the tenants, the military families especially, took good care of the property, but others were destructive—especially the kids. The Syphaxes had tried to solve the problem by evicting destructive families, but some were troublesome to budge and others, equally destructive, kept moving in.

Mrs. Syphax told of liquor sales and traffic in stolen goods in the apartments. There were crap games with many outsiders. Non-residents were using the laundry rooms and other apartment facilities. The manager said good tenants were intimidated and afraid to report specifics to him. There were many rumors of narcotics.

To make matters worse, trouble wasn't confined to the apartments. The old guard in the older black community resented the new buildings and the trouble and noise they brought. The owners and well-behaved tenants naturally were concerned about this resentment, the well-behaved tenants, of course, feeling it unjustified in their case.

Our team explored the situation with a group of people who seemed to be keys to the situation: Mrs. Syphax; the resident manager of the apartments; some of the residents; people from the community Civic Association; people from the Community Action Program which had an office in the apartments and contact with the hard-core troublemakers; workers in that area in basic education, and the day care center.

These people decided that two different groups should be formed to attack the problem from two different directions, a sort of pincers movement. We would work with both groups:

1. With the Community Action staff to explore ways that staff,

through its contacts with hard-core people, could help solve the problem.

2. With the community group, which we already had formed, to train the existing leaders in more effective leadership and in problem-solving techniques while working toward converting troublesome tenants into more civic-minded citizens and promoting better community understanding.

Alas, we never had a chance to use plan number one. Before even one meeting with the Community Action staff could be set up, the CAP office fell apart with internal strife that resulted in the firing of two key people. There was so much chaos we never could get CAP co-operation, and our hope of reaching the hard-core troublemakers was doomed. Only CAP had the contacts to reach the people we had set out to reach. When we lost their help, we had to chalk up complete failure for that half of the program.

The other half went beautifully from the beginning. In October of 1966, we conducted leadership training sessions during which we developed goals for community leadership.† The setting for these sessions was the basement of a small frame church. The basement was large since it covered the same area as the church itself, and we gathered together in one section. High windows let in little light, and the pipes made a network over our heads. We were too engrossed to care.

In November, we learned that the Civic Association had few members who lived in the apartments, and the group talked of the value of drawing into the Civic Association the people who lived there. Then we role-played ways to approach these people.‡

Next we discovered that the Senior Civic Association had started a Junior Civic Association, but that the members of this younger group were now turned off because the seniors didn't pay any attention to them. Our community group agreed that the seniors should do something immediately to mend the rift, and the senior group agreed to invite the juniors to the next senior meeting, let the kids sound off and then calmly start exploring problems.

The day after the meeting in early December, we called the president of the Civic Association. How did it go? "Fine," he said. "We kept our cool and when the kids calmed down, we planned two joint projects. We're going to have a joint paper drive and the proceeds

† See Appendix, Chapter 2, for a list of the goals developed.
‡ See Appendix, Chapter 2, for the suggestions to interviewers.

will go to the church. And we're going to have a community Christmas tree, with us buying it and the kids decorating it."

We saw Mrs. Syphax a month later. She was ecstatic, said her problem was solved. After the January Civic Association meeting, we again called the association president, who reported that the seniors and juniors were still getting along fine. The paper drive and Christmas tree were both successes, and another paper drive was planned. There didn't seem more that the community group wanted so we moved on to other matters with a partial feeling of accomplishment. At least, we had greatly increased communication in the community, we had helped mend a rift between generations and, incidentally, we had given some training in leadership and in useful methods of problem solving and group participation.

We had failed, however, to establish contact with the real troublemakers. The kids of the Junior Civic Association were the "squares" who related with their elders in the Civic Association. They had been disaffected to be sure, but they hadn't been the cause of any major problems.

In the spring, we began to hear rumors of trouble in the apartments and trouble of various sorts persisted, but our program never got reinvolved. The Syphaxes solved part of the problem by putting in a swimming pool, and the Civic Associations worked together to solve other parts. They organized basketball and baseball games, skating trips. The county got into the act, too, turning the playground of a pre-integration Negro school into a park and opening a small recreation center with a full-time staff. How much our efforts had to do with all this, we're not sure, but we think they helped. In problem-solving work, it's important to remember that goals are seldom reached in one step. The important thing is to start toward the goals and get into the constructive thought and action that leads to worthy change.

Letting Youth Help Train Chaperones

We find that the best results on all problems come only when we include people who are causing them. This happened successfully in the fall of 1967 when the director of the Vienna, Virginia, Teen Center asked us to help write guidelines for chaperones and then conduct training sessions in using them. From the beginning, the youth of the center were in on the planning and as a result, *with* the project all the way. It had to be so. Nothing can make or break a teen activity as fast as the adults in authority. If the kids, themselves, have helped set the guidelines for these adults, they respond with respect and support. Otherwise . . . well, who wants a teen center either empty or in such dangerous chaos there's nothing to do but call the cops?

Vienna, an old rural town, has grown rapidly in recent years into a thriving suburb, but most of the old part, with tall trees surrounding rural style houses on well-kept back streets, still has a turn-of-the-century feel. The streets with heavy traffic, though, have a run-down look. An old white frame house on one of these streets had been converted into the Teen Center.

Helping the center with its chaperone-training project was one of our favorite endeavors. The adults who ran the center and the kids who used it were a warm, intensely alive, experimental, likable bunch. Joe Killeen, founder and director, and his wife, Kathleen, were obviously more than mere authorities in the kids' eyes. Kathleen was Center Mama, understanding but firm. Joe was the big brother or father image, a guy to love and respect, who knew all about the ghetto and the drug and crime scene, had even served time before he decided to go straight. Joe made going straight look attractive to even the toughest kid.

Tough kids indeed were at the center. Some were dropouts. Some had police records. About three fourths were black and among the blacks were more boys than girls. In the white quarter, females greatly outnumbered males. Very few of the two hundred or so members related to "the establishment."

The place always seemed to be full of motion and racket. Players and watchers moved constantly around the pool table. The jukebox sprayed out ear-shattering tunes. Kids wandered about noisily, borrowing dimes from each other to use in the vending machines.

There was psycho-drama, conducted by one of two psychodramatists on Monday nights, to help the kids get rid of some of their hostilities short of mayhem. Court was on Wednesday nights for members to bring up complaints against other members, and while the kids could dance to the jukebox any night, they "made a thing of it" on Friday and Saturday nights. By agreement among themselves, Friday night was "folk night" and for the whites. Saturday night was "soul night" and for the blacks. The kids devised the separate black and white dance plan because of space not race. The living room of the old house just wasn't big enough for everyone to dance at once.

The night Martin Luther King died, however, they tried. It was "folk night" at the center but the white kids, wanting to show their sympathy, went out to round up the black kids, bring them to the center and convert "folk night" into "soul night." As Joe Killeen enjoyed telling us, Vienna was the only community in Northern Virginia that didn't have a problem with its blacks that night.

The kids were proud of their center and, for the most part, extremely careful not to do anything to reflect on its "image." Anyone who did was likely to be in disgrace with the group, and this peer group pressure was worth more than cordons of police at keeping the kids in line and getting across lessons of acceptable and unacceptable behavior.

For example, at one time an outside group asked the center to send several of its teen-agers to describe its activities to people discussing youth problems at a large suburban church. The kids were flattered that their center had been chosen as an example of effective action, and their thoughtfully selected spokesmen made careful plans to sell the center.

All was going beautifully at the meeting when a dreadful thing occurred. While the spokesmen were in front of the audience doing a great job (especially one who could have rivaled Bill Cosby for wit and charm), a couple of others from the center who had come along for the ride were in back of the audience undoing all the good. Something about the white man's church sent them berserk and, with magic markers, they began writing obscenities on the walls leading to the meeting room. "You wouldn't believe what obscenities," according to Joe Killeen.

The others from the center discovered what had happened. Horror-stricken, they raced to the men's room for soap and paper towels to try to wash off the offending marks. As people began to leave the meeting, they tried to cover the marks with their bodies. They were furious, too, willing to kill these "stupid apes" who had so disgraced them all.

When scrubbing wouldn't bring the walls back to their previous purity, the church figured out a bill for repainting and the kids at the center assessed all their members to pay it. The offenders got the message. What they had done had hurt everybody at the center and everybody had to suffer for it.

There was a happy ending when the church, figuring the lesson had been learned, returned the money for painting to the center.

Upstairs at the center, in what had been the master bedroom, the pool table reigned. There were three other small rooms upstairs, and in one of these, we held our conferences about how to train chaperones. The room was just big enough for a ring of chairs around a table about three by five feet and we put our flip chart in a doorway because there wasn't room for it in a corner. Officially, the group consisted of a staff person, one of the psycho-dramatists, two people who had served as chaperones and two teen-agers. We say officially, because other teen-agers continually darted into the room, listened for a while, contributed their thoughts to what was going on the flip chart, then darted out to be replaced by others. At times, six or eight sat on chair arms or on the floor or didn't sit at all. With this constant turnover, was a background of shouts from the pool room and tunes from the jukebox. It was pure chaos, very different from the atmosphere in which we ordinarily work, but we found it fun and were delighted to have so many teen-agers participating, getting the feeling that the result would be their own and not something imposed on them.

We held three sessions, each lasting about two hours. Generally, we were trying to answer three questions:

1. How should a chaperone handle himself?
2. How should we go about getting chaperones for training and regular participation?
3. What would be the best way to train the chaperones?

What was produced, we think, was good. We knew what sort of chaperones the kids would support—those who would join in the activities and know how to use the kids to help control trouble-makers.

With the guidelines ready, the center issued a press release hoping to attract volunteers.*

The staff and the kids also threw the challenge directly. They talked to parents, to the social action groups of churches, to blacks from the community at large. It was a wise move. While press releases reach the many, the person-to-person approach can be concentrated on the most likely. Even these most likely people are much more inclined to respond with a "yes, I'll do it" if they are personally approached. It is much easier to say "no" to a press release than to a person who is looking at you, making you feel singled out, personally needed.

* See Appendix, Chapter 2, for news release.

Soon, with a handful of volunteers, we were holding training sessions in the basement of a nearby church. The training, mostly by role playing† put the trainees through situations likely to confront them at the center. Playing the role of center kids were youths who had been center members. Most had just turned twenty and been "graduated," since top age for center participation was nineteen.

These youths played typical problem situations they themselves had witnessed or, sometimes, even helped make. Chaperone trainees acted out ways to cope with kids trying to come in with pot or beer and over-age youths trying to start trouble.

Playing an over-age youth one night was a big, bulky black, recent center "graduate," who brushed right past the much smaller white man training to be a chaperone, entered the center and began talking noisily with friends there. It was the future chaperone's assignment to get him out. He kept telling the big youth that he was over-age and would have to leave. The youth kept ignoring him. The future chaperone, actually a sweet, mild man, got more and more flustered. "You mean you're not going to leave?" he demanded.

The big youth, looking down at the chaperone, replied, "No, I'm not going to leave. You going to put me out, baby?"

Another chaperone trainee tried with the same results. The youth got more and more insolent and abusive. Both trainees ended by calling the cops, exactly the wrong thing to endear them to center members.

Joe Killeen cooled the situation by asking the invader, "Having trouble, man?" That friendly question, asked in the mildest possible manner, got a reasonable answer and led to a reasonable discussion. The intruder finally agreed to leave.

Joe was the source of many valuable pointers. For instance, to enter the center, people had to go through a door at the top of narrow steps. If the chaperone stood on the top step, he could put a knee in a face if necessary to keep someone out. What's more, he looked tall to people coming up those steps. He loomed over them.

"It's easier to keep the wrong people from ever entering than to get them out once they're in" was one of the lessons.

There were arguments, too, that would speak to the over-age and the rule breakers as well as bring reinforcements from the peer

† For more information about role playing, see Chapter 16, "Help for Continuing Groups."

group. "What you trying to do, Duke? You trying to get this place shut down on these kids?" And when the peer group realized that the misbehavior, whatever it was, threatened the existence of the center and their good times there, they would gang up and do the chaperone's job for him.

Chaperones, during the training, learned to force responsibility on center members. Questions like these helped:

"Who let him in?"

"What are *you* going to do about him?"

Situation after situation was enacted—the cops coming after some kid or accusing the center of hiding some kid in trouble, or a youth flirting with a female chaperone while her husband (also a chaperone) pondered how to act.

Reversing roles proved very helpful. The kids, while playing chaperones, could demonstrate the sort of talk, attitude and action that would get the desired results with them.

All the trainees survived the tough preparation—except one. She was a white mother with two small children. She was also only twenty-six years old and attractive. When one of the black youths responded (as some kid at the center was sure to, sooner or later) by putting his arms around her and kissing her, she was totally embarrassed. She ran out of the room and never returned.

Role playing often can eliminate in advance those who are not fitted for a particular role—or committed enough to learn to be. It can save future embarrassment for these square pegs in round holes. It also can save future woe for the cause you are trying to serve.

The rest of our student chaperones practiced coping with every variety of situation. When they went to work at the teen center, they already had tasted experience and success. And, once at the center, they had the reward of seeing practice success repeated in actual situations.

Especially for people who are going to work outside their usual experience, preparation through well-directed role playing, with the opposite roles played by those well acquainted with the potential situations that will face the trainee, is unbeatable. It enables trainees to test various approaches realistically and without loss of face when they fail. Moreover, each trainee learns from the others' experiences.

Also useful in effective role playing is reversing of roles. When the trainee steps into the shoes of the sort of person he will be confronting, he gains understanding of that person and his reactions. At the same time, his opposite, now in his shoes, can demonstrate what *he* thinks will work. It brings an added illumination neither lectures nor discussion can get across. It is very satisfying, when training people through role playing, to see that abrupt dawning on faces, the brightness of a wanted mental breakthrough, that look that says, "So that's it! Why, sure, sure. I see. I get it. Of course. Of course."

3

A MEETING ON JOBS—AND WHERE IT LED

In every conference the Program team conducted that summer of 1967, sooner or later, and usually sooner, people raised the problem of school dropouts. What to do about these young people, sixteen to twenty-one years old, who were unemployed and poorly equipped for employment? Something had to be done. It was a question not only of combating poverty but potential crime, drug abuse, racial unrest, rioting.

Many Northern Virginia agencies, civic groups and individuals were concerned with the problem and making efforts to alleviate it. But these efforts were not co-ordinated. Communication among those trying to help was on a fragmentary now-and-then basis. The needed exchange of information and unifying effort toward specific goals just wasn't there.

The time seemed overdue for a comprehensive approach to the problem. The Program team got in touch with Huston Martin, then Co-ordinator of Human Resources for the state office of the Virginia Employment Commission. With his support, we began working with concerned agencies and organizations, and with their help, recruited a planning and advisory group to determine the best approach.*

* This advisory group included a representative from the Alexandria branch of the Urban League, the chief of the Guidance Department of

The group worked long, hard and well to set up a large, all-day meeting for Saturday, April 6, 1968. Its purpose: to study job problems of Northern Virginia people, aged sixteen to twenty-one.

Compiling a list of others to invite, the planning group included people from every type of agency involved in preparing youth for jobs or in helping young people and employers get together, personnel people of companies which needed employees and people sixteen to twenty-one who needed jobs. The planners also analyzed various services the sixteen–twenty-one group needed and prepared an outline of background information for participants.

The invitation, enclosing the agenda and the outline, was mailed on March 22 and contained these two paragraphs:

We are inviting, as participants in the study, people from every type of agency involved in helping young people and employers get together, personnel people of companies which need employees, and people 16–21 who need jobs. We believe that the study will help all of them by improving their understanding of each other's problems, strengthening communication among them and providing both new and better ways of helping people qualify for jobs, get them, keep them, and grow with them.

We plan to establish a study group for each of seven services these people need: preliminary counseling, training, job counseling, day care, health, financial affairs and job development. We have outlined briefly, as jumping off points for the study groups, some of the ground each might cover. These outlines, however, were intended only to clarify our own thinking, and the study groups will be free to explore whatever ground they think may be useful. [For the agenda and outline, see Appendix, Chapter 3, "Advance Information for April 6, 1968, Conference."]

Our plan for facilitators was to use members of the planning group, each assigned to one of the subgroups. Although there were no written agreements, each facilitator expected to be part of the continuing effort this one-day meeting was intended to kick off, staying

the Arlington Public Schools, the director of Fairfax County Public Welfare, the executive directors of the Alexandria, Arlington and Fairfax Community Action Programs, the director of the Vienna Teen Council, representatives of Alexandria's Department of Vocational Rehabilitation, Falls Church's Juvenile Court and the area's Basic Education Program, the superintendent of Prince William County's Welfare Department and three officials of the local offices of the Virginia Employment Commission.

with his subgroup, sparking and helping it through as many more meetings as were necessary for the subgroup to reach its goals. It was a good plan, with only one major weakness, and it worked in a couple of instances. It would have worked for all subgroups if— but we'll go into that later.

Getting Started

Well before the appointed hour of 9:30 A.M. on that Saturday, several of the facilitators, a few others of the planning group and our Project team arrived at the conference site, a school cafeteria, to make preparations. The scene was soon frenzied. One man was plugging in the coffee maker and unwrapping plastic cups. One woman was unpacking lunch boxes and another was setting up the registration table with lists of invitees and adhesive-backed name tags. We were answering questions of "What shall we do about this?" and "Where do you want that?" and greeting early arrivals and enlisting helpers to affix a pad of four or five flip chart sheets with masking tape to the wall beside each of the tables we were to use for the discussions.

This Saturday was April 6, 1968, two days after Dr. Martin Luther King was assassinated. Riots were still going on in Washington and the black sections in Northern Virginia were tense. Our two black facilitators were engaged in more urgent duties. Nothing to do, here at the last minute, but fill their places with other planning group members who were willing but untrained.

Perhaps because of the tension attendance was exceptionally good, and the subgroup tables quickly filled. Each group included two teenagers—some white, some black, some girls, some boys. We had avoided confusion by pre-assigning participants to their subgroups according to their professional expertise or interest. Since each was wearing a name tag, necessary introductions were quickly over, and those not good at remembering names needed only a glance to say, "What do you think, Bill?" or "I agree with Mr. Jones." People everywhere were meeting others they had heard about and long wanted to know. This establishing of communication alone would have made the meeting worthwhile.

It was a good morning for most groups. They tackled their assigned work with interest, spreading needed information as they explored their subjects and set their goals. A couple of groups ran into trouble, however, largely because their substitute facilitators didn't understand their job.

In one group, one participant repeated over and over again that nothing could be done and this effort was a waste of time. Neither the substitute facilitator nor the other participants knew how to handle him, so that group's effort could amount to little. This can happen in any meeting tackling any problem and there *are* ways to handle it. One is to give the troublemaker a specific observer assignment which flatters his ego yet removes him from the discussion. For other ways, see Form 7, "Some Clues to Facilitating," and Form 8, "Cutting in on a Long-Winded Speaker" (Appendix, Chapter 14).

The afternoon, during which subgroups reported and then received comments and suggestions from all the other groups, went well, too. The enthusiasm of other groups seemed to sweep into even the bogged-down ones and all set times and places to meet again and proceed with their work.

With one exception, these groups did meet during the rest of April, May and early June although attendance at most of the meetings was lower than on the opening day and in some was only a fraction of the original group. Even so, a lot of useful work was accomplished, especially work of compiling needed background information, discovering who was already doing what and assessing problems. We had high hopes that all this would lead to useful action and set a meeting for all participants for June 18, mailing out an interim report on the various groups at the same time as the meeting announcement. (For examples from the "Interim Report," see that title in the Appendix, Chapter 3.)

Appraising Progress

Attendance at the June meeting for all participants was good enough, but we sensed a weariness and frustration among a lot of the people, a feeling of being tired of all these meetings, of not really getting anywhere, of what's the use? It didn't take long during the small group discussions that day to realize where the fault lay.

Most facilitators were carrying on because they had said they would and they weren't the sort of people to renege, much as they would have liked to be free of it all now. They were planning group members who weren't intensely interested in their groups' subjects and hadn't sparked the groups as we had planned.

That was our major mistake, using some facilitators who weren't enthusiastic enough about their subjects. They didn't transmit to the group members the zeal needed to get assignments carried out, to add other members who could fill information or skill gaps, or to provide challenging summaries of progress (or lack of it). (See Chapter 16, "Help for Continuing Groups," for suggestions on how to help a group keep going strongly.)

We were discouraged. It had seemed an excellent approach to an important problem, but it hadn't developed as we had envisioned. We felt that if we ourselves had worked with each group things would have been better. For one thing, we would have been enthusiastic and willing to plug hard. For another thing, we were old hands at facilitating. But our role is to stimulate needed activities, not conduct them.

Fortunately, there were a few bright spots. One young woman in the day care group, not the facilitator, radiated enthusiasm and hope. She already was working with a day care center and knew a great deal about it. We asked her if she would take over that effort. She said "sure" and the result in a few months was the creation of the Northern Virginia Day Care Association, which has been very useful in helping members share solutions to operating problems and in giving guidance to groups forming new centers.

Job development, too, seemed very much alive that day in June and it, too, continued during the summer. The Arlington and Fairfax County Community Action Programs (with people from Alexandria's CAP frothing at the mouth because their power structure wouldn't let them join) provided the breakthrough when they persuaded the Office of Economic Opportunity to provide funds and a special employee to help them find jobs for a number of hard-core blacks sixteen to twenty-one.

Another bright spot. The job coaching group displayed not only enthusiasm but confidence. If only the job development group would come up with some jobs for hard-core youths, they said, they would train the coaches.

Job Coach Training

We asked the director of the Arlington CAP, a personable black man in his forties and highly regarded for his work with hard-core people, whether middle-class whites could successfully coach young blacks.

He replied, "They can if I train them."

What he meant was that they could succeed if they had tough, realistic training from someone with an intimate knowledge of the hard core. In preparation for that training we developed with him a set of guidelines for training job coaches and job counselors. (See

Appendix, Chapter 3, "Job Coaching and Job Counseling, Training Guidelines.")

Knowing he already was overworked and fearing there might be times when he couldn't be on hand, we recruited three others who knew the hard core well to join the "faculty" for our training course. Backup. Insurance. A good thing, too, for the CAP director actually was able to attend only two of seven of our training sessions.

By the time we received news that seventeen job coaches were needed, we had set to work to recruit middle-class whites for job coach trainees, each to work on a one-to-one basis with a hard-core black. We talked to our job coach study group; to a number of church groups who had dedicated themselves to action, not just talk and donations; to people who had supported Resurrection City† in Washington the summer before, and, after it folded, helped provide care for the stranded; to known civil rights and anti-poverty workers. We stressed that, of course, there was nothing new about job coaches but the idea of using volunteers for this work instead of professionals was new in our area. Here was a chance to be a pioneer.

The list of interested people grew. In fact, thirty "students," twenty-nine of them white, appeared at the YMCA in one of Arlington's black neighborhoods for our first training session in late January 1969, thirteen more than we had been told to train. Should we set up some criteria that would eliminate the excess? No, we decided, suspecting that some had come only out of curiosity and would drop out as the training progressed. The course would be tough. Let survival be the only screening device. Meanwhile, at this first session, we would use all available heads to help us outline the work that should be covered in the training.

We divided the thirty into small groups, asking them to talk about their concerns as potential job coaches. We then organized the material they produced into the following lists which provided the basis for training, largely by role playing, in future sessions:

Making Contacts
1. Where are you going to meet this person?
    —Not supposed to in your own home? May be tempting to meet in own home—in drugstores—not about to go out to a movie or bowling—have a husband and children—Can you talk to them on the phone? Do we have to spend a lot on personal contact?

† In the summer of 1968 a poor people's march to Washington occurred. Resurrection City was the tent camp erected to give them shelter.

2.   Breaking the racial barrier.
3.   They have a feeling of why are we qualified to help them—resentment.

Coach-Employee Difficulties
1.   What if there is difficulty in understanding the employee? Communication?
2.   Communication—especially with the very reserved.
3.   Reluctance to reveal real problems.
4.   When you aren't on the same social level (example: person had a cleaning woman who used to keep coming up to chat —and for clothing and money), how do you disengage yourself?
5.   Black militant using militancy as basis for all problems, answers, difficulties.
6.   Lack of employee co-operation with coach.

Coach-Employee Involvement
1.   Getting too involved with employee emotionally.
2.   Problems recurrent from development of personal friendship.
3.   How do you help the employee help himself instead of "giving" the wrong way?
4.   When you are sympathetic toward the employee, how do you disengage yourself gracefully?
5.   Backing off, being unable to meet a need.

Employee's Personal and Family Problems
1.   How deep do you go into personal problems—i.e., sick child?
2.   Family involvement, how far?
3.   Drugs, drinking.
4.   Psychological problems—knowing degrees in which to involve ourselves.

Employee-Employer Difficulties
1.   Proper dress with employers and employees.
2.   How handle employee's dissatisfaction with the type of job he qualifies for?
3.   How handle gripes that are not legitimate?
4.   Insurmountable attitude in supervisors.

The next session proved that we were right not to have worried about numbers the first time. Only eighteen were back. It was an excellent session, however, that set the pattern for all other sessions. First came role playing, then brief discussion of the truths unveiled, the lessons learned, with use of the flip chart, of course, to record highlights. These included some of the many barriers between coaches and employees and suggestions for handling them.

On we went, through six sessions, and what a cast for the little illuminating dramas we enacted! Playing the hard-core youths whom our job coach trainees would be trying to help were the three backup "faculty" members we had recruited. These three knew how hard-core youth could be expected to talk, think, feel, react in the very situations most likely to arise. One was a white ex-convict, ex-holdup man who had organized and run a successful, integrated teen center. What's more, he was superb at role playing. (See the story of training chaperones at the Vienna Teen Center, Chapter 2, "Approaches to Problems of Youth.") The other two were blacks, employed at the time in poverty programs, but both one-time high school dropouts and graduates of the ghetto. These three never failed to play it "like it was."

Training session after training session, in one projected job coaching situation after another, the trainees acted out their approaches and our three hard-core actors acted out the reactions these approaches would bring. They were tough and real, pulling no punches. The role playing showed that working with hard-core was going to be difficult. Hard-core youth was not often reasonable, pleasant, appreciative.

Gwen, for instance, who spoke the ghetto's salty language, gave one middle-class white matron a jolting indoctrination. Gwen was playing a high school dropout with a job. The matron playing her job coach was nervous and unhappy about Gwen's attitude. Gwen retaliated by calling her a "honky bitch."

The white matron was even whiter.

"That's what you'll be up against," Mac, the other black hard-core actor commented. "Be glad she didn't call you a mother-fucker."

So it went. We could see people changing, more understanding appearing in their faces. The heat was too much for several more and by "graduation" we were down to ten, eight ready to be job coaches and two ready to be job counselors. We decided the best way for these graduates to meet their "clients," the people they were to coach, was to give a party for coaches and clients.

These graduating coaches were well trained, capable of working with understanding, intelligence and patience with hard-core youth. Our training sessions had been a success.

Meanwhile, the job arrangements department was unintentionally letting us down. One employer had his own training program and that took care of the people hired to work for him. The remaining six or seven "clients," five of whom came to our party to meet our coaches (coaches trained to work with the roughest and toughest), turned out to be not hard-core at all. They were people who had been employed before and who were now being given upgrade training for computer jobs. Disappointment among some of our coaches was pretty evident. We had to fight disappointment ourselves.

How often it happens. One part of a plan comes off beautifully. People give their all and reach their objectives. But the overall goal is doomed because some other vital part of the plan is muffed or carried to an unplanned conclusion. All one can do is salvage what can be salvaged. In this case, half a dozen of our coaches actually went to work—and learned that they weren't really needed. All of them could only console themselves with the fact they had learned a lot and the thought that someday they might be called upon to use their hard-won education in other activities. Who could foresee when it might prove valuable?

Using Our Experience

We still like the idea of a large conference on a large problem sparking continuing efforts by study groups, each devoted to solving a part of that overall problem. Our next opportunity to use this kind of study came with the Fairfax County Goals Program (Chapter 6, "Tackling Problems of Community Growth"), and with it we learned how such a comprehensive effort can work successfully. For it to succeed, each group needs interested participants, with a dedicated and enthusiastic leader, one able to spark his group, be willing to ride herd on it if necessary and to see the program through. Beyond that, there must be a devoted sponsoring group or organization which can keep the study groups going well and in touch with each other so one doesn't let others down.

4

A SUCCESSFUL SERIES OF
JOB FAIRS*

We of George Mason College's Community Education Program had
no idea of going into the employment field when we met, in the board
room of a Leesburg, Virginia, bank in February 1969, with a little
group of Loudoun County citizens interested in discussing the problems of Loudoun blacks.

A conversation with Clarence Mitchell of the NAACP national
office had sparked the meeting. Mr. Mitchell had talked with us about
the migration of blacks to the District from rural areas, including the
rural areas of our region. This influx, he said, was only compounding
the many problems already existing in the Washington ghetto. The
greatest help we could give would be to improve conditions for the
rural blacks of our region so that they would be less tempted to move
to Washington, full of hope, of course, but, for the most part,
doomed to suffer the tribulations of urban poverty and overcrowding
that he knew so well.

Since Loudoun County was the most rural county in our region,
we decided it was the best place for the Program to explore ways
to make home more attractive to black citizens.

* A 1970 publication of the School of Continuing Education of the
University of Virginia, "People Needing Jobs—Jobs Needing People," contained some of the material in this chapter.

The First Fair—How It Started

Our Loudoun consultant, who knows the leadership of the county's various segments, interested ten key people in coming to consult with us. These ten were all known to be concerned with improving the conditions of black citizens.†

We were there before the first participant so no one would arrive without a welcome. We seated the arrivals around a large table where every one could see everyone else, each with a name tag upon which his name was printed in magic marker in letters large enough for all to see. When all were there, we asked each person to tell who he was and why he was interested in this particular meeting.

The discussion began with a quick listing on the flip chart of the matters of concern to those present. Of these, the group agreed that Job Opportunities and Transportation should receive their first attention. Talk then concentrated on that subject.

Time ran out with only token discussion of the other matters of concern. The participants asked the Loudoun County consultant to set up another meeting for them, plus several other people the group felt should become involved.

Three potential employers and two more black leaders attended the second meeting of the group in March. The discussion, quickly focusing on jobs and proving extremely creative, led directly to plans for a Job Opportunity Night to be held in less than a month and to demonstrate that Loudoun blacks could get jobs with a future while still living in Loudoun County. It was a first for the county and a plan that could be duplicated anywhere in the country.

Negro members of the planning group were to make arrangements for use of the black community center in the town of Middleburg for the night of April 21. They were also to get out as many of their people as they could, people needing jobs or better jobs. Meantime, the Community Education Program was to invite several

† They included a black builder and civic leader; the vice-chairman of the Board of Supervisors, who was also serving as chairman of the county's Community Action Committee; a Catholic priest also serving as chairman of the county's Ministerial Association; the League of Women Voters' representative on the Community Action Committee, who also had been active for years in the Human Relations Council; the black president of a group working for low cost housing in the county; a Methodist minister serving as co-ordinator of the Loudoun Methodist Reconciliation Projects; and a woman realtor and civic leader who had organized the effort for low cost housing.

employers in addition to those already represented, employers receptive to the idea of hiring blacks and with jobs to offer. At the meeting, each employer representative would make a brief statement about his company, its current job opportunities and possible future needs. Then each employer representative would take a position in an assigned part of the room to talk to people interested in working for his company.

It was a simple plan that we felt would work, provided:

1. Enough unemployed and underemployed blacks could be persuaded it was on the level and worth the effort it would take for them to come.

2. Enough potential employers would be there to greet them and make concrete offers.

The First Fair—Carrying On

Fortunately, both the black leaders who assumed the task of getting black job seekers to come and we of the Community Education Program were willing to work hard for success. The black leaders spent hours on the telephone, drove untold miles to spread the word of the meeting, organized car pools. White members of the group pitched in, too, to inform the black community and arrange transportation.

We of the Program also were busy. First we determined which of the employers in the county and in the areas toward Washington, but near enough for commuting, actually had equal job opportunities to offer. Next we wrote letters of invitation to these employers. Then, as the meeting time drew near, we telephoned to make sure how many actually would appear. Of twelve big employers invited, eight assured us they would be there and gladly.

We prepared signs in magic marker with the various employers' names and affixed these signs with masking tape around the room so each employer could have a station for talking with people. We also made name tags for employer representatives so job seekers could quickly identify them.

The big night came. The planning group members were there early, an anxious little black and white knot of people, watching the entrances. No one really dared expect more than a small gathering. Our Program team tried to cushion us all for the disappointment. "Well," we said, "if almost nobody comes, we'll have a meeting on why almost nobody came and what we can do about it."

Fortunately, there was no need for such a meeting. People were soon hurrying in out of the rainy night, employer representatives and over ninety people interested in jobs.

We got the white men in their executive suits up onto the wooden platform and showed them their signs taped to the walls around the room, signs with the names Melpar, DECO-Westinghouse, Drug Fair, IBM, Highway Department, Levitt, Atlantic Research, Farrington.

"This is great," one of them said, "really great. I'm glad I brought some application forms with me."

"So'm I," said another. "Look at all those people."

To understate it, we were proud. All their company advertising hadn't reached Loudoun blacks but here was a roomful and more coming.

"Man, we're really out tonight," commented one of the blacks just arriving. "I didn't think we'd get half so many out." And then, as he saw the men on the platform and the signs around the walls: "Looks as if they're out, too. And the man told me about the meeting said they'd do more than just talk to us. Said they'd really offer some jobs."

That was exactly what the men on the platform were waiting to do.

We opened the meeting, explaining that each employer representative was to be given five minutes (to be timed with a kitchen timer) to tell what jobs his firm had open now or would soon have open, what starting salaries would be, what qualifications were required, what training, benefits and chances for advancement would be offered. Then we called on the employer representatives in the order of their acceptance of our invitation, and as each spoke, wrote on a flip chart sheet the highlights of what he was saying. A couple of our Program staff members took these sheets and taped them by the appropriate employer's sign already affixed to the walls.

The people applauded each speaker. When the sales talks were over, they hurried to one station or another. For an hour and a half the interviews went on. Then the room began to empty, but eighteen people had been hired, eighteen people who had needed work or better work now could look forward to a brighter future. (And later hirings from contacts made that night would raise the total to thirty within a few weeks.)

The Second Fair—Planning

It was a heady thing for our little group of planners. We met two days later for evaluation and decided to do it again. There were several reasons, we felt, to plan a second Job Opportunity Night:

1. Loudoun County covers 516 square miles with Middleburg at one edge, and many people needing employment or better employment had been unable to get to the first meeting.
2. Too many people had not even known about the first session. Publicity had been limited to word-of-mouth and a notice in the black social column of the county paper, to which most blacks needing jobs didn't subscribe.
3. A number of potential employers had not even been asked to the first session. Emphasis had been on big employers and those known to be committed to offering equal opportunity.
4. Whites needing jobs, and there were many in the county, had not been asked to the first Opportunity Night because it had been an outgrowth of discussions on problems of blacks. Yet a second night could benefit the unemployed and underemployed of both races.

So plans were made for an all-out effort, one that would reach as many job seekers and employers as possible and also demonstrate to the county how a job fair could be organized and what it could accomplish.

With these goals in mind, we decided to enlarge our planning group to include leaders of several black segments not previously represented and, also, a white minister who had worked closely with white poverty people.

Our enlarged group met in a black church in the small town of Purcellville, Virginia, in early May. Two new black leaders had been persuaded to come, and we met them with interest. Both were exceptionally attractive. The woman, slender, tall, soft-spoken and smartly dressed, possessed exquisite features. The man, also tall, well-groomed and handsome, had an equally quiet voice.

More militant than the four in the original group, these two had given little or no support to our first Job Opportunity Night. They had been contemptuous because they considered the other blacks working for it "Toms" and because only three of the employers represented had been in-county employers. Now they insisted that more Loudoun employers be asked to co-operate.

"All right," we agreed, turning to the flip chart, "let's get a list."

Soon the sheet was filled with the names of suggested companies. Some of them, our Loudoun consultant knew, were hard-line old guard.

"We'll write them all the best letter we know how to compose," we said.

"All of them?" the woman challenged, and the man mocked us with his smile.

"All of them," we repeated.

The two looked at each other (and, incidentally, later gave strong support to the undertaking).

The earnest young minister who had worked with white low income people pointed out the difficulty of getting word to them. Few of them attended churches or meetings, read the county newspaper or even listened to the radio, preferring TV. Loudoun County had no local TV station for TV announcements. To get word to these low income whites, he suggested sending announcements home by their school-age children. But it didn't seem either democratic or feasible to single out low income children. We decided to solve the problem by giving all school-age children announcements to take home. The IBM personnel director agreed to run off 8,000 announcements for the purpose, permission was obtained from the school authorities, members of the planning group agreed to deliver the announcements to the schools, and two days before the second Job Opportunity Night, 8,000 school children were handed our flier to carry home to their parents.

The Second Fair—The Happening

We had planned well for Job Opportunity Night No. 2. Leesburg, the county seat, was centrally located so that the greatest number of job seekers would find it convenient to get there. The auditorium of the school (which before integration had been all black) was roomy and well adapted to such a meeting. Of fifteen employers there, not three, but ten were Loudoun employers, several of them real surprises who had searched their consciences and decided to make this their debut into the world of equal opportunity. A surprise, too, was the number of white job seekers who came to the meeting even though they knew it was to be integrated. Traditionally, most of Loudoun's low income whites had spurned efforts for their betterment which involved blacks. Yet, on this night, fifty of the 120 job seekers were white.

Sitting at student desks or in folding chairs on the floor of the big school auditorium, the potential employees listened attentively while the fifteen employers gave their brief, timed talks and we wrote highlights on flip chart sheets to be taped beside employer signs on the walls. The Middleburg format progressed smoothly with the people moving to the various employer stations when the employers had finished talking to the whole group.

A happy hubbub. Earnest people speaking to equally earnest employers. Smiling people, black and white, walking out into the spring night clutching application forms.

One employer hurried up to us, beaming. "Thank you. Thank you. I needed five people in the worst way, and I've got them all, all hired, all ready to start."

"It wasn't an easy decision," the president of a Loudoun bank said. "We have many old guard depositors who still have old guard ideas, but when you put it to us so we had to say either 'yes' or 'no,' we decided on 'yes.' And I'm glad we did." He added with pride that he was hiring a black girl to train as a teller.

"When are we going to have another Job Night?" inquired one of the original black planners. "I think we ought to have one every few months."

One of the more militant black planners heard him and nodded solemnly.

"Well," we said, "you know how to do it now." And we hoped that these local people actually would do it again and again. They had a successful format to follow. They knew all about getting the right people together to plan, how to approach employers, how to reach people who needed jobs, how to conduct the actual event. Now that they knew what could be done and how to go about doing it, they didn't need the Community Education Program—unless it was to get them started, get them moving out of apathy and into useful action.

Alas, as this book goes to press no one has picked up the ball in Loudoun County. As in the beginning of our youth activities, we lacked a sponsor to carry on. It's too bad, job fairs can help solve the problems of unemployment and underemployment. They can be useful to the people and businesses of any community. Properly handled, they also can serve as a useful tool in increasing racial understanding.

A Somewhat Different Fair—Also Successful

The IBM personnel director who had participated in Loudoun's

Job Opportunity Nights said he would like to do something similar in Prince William County, where IBM was about to open a new plant. We of the Community Education Program agreed it would be a fine idea to do for Prince William what we had for Loudoun, spark an effort that would serve as a demonstration of what local people could do for themselves in the future—if they only would.

We had another purpose, too. We hoped to inspire the Virginia Employment Commission to adopt some innovative concept of bringing together people who needed jobs and employers who needed workers. The VEC's traditional policy was for its employees to sit in their offices and wait for employment problems to come to them. This centralized clearing house approach just wasn't meeting enough needs in a fast-changing world. Both employers and job seekers were complaining. We wanted to give the VEC an alternative approach or two to ponder. After all, the Community Education Program in the future had other fish it should be frying. Our job was to show effective ways of approaching problems to established agencies and concerned citizens. There just weren't enough of us with enough time and funds to carry on everything we started. The VEC, working with employers and citizens, was the logical agency to take over from us.

We had invited a VEC official to observe the Job Opportunity Night in Leesburg, and he had been impressed enough to speak favorably of the concept to other VEC officials. As a result, a VEC representative attended planning sessions, and when the actual event was held, the VEC was there, staffing a room to which people could come for information, where they could talk about jobs and apply for them.

Our first problem in planning was to establish contact with Prince William blacks. In Loudoun, our consultant had known black leaders who could reach the black population. In Prince William, we had no consultant, but our IBM friend had established good relations with a black group called the Concerned Citizens, and the president of this group was among those who met with us at the first planning session in the autumn of 1969. Also, at that session were representatives of several big employers besides IBM, the VEC representative, and, very importantly, the executive secretaries of the county's two influential Chambers of Commerce.

Now that we had contact with the black community, we had everything going for us. We could begin with a built-in momentum the Loudoun effort had lacked (but certainly made up for). Thanks to the work in Loudoun, powerful employers were acquainted with our methods and enthusiastic about them. The VEC was working with us. The inclusion of the two Chambers of Commerce promised to be of tremendous help. They not only could tap many employers for us, but they were willing to handle announcements and mailings, an expensive and time-consuming job sometimes difficult to assign. What's more, we had the Loudoun County experience to provide both inspiration and guidance.

Planning progressed smoothly although along somewhat different lines than in Loudoun. The Prince William people decided against a one-night affair. They felt they could reach more people if their event gave a choice of times to come. So they planned to forgo the five-minute talks by employers and conduct their event on an open house basis, with no starting time. There would be a Friday night session and a four-hour continuation on Saturday. Each participating employer would set up a booth and job seekers could shop around among employers, coming and going from the job fair as they wished.

We were negotiating for use of the only place big enough for such an affair, the armory in Manassas, when we were dealt a blow. Our principal black contact, the president of the Concerned Citizens, was found shot to death. Our plans came abruptly to a halt. We searched for someone else who could reach the Prince William blacks and suddenly found him in our planning group, a quiet black undertaker, who agreed to fill the breach and did an admirable job.

We moved ahead once more and by our January 1970 planning session could report on the flip chart a number of decisions which were then transcribed and mailed to all participants. On February 16 came the welcome news that we had obtained the Manassas Armory for the evening of March 20 and the morning and afternoon of March 21.

Now, with the date firmly set, we could do the final planning and make firm assignments. All fell neatly into line at the final planning session on February 27, and soon thereafter a flier was ready for wide distribution.

The Job Fair itself was a smashing success, with twenty-five employers participating and 400 people drawn to the armory. Some of these, inevitably, were merely the curious but others were there on serious business and fifty-five jobs were nailed down.

The planning group members were gung-ho for another and made excellent specific plans to hold it in about six months. However, in

THE CHAMBERS OF COMMERCE OF GREATER MANASSAS AND EASTERN PRINCE WILLIAM COUNTY

PRESENT

A JOB FAIR

WHEN? — FRIDAY, MARCH 20, 6 – 10 P. M.
SATURDAY, MARCH 21, 10 – 2 P M.

WHERE? — MANASSAS ARMORY, ROUTE 234

AVAILABLE JOBS

MANAGEMENT TRAINEES
MACHINE OPERATOR TRAINEES
CLERICAL
TELEPHONE LINEMEN TRAINEES
AIRPLANE LOADERS
SALESMEN
HEATING AND AIR CONDITIONING TECHNICIANS
ELECTRONIC TECHNICIANS
FIREFIGHTERS
FURNITURE HANDLERS
HOSPITAL ATTENDANTS
CHEFS/COOKS
BELLMAN
WAITERS/WAITRESSES
DISHWASHERS
HOTEL WORKERS
STORE CASHIERS
OPTICIAN TRAINEES
. . .AND MANY MORE

This is a chance for local employers and
employees to come together to explore,
and better utilize, the job resources of
Prince William County and adjacent areas.
We urge you to take advantage of this
opportunity. No cost to you.

FOR FURTHER INFORMATION CALL:
WOODY BROWNE – 368-4813, GREATER MANASSAS
OR
GEORGE BROWN – 494-4400, EASTERN PRINCE WILLIAM COUNTY

PARTICIPATING EMPLOYERS

IBM
MARRIOTT
MELPAR
BELTONE HEARING AID CO
VEPCO
GIANT FOODS
MANASSAS TRANSPORT AND DELIVERY
B&B SUPPLY
COLGAN AIRWAYS
C W STEWART AND CO
F.W. WOOLWORTH
HILLDRUP STORAGE
LEGGETT S
PRINCE WILLIAM COUNTY GOV'T
PRINCE WILLIAM COUNTY HOSPITAL
...PLUS MORE

SEE YOU
AT THE JOB FAIR

FRIDAY, MARCH 20,
6 – 10 P.M.
AND
SATURDAY, MARCH 21,
10 – 2 P.M.

that interval a number of factors far beyond their control were producing an unfavorable climate. A cutback in military and space program spending was reducing greatly the number of jobs many of our
participating employers could offer. Some of these companies, in fact,
were squeezed into a firing rather than a hiring situation.

The planners met in October 1970 and again in January 1971 to
consider repeating the fair. Each time the members decided that,
because very few job openings existed, a repetition would frustrate
everyone concerned. Instead, they decided to organize themselves as
the Prince William Area Employment Advisory Committee and began discussions with the Northern Virginia district representative of
the Virginia Employment Commission to learn in what other ways
they might help the employment situation. At subsequent meetings
the county agreed to provide space for a long-sought Virginia Employment Commission office in Manassas, the county seat, and the
VEC district representative promised to obtain personnel for such
an office as soon as feasible. The office was opened in a trailer January
1, 1973, and moved to permanent quarters June 1, 1974.

5

HELPING CITIZENS COMMUNICATE

The right people—representing all the viewpoints of consequence —must get together in the right way to discuss the right things and then follow through on a right action before any problem can be solved. We are convinced that this is a cardinal rule and relate the examples in this chapter to prove that no part of the rule should be ignored.

When Some of the "Right People" Drop Out

The scene for example number one was Alexandria, that once colonial city on the Potomac just a few miles south of the District of Columbia. We were called there by our friend Joe Killeen, formerly of the Vienna Teen Center (see Chapter 2) but in the spring of 1969 with Alexandria's poverty program.

As always, the old city presented a mostly charming face as we drove toward Joe's office in the City Hall. We admired the many large well-kept colonial brick homes with their boxwood and gardens, the streets with carefully restored narrow row houses sometimes painted in attractive pastels, the quaint courts, gift shops, undulating old brick walks. We also shuddered at what else we were seeing—the dingy, decrepit sections where there had been no restoration, where only the poor and the rats lived.

Joe got quickly to the point. In his job, he had met some church members who said they were fed up with the way their group tried to salve their consciences by playing Lords and Ladies Bountiful with Christmas and Thanksgiving baskets. These church members, Joe said, wanted to get their fellow members involved and change their whole approach from these biannual bursts of charity that really accomplished little to providing the kind of real support the poor needed to help themselves. The trouble was none of these "do-gooders" had any idea how to work effectively with the poor. Why didn't we hammer out a training plan for them as we had for the Vienna Teen Center chaperones?

Fine, we agreed. He would bring in all the needed viewpoints and together we would see what could be done.

So Joe set up a meeting with church members who said they wanted to learn, representatives from the Community Outreach section of the Economic Opportunity Commission, representatives from the Welfare Department and three poor people to tell the rest of us what the poor needed to help themselves and how we could help them get it. All the people vital for success were there.

First we made a list of "hang-ups" to use in warnings for our trainees:

1. Most volunteers have never been poor and are unaware of how to start helping the poor.
2. People are afraid of having to give money or time, or of getting into something with unknown limits.
3. Volunteers can do more harm than good through lack of knowledge. They tend to make people more dependent.
4. Volunteers have little knowledge of the background of the families in need.
5. There are different value systems between people who need help and those who might give it.
6. Volunteers may get more satisfaction from activities that make others more dependent than from helping them become independent.

To let the trainees know that their reception would not be roses, we then outlined typical difficulties volunteers and clients encounter with each other:

1. Clients who play games with volunteers:
   a. Lying.
   b. Seeking pity.

   c. Making threats (suicide, running away, desertion, giving
       child away).
   d. Agency hopping.
2. Parents who give a child no emotional support.
3. Volunteers, pros and semi-pros who invite clients to play
   games:
   a. Gullible volunteers who don't know when they are be-
       ing conned; believe fabulous stories kids tell about their
       families, etc.
   b. Volunteers come in looking for situations they have read
       about and clients play up to them.
4. Clients who pit volunteers against other family members or
   agency people.

The group went on to list the type of volunteers to try to reach,
possible approaches to those people and suggestions for training
them. Next came what volunteers could do to help clients increase
their independence and advice on "How to Separate Filling a Client's
Needs (which helps) from Filling Wants (which hinders his achieving more independence)."

There was only one thing missing. The people who had said they
wanted to learn stayed politely through the first meeting, even made
worthy contributions to it, but at later meetings, although we watched
the door hopefully, they never showed. Apparently, they really didn't
want to work *with* the poor, after all. It was easier just to do something *for* them, like those Thanksgiving and Christmas baskets.

Having had our interest aroused, those of us left in the group
ignored their absence. We wanted to devise a Volunteer Aide Training Plan with or without those particular volunteers. We had representatives of the poor to guide us and if we created a good plan, we
would find people to use it. So we plunged on, and the result was,
indeed, good.

The only trouble was that our ex-members had left us no contacts
with volunteers who might use it. We had lost some of our "right
people," so, as a particular group, we could not go ahead with the
"right action."

However, the plan was by no means dead. We had failed to get
it off the ground in the form we intended, but there were other groups
to use it and people in our group determined to see that these groups
got it.

Joe Killeen had several hundred copies of the plan reproduced.
One of our group members sent copies to all the Alexandria churches.

The plan was used by ALIVE, an organization of Alexandria volunteer citizens who built a record of working very effectively on a one-to-one basis with Alexandria's poor. Other copies went to poverty-fighting groups and agencies all over the state.

In 1973, we talked with Joe, who, since those Alexandria days, had moved to the Maryland suburbs but was still attracting interesting assignments. One he told us about was putting together what he called a "training package" for young members of the American Bar Association in Maryland who had volunteered as parole assistants. Another was work on a special six-man task force appointed by Governor Mandel of Maryland to study Maryland prisons with the idea of decentralizing the system and finding alternatives to incarceration.

"Don't worry about that Volunteer Aide Training Plan being used," he said. "It was used. It is used. I, for one, am still using it. All the time. I use all the material I got from working with you people—Teen Center, the Volunteer Aide Plan, the Jobs Now and Mental Health stuff. I keep it in a notebook and use it like a Bible."

So, thanks to Joe and his cohorts, we reached some of the other "right people" in spite of ourselves.

Helping a Group Discuss the Right Things

Another part of the cardinal rule was being violated by the Loudoun Association for Retarded Children (LARC). It was an intensely human, completely understandable violation and that made it all the harder for the president and the several other members who were aware of the trouble to do anything about it. They were too filled with compassion for the offenders, parents or close relatives of retarded children, who were using the meetings to unburden themselves of their personal woes. One would relate worries about his or her child, another would sympathize, then add a personal anecdote and so on. This, of course, was useful in one way, a form of group therapy that made members feel not so alone with their problems. But it didn't do much for the retarded children the association had been formed to help.

At every meeting, there had been efforts to move the group on from this mutual crying on sympathetic shoulders, but attempts to get down to business always had been frustrated before much concrete action could be planned.

Two members of the group had worked with us on other projects and were acquainted with our techniques. After "selling" us to the newly elected association president and giving us the background of the problem as they saw it, they arranged for us to conduct an association board meeting in February 1968.

The meeting was in a small, bare room above a drugstore in downtown Leesburg, the county seat of Loudoun County. We lugged our flip chart up the steep wooden stairs, shook hands with a dozen people, some of whom seemed a little curt and suspicious at the presence of outsiders, then added our coats to those piled on a couple of chairs in a corner and set up the flip chart.

The newly elected president, an attractive sweet-faced young woman with a retarded brother, called the meeting to order and introduced us by saying that we had been recommended by Helen and Anne as knowing ways that might get the group off to a year of real accomplishment.

It was a helpful introduction and we gladly took our cue from it. "So let's plunge right in," we said. "What *do* you want to accomplish this year?" For emphasis, we turned to the blank flip chart sheet and wrote:

What do we want to accomplish?

Suggestions came quickly:

1. More participation from general membership (25 to 30).
2. Find what projects need immediate attention.
3. Improve relations with county officials so they will listen and come with help.
4. Locate the children who have need.
5. Reduce parents' reluctance to accept idea of retardation in the family.
6. Educate public to problems of retarded children.
7. Transportation—the problem is the size of county and lack of public transportation.
8. Reach conclusions in Executive Committee and follow through with action.
9. Set goals for a year so we can all work for the same thing—concentrate on just a few activities instead of moving from one thing to another.

The sheet was filled. We waited briefly for additions but none came. We tore off the sheet and taped it to a nearby wall saying, "Maybe next, we'd like to go on with number nine, decide what those activities should be." (Notice that almost immediately we had stopped saying "you" and "your" and quietly included ourselves in the group by saying "we," "us," "ours." This is a technique we always use to break down barriers and help the group members know we are with them.)

All agreed the next step should be to decide on a program for the year ahead. We wrote on the flip chart:

Possible One-Year Program

Then we waited—but not long. This sheet, too, was soon filled:

1. Locate the children in the county who have needs, define the needs, catalogue the information, make a map showing location by age group, sex and need.
2. Develop a long-range program with beginning action steps to meet the children's needs.
3. Get support for and participation in the program (parents, officials, public).
   a. Get parents' acceptance.
   b. Get public's acceptance.
   c. Get support of County Board and School Board.
   d. Get the children.
   e. Get member participation.

The group was going strong. Obviously its members, even those who had seemed wary about us at first, were glad to be getting down to business. There were no personal anecdotes. We had no need to cut anyone short. Everyone seemed to share a sense of urgency as the group decided to forget everything else for the time being and work on step number one (above) actually assigning people to be responsible for the necessary action. Our flip chart recorded it:

How Do We Do Step 1?

Concentrate on it for two months, do no other activities. Get names.

Send out newsletter—Bornarth.

Send out special letter to ministers, doctors, health, welfare, speech and hearing—secretary.

Contact doctors.

Get a doctor on the board.

Dr. Maganies—Consagra

Dr. Nichols—Bornarth

Speak to Medical Association—Parsons.

Contact ministers—Hobson—each member talk to his own minister.

Contact Community Action staff—Devine.
Contact schools—Nichols, Hobson (homebound program)
    (school superintendent, Special Education teachers for present and recent children).
Contact Welfare—Parsons.
Contact Speech and Hearing—Wallace.
Contact Health Department—Consagra.

Methods

Newsletter—Bornarth.
Informative letter to parents—Nichols and Devine.
Radio program, monthly—Boulter.
Speakers—Simons, Devine, Consagra (speakers bureau).

It was late. We closed the meeting by explaining to the group how they could carry on by themselves at future meetings. The final flip chart sheet said:

To continue action get *AGREEMENT ON:*

1. The problem—the situation to be changed.
2. The goal(s)—the situation(s) we would like to have exist.
3. Barriers that need to be reduced.
4. Recommendations.
5. An action plan.
6. Assignments to carry out the plans.
7. Evaluation plan.

We seldom have left a single meeting feeling so good, feeling we had accomplished so much in so little time.

Since then we have tried to analyze exactly why it went so well that night. Basic credit, of course, must go to our problem-solving process. That approach first forces the discussants to think about the problem in a fresh way, replacing habitual thought patterns with ones that open new vistas. At the same time, it gives a logical pattern to follow. We had, with this group, ideal conditions for using it. But we know there were other things going for us, too. The two members who had invited us knew how to help the discussion. We were outsiders and no one knew us well enough even to think about crying on our shoulders. Maybe our experience showed and our calm, let's-get-on-with-it no-nonsense approach was contagious. Maybe it was the relief of seeing a concrete plan finally go down on paper for all to see—and with no single person making the plans. The group was working together toward what they all so fervently wanted.

In any event, we felt we had helped these good people accomplish a needed breakthrough.

Five years later, we checked back with the young woman who had been association president the night we were there.

"We were floundering and you put us on the right track," she assured us. Then she went on to list some of LARC's accomplishments since that time: county funding, a bus to transport retarded children to the LARC school, a summer day camp for retarded children lasting six weeks, a youth auxiliary that provided special treats for the children, such as taking them bowling, enlistment of the Soroptimist Club and the Jaycees to drive retarded young adults to a Sheltered Workshop, special education classes in the public schools. Even the census of the retarded was ever more complete, thanks to cooperation from the public schools, the Health and Welfare departments and the general public, who began to report cases of the retarded as LARC became better known.

"You deserve a lot of credit," she said.

"So do you," we replied. "You gave the group its chance to discuss the *right* things."

For some reason that we'll never fully understand too many leaders feel threatened by the very thought of doing that.

Mutual Suspicion in an Organization—and How Discussing the Right Things in the Right Way Helped Overcome It

Any continuing organization has to be on the alert for hard feelings that may develop between groups of members. The cause may be almost anything. One group is more conservative than another group would like—or more liberal. A number of PTA members decide the school's principal is incompetent or too permissive or too harsh with students and want him ousted or, at least, chastised. Another number of members rally to his support. One part of a Chamber of Commerce would like to work for new industry and business. Another part presses for preservation of the status quo. Some of the members of a church are filled with activist zeal. Others want the church to stick to the salvation of its members' souls. Examples could go on endlessly of the potential for trouble in all-volunteer organizations.

Now, consider the potential in another type of organization, one in which part of the work is done by an unpaid Board of Directors, part by a paid professional staff and part by volunteers from the community. Not only is there the possibility of trouble over direction or method of operation, over who has authority over whom about what, but the very fact that some are paid and others aren't may produce a real or imagined sense of class difference with all its attendant problems.

The two-county Fauquier-Loudoun Day Care Association with day care centers in Upperville (Fauquier) and Leesburg (Loudoun) is such a three-part organization.

It was a grass roots accomplishment, the result of careful and enthusiastic planning by about a hundred concerned citizens, a number of whom were from the wealthy, socialite set of that section of Virginia's hunt country. These wealthy people contributed so much time —and money—to the job of starting the first day care center in late 1969 in the old Upperville elementary school that, naturally enough, when the Board of Directors was named, about half the directors were from their group. The other half of the Board consisted of a wider range of community people, citizens from other areas, clergy, blacks and an educator who called us in late 1970 to ask our help in overcoming friction between some members of the Board and the staff. This woman, who had worked with us on other projects, was serving as Board personnel chairman and worried that the friction would lead to real trouble.

She arranged for us to meet with her and the center's paid executive director, an attractive young professional with long hair, mini skirt, white stockings, the very sort of young liberal intellectual most likely to clash with the attitudes of wealth.

These two women explained that they hadn't invited the president of the Board to this meeting because they wanted to level with us. Level they did: The staff resented several Board members, wealthy women who dashed into the center whenever they chose, interrupting the staff's work with the children, giving directions to the professionals although the professionals were trained and they weren't, expecting the professionals to give talks to civic groups on their free time, just generally "throwing their weight around." The staff couldn't complain, of course. They wanted their jobs and feared instant firing.

The personnel manual outlined rules, regulations and procedures for the staff but lines of authority weren't drawn as sharply as they should be. Moreover, there was little to tell the Board members the limits of *their* roles and responsibilities. What could be done to keep the Board in line? Without offending them, of course. They really meant well. They loved the center and worked hard to raise the money for it. They just didn't understand that they were making pains-in-the-neck of themselves. At the same time, what could be done to involve the parents of the center children more actively? And draw up guidelines for volunteers so that they, and everyone else, would know what was and was not expected of them? The trouble was aggravated because some of the Board members also served as volunteers. As volunteers, they should be under the authority of the staff but they were more likely to act like Board members. What's more, they were likely to wear clothes that were too nice for dirty jobs and to chat about horses and social affairs, making both the staff and the other volunteers uncomfortable.

We clucked sympathetically as we heard all this background and felt that if we accomplished nothing else, we, at least, had let the executive director unburden herself. We were sure, however, we could accomplish more and suggested a session with the association president to plan a meeting of all the right people, a meeting that might eliminate a lot of the problems without offending anyone. Obviously there was legitimate need for guidelines on the responsibilities of Board, staff, volunteers—all three. To draw up such guidelines was certainly an acceptable purpose for a meeting. Moreover, a new year was about to begin. The timing was ideal.

The two women agreed to try to sell the idea, and about a month later we were invited back, this time to meet the vivacious, tweedy president. She was waiting for us in her office at the center, a trifle skeptical but willing to help us plan a January meeting with Board and staff. We wouldn't try to have volunteers who weren't Board members, she decided, but it would be all right to work up guidelines for them.

We agreed, feeling the principal difficulty was not with all the volunteers anyway—only with those who were also Board members. Then, with her help, we worked out a meeting plan:

First, Board and staff would meet together for explanations. Then the Board would meet in one room with one facilitator (Strauss) while the staff met in another room with another facilitator (Stowe). Each group would have three jobs: to list the responsibilities of the other, suggest how the other could improve, and outline responsibilities of the volunteer. At the end of an hour, both groups would meet together again, examine each other's work and ask questions, suggest additions or comment as they chose.

"Fine," said the president. Then she grinned. "And I'm fascinated by that word 'facilitator.' I think I'll name my new horse that."

The January wind was howling outside the old schoolhouse the evening of the meeting as eight staff members met in one room and fifteen Board members in another.

In both rooms, there was obvious effort to make the suggestions as inoffensive as possible to the other group. People worked carefully on wordings. Even so, underlying meanings were plain enough in responsibilities such as these which the Board members put down for the staff:

Teach children respect for property. [A number of Board members felt the staff was too lenient when children abused school furnishings and materials.]

Serve as children's example of a healthy adult—physical and emotional.

Refrain from political activity—leave partisan political activity at home.

Be friendlier—gracious.

The staff, too, put its points across. For instance:

Board members should accept primary responsibility for public appearances—speaking at meetings, etc.

Board members, when working as volunteers in the center or in the community, should endeavor to demonstrate by their actions the distinction between the rights of their respective roles.

When the two groups met together and the flip charts of both were hung for all to see, the Board accepted all that the staff had to say. If any of it rankled, there was no sign. The Board's suggestions, too, were apparently acceptable—with one exception. The young executive director did not like *Teach children respect for property.* She argued heatedly that the staff's purpose was to help the children overcome a sense of inferiority.

"Let's teach them consideration for others," she said, "but let's not call it 'respect for property.'"

Now there were whispers and murmurings in the room, nudges of a neighbor, glances back into the next row. An elegant-looking matron lifted her head from her knitting. "All of us have had to learn respect for property," she said firmly. "We have had to learn how to take care of our own things and to leave what isn't ours alone. The fact that some have more than others has nothing to do with this point. This point is basic to everybody's good citizenship."

The debate was on. Some, including a couple of Board members, sided with the executive director—surely to teach the children consideration was enough. Others said "no!" Consideration was *not* enough. The lessons the center should teach above all were the lessons of how civilized people behaved. And that included respect for property.

We let the two sides go to it for about ten minutes. Then we cut off the argument by asking for a show of hands. (Although we try to avoid voting, sometimes it is the only quick way out.) How many wanted to keep it *Teach children respect for property?* Twelve hands went up. How many wanted to change it? Eight hands.

Even so, the young executive director was happy about the meeting. "I just wish it could have gone on longer," she told us as we rolled up the flip charts. "I wish we could have had role playing, too."

A number of Board members, too, including the president, told us they thought the meeting had "cleared the air."

But was this mere politeness? To find out, we checked back a few months later with the Board personnel chairman who had sympathized with the staff. How were things? "Oh, much better," she said. "Your workshop really helped a lot."

A year later, however, there was trouble again, this time division within the staff after it had experienced some natural turnover. The new Board chairman called us several times to discuss the difficulty. We suggested a meeting of all the people involved, and she, at first, asked us to conduct it. Then she reported that she and others who had participated in our sessions the previous year had decided they really shouldn't bother us. We had given them a pattern and surely they were competent now to handle the meeting themselves.

We were busy and glad, as always, when those with whom we've worked feel confident to carry on without our help.

Nor were we surprised to learn of new problems. Troubles of some new sort (or old sort) do keep arising in all continuing groups. The important thing is knowing how to meet them by getting the right people together in the right way to discuss the right things.

A Day of Communication

This story is a classic example of how a very few right people can provide the right momentum for a successful large conference on a subject very much needing exploration.

It began with three or four members of the League of Women Voters of Fairfax County wishfully thinking to one another about how great it would be if all those Northern Virginians interested in school volunteer work could get together to hear some experts in the field, share information about what was being done in the area and plan together for improvements.

"Let's not just talk; let's *do* it," said Sarah Lahr, who was active not only in the LWV but was chairman of the Childhood Mental Health Committee of the Northern Virginia Mental Health Association, and very much a ball of fire.

So the little group got in touch with us and we readily agreed to facilitate the planning sessions, train facilitators for small group discussions, provide use of lecture halls and classrooms at George Mason, whatever.

Then came the job of pulling in other right people to sponsor the conference and help with the planning. The result was an impressive quantity and quality of participating and supporting organizations* to list on our conference invitations.

Of these, enough for a wide base of representation worked actively in the planning. Others gave only passive support (the use of their names, announcements to their members, help in providing needed background information, representation at the conference itself). The important thing was that all the "right people" in one way or another were included. Finally, anyhow.

The truth is we overlooked some very important "right people" in the beginning. We were planning away one day when one of our group looked around and said, "Oh, my God, where are the teachers' associations?"

It was a grave omission but we quickly remedied it by inviting all the teachers' associations of the area to join us. Some did quite actively while others merely said, in effect, "Good luck." Those who worked with us actively provided much needed input. The others at least didn't sabotage our efforts. All was well.

As planning session followed planning session in the Northern Virginia Mental Health building in Arlington, the conference program took shape. We booked the speakers and panelists for the morning session and outlined potential topics for afternoon discussion groups:

I. Pre-school programs
II. Elementary (including kindergarten)
    1. Disadvantaged children.
    2. Slow learners.
    3. Office—clerical aides.
    4. Teacher aides—assist classroom teachers with routine chores.

* See Appendix, Chapter 5.

5. Instructional aides—work with children in teaching situation.
6. Field trips, special events.
7. Educational resources (speakers, experts in community).
8. Cafeteria aides.
9. Library aides.
10. Special needs (extended day care, breakfast, clothing, shoes).
11. Physically handicapped; special education.
12. Emotionally and mentally insecure.

III. Secondary (intermediate and high school)
13. School dropouts and pre-dropouts (behavior problems).
14. Pregnant girls (homemaking skills, vocational guidance, health education).
15. Educational resources (speakers, etc.).
16. Drug abuse.
17. Vocational guidance (community experts).
18. Emotional problems.
19. Social activities.
20. Teacher aides (grading papers, etc.).
21. Clerical aides.
22. Instructional aides.
23. Continuing education.
24. Student volunteers.

IV. Volunteer Programs in General
25. How to interest volunteers in service recruitment.
26. How to organize and administer a program in a school system.
27. How volunteers work, guidelines.
28. How to train volunteers.
29. Teacher-volunteer relationships.
30. Administration-volunteer relationships.
31. Evaluating volunteers.
32. Co-ordination of volunteers in a local school.

The planning group also discussed the value of a kit for all participants and what should be in it. A special kit committee then ordered materials from all over the country.† By conference day, the bright red cardboard folders were fat with reading matter.

Meanwhile, we of the planning group prepared the invitation and a list of several hundred invitees, planned for and assigned the duplication and mailing, made arrangements for the college facilities, for coffee breaks, for lunch.

It was a massive job but approached with the relentless enthusiasm necessary for a smoothly run, well-attended conference significant in content.

On the side, we of the CEP were training facilitators (see Chapter 14) and since they were mostly people interested in the subject, we put them to work discussing it in practice sessions. This not only helped to hold their attention but served to let them unburden their own minds in advance so that, at the conference itself, they could listen better to others. Also in advance, we provided them with written guidelines intended to answer most of their questions, for we knew that, during the heat of the conference itself, there would be little time for the giving of instructions, advice and counsel.

While we were at it, we prepared written guidelines for the resource people, too, asking them to limit themselves to three types of activities:

1. Recognizing the facilitator as the discussion leader.
2. Answering (briefly) specific questions from the facilitator or other group members.
3. Intervening (sparingly and briefly) when they thought they could give helpful information or suggestions.

All three of these rules were designed primarily to keep the resource people from monopolizing the discussion of the groups to which they were assigned.

Registrations for the conference poured in, with each registrant giving a first and second choice for the afternoon discussion. Thus, before the conference, we could form groups of manageable size.

Everything we could do in advance, we did. Even so, the CEP

† "Educational Strategy & Practice" from the Center for Effecting Educational Change; the Portland, Oregon Public Schools' pamphlet on VIPS (Volunteers in Portland Schools); a reprint from *Reader's Digest*, "We Can End Juvenile Illiteracy"; the U. S. Department of Health, Education, and Welfare's publication "Volunteers in Education"; the American National Red Cross's booklet "Red Cross Volunteers in the School Health Program"; the information kit and forms used by the School Volunteers Program of the New Hampshire Council for Better Schools; reports from Northern Virginia schools on volunteer work already under way, etc.

staff, the planning group and several volunteers needed to set alarm clocks for an early hour on April 11, 1970, and hurry to George Mason to prepare the registration tables in the lobby of the lecture hall, hang flip charts in the various lecture rooms that were to be used for afternoon discussions, lay out the bright red kits of background materials, make sure the coffee was ready, tend to a multitude of last-minute details.

Participants began to arrive to check in and receive their name tags and kits. Soon the babble of voices was deafening and the taps of the giant coffee makers had no rest until it was time for the 251 participants to file into the lecture hall for the morning session.

The talks were stimulating, the questions were pertinent, the lunch, which never pleases everyone, pleased some and not others. Then the afternoon discussion was under way in nearly forty small groups. (Some topics had interested enough people for several groups.)

In follow-up work afterwards, a committee consolidated the flip chart records and sent them to all participants with other materials and a summary of the ratings given the conference by participants, showing that more than half rated it excellent, with such comments as "common ground for exchange of ideas," "encourages well-planned volunteer programs," "brought more awareness of volunteer possibilities in the public schools," and "interesting speakers and well-planned meeting." Another third rated the conference "very good." Even these comments gave weight to the value of "exchange of ideas" and "learning of effective volunteer programs." Reasons for the "very good" instead of "excellent" rating centered on the lack of time in the afternoon discussions to answer questions or pursue thoughts, or the feeling too few questions could be covered in the time allotted in the general sessions. A small group of evaluation sheets said the participants had gained little from any session not already known to them, commenting that specific volunteer experience of "working volunteers" in the Northern Virginia schools systems would have been very helpful to them. One sheet rated the conference "poor" and another "very poor."

Well, you can't please all the people all the time, and, on the whole, we felt good. Our group member who prepared the analysis of registration data for the mail-out after the conference had this to say:

An outstanding feature of this Conference had nothing to do with numbers of people to be totted and charted. This was the very palpable, permeating *interest,* emanating from all those in attendance, that charged the meeting with electrifying enthusiasm. In such an atmosphere, when a steady crackling of stimulating ideas falls on eager ears, it's almost impossible for a Conference to fail to be productive.

But productive of anything besides a lot of needed communication? We weren't sure until we checked back with two of the most active planners enough later for some action to have surfaced. One planner was discouraged because the conference had led to no centralization or administrative structure for the use of volunteers. The other credited the conference with several specific results. For instance:

1. The institution of new programs for volunteers in several schools, thanks to the inspiration of the conference.
2. The improvement of a number of other volunteer programs already under way, thanks to the exchange of information and ideas the conference had provided.
3. The giving of status and respectability to the idea of using volunteers in several additional schools where administrators previously had been skeptical.

Letting Citizens Decide on Pocket Parks

When Mrs. Lyndon Johnson was First Lady, she sparked an effort to beautify the nation's capital city. Among the plans was the idea of converting into small neighborhood parks a number of vacant lots owned by the city in its predominantly black residential sections.

Under a grant from the General Electric Company and working in co-operation with the National Park Service, the School of Business Administration of American University in 1966 completed a study of a variety of small parks, including the proposed pocket parks. Architectural consultants prepared graphic sketches of alternative plans that might be used for several chosen Northeast sites. The project had two goals:

1. By creation of parks on these sites to demonstrate what could be done elsewhere.
2. By enlisting the fullest possible participation from the people in the neighborhoods to be served, to prove the value of consulting the citizens and letting them help decide what kinds of parks they would most like and would use.

To gain this neighborhood participation in planning, the School of

Business Administration then enlisted the help of the Northeast Neighborhood Council in conducting a survey of what the people in the neighborhoods around the proposed parks would most prefer. Armed with sketches of alternative plans, interviewers went from door to door in two of the areas and, in another, the council mailed questionnaires.

Typical was the questionnaire used for a proposed triangular park bounded by Bladensburg Road, Douglas Street and Thirtieth Street, N.E.:

1. Which of the two designs would you prefer?
    (*Check one*)   Plan A_____
                     Plan B_____

2. What changes would you like to have in the design you se-
    lected?

    _____

    _____

3. a. How would you and other members of your household
        benefit from the development of your choice?

        _____

        _____

    b. How many people are in your household?
        (*Circle one*)   1   2   3   4
                          5   6   7   8
    c. What are their ages?   ____ ____ ____ ____

                                 ____ ____ ____ ____

4. Would you like to attend a meeting to discuss the design?
    (*Check one*)   Yes _____
                     No _____

When the survey was completed, the School of Business Administration asked Strauss to conduct meetings of all interested neighborhood people in two of the chosen areas and set the first meeting for
early March 1967 to discuss a proposed park at Perry Street and
Thirtieth Place, N.E.

The Neighborhood Council then mailed invitations that stressed
the open nature of the meeting, saying: "Please come and bring your
family and neighbors, including our youth and senior citizens."

Only thirteen adults and three boys (about thirteen, ten and eight
years old) were present at the appointed hour and appointed place
(St. Joseph's Home for Boys on Otis Street, N.E.). However, others

kept coming in and eventually there were twenty-five, twenty black and five white.

The chairman of the Neighborhood Council described what the meeting was all about, then introduced Strauss, who explained that the Park Service wanted to put in a park tailor-made to fit the needs and wants of the neighborhood people so they would use it. Somebody asked if the park would be supervised and Strauss had to break the news that there were no outside funds to pay for supervision. If parents wanted the park supervised, they would have to do it.

Then he divided the people into four groups, having them count off one, two, three, four in order to break up the women, who were all in one spot, and the boys, who were all in another. The idea was to make a group of the number ones, another of the twos, and so forth. A knot of people in one corner put their heads together and one of them said, "We people from Perry Street want to stay together."

Strauss explained that the purpose of mixing people up was to get a cross section of people.

Perry Street people were not convinced of the desirability of that. An elderly white woman said, very firmly, *"We people from Perry Street want to stick together."*

Strauss could only surrender. The result was three mixed groups, with the Perry Street people sitting apart.

As soon as the discussions had started, Strauss walked down to the Perry Street group at the far end of the room. They told him they were against this park. "We came here to fight."

Strauss suggested that they put down their reasons for not wanting a park on a piece of paper. Eventually they did and their reasons were that stragglers and bums would hang out there in the late hours of the night. There would be loud noise, littering, etc.

Strauss then visited the other groups. Five people who lived next to the proposed park were saying that they thought this space was not big enough for a park of use to larger children. The only practical use would be for tots who would be taken there by their parents, particularly mothers, and the mothers were already getting their tots outside in their backyards. The other people, having no unity among themselves, were saying, in effect: "It would be nice if we could have a park here to make this lot a pleasant place. But we don't think it should be here if the people right next to it don't want it." The Perry Street and third groups concurred.

Strauss could only go along with the consensus that the park seemed inappropriate because of the feelings expressed.

In something of a state of shock at the turn of the meeting, especially since advance interviews had indicated that most of the people would be delighted to have a park of some sort, he drove the chairman of the Neighborhood Council back to his office.

The chairman was not depressed. In fact, he said he felt very good. This area had never had any kind of group, so it had been wonderful to get these people out, get them talking to each other. "This is going to help me a great deal in trying to get the neighborhood organized," he said. "And I'll bet you that it won't be too long before these same people who said that they didn't want a park will be making a park there."

The other meeting of citizens to talk about a proposed park in their area: Sixth and Evart streets, N.E., brought the same surprising result. The majority of the people didn't really want a park. They said, in effect, that a park would be nice if it could be kept clean, taken care of and supervised—by someone else. They said, in effect, they didn't want to do all that themselves. They worried about disorderly conduct, litter, noise, bums and hoodlums using the park as a hangout. Several said, just give us playground equipment for a larger park already in the area.

The School of Business Administration, under pressure for decisions, tried hard with further surveys, further meetings, but the necessary enthusiasm could never be engendered.

The chairman of the Northeast Neighborhood Council had been wrong when he prognosticated that a park at Perry Street and Thirtieth Place would soon be forthcoming. We drove by the proposed site in the spring of 1974. Nothing had happened. We drove by the other proposed sites, too. No parks.

Real participatory democracy can bring many surprises to the experts who sit in their offices deciding what would be nice for other people. Fortunately, in this case, the concerned people were consulted before they had things they didn't really want foisted upon them.

Once again, bringing the right people together in the right way to discuss the right things had brought the right action. In this case, for these people, it was no action at all.

6

TACKLING PROBLEMS OF COMMUNITY GROWTH

Ways to Focus the Power Structure on New—and Better—Ideas for Control of Development

We don't recommend that other areas tackle their growth problems for the same reason that Fairfax County finally did. Unfortunately, that fast-developing county's motivation was a juicy scandal. What happened in its wake, though, is worth emulating.

The scandal, briefly, was this: Back in 1966, federal income tax checks disclosed that several members of the Board of Supervisors had taken bribes in zoning cases. Press, radio and TV were full of it for weeks. Five supervisors and ten other influential persons, including several former supervisors, were indicted by a federal grand jury. Three of the supervisors were convicted. The other two resigned. Replacements were named to the Board.

The new Board moved quickly to placate the outraged public. It appointed a nine-member, blue ribbon Zoning Procedures Study Committee to recommend improvements so a similar scandal would be unlikely to occur. The committee, in turn, hired Fred Mauck, of one of the most qualified law firms in the country on zoning matters, to head its staff. The resulting report, made officially in September 1967, constituted such advanced thinking that both Mauck and the

committee members were afraid the county Board would sweep it
under the rug.

That is where our Community Education Program came in. The
committee asked the CEP to take the job of making sure the "right
people" would not only know of the report's existence but would
study it, come to understand its innovative proposals and, hopefully,
decide to push for its suggested reforms.

Working with a small planning group that included the vice-
chairman of the committee and Mauck, the CEP set up an all-day
meeting for topside county officials, state legislators, leaders of
business and civic organizations. The invitation to these "right people" stressed that the purpose of the conference was "to promote
understanding of the complex aspects of land development," that
the report "deals in some depth with the institutional arrangements
of local government to regulate land use, not only in Fairfax County,
but in all local governments. The report is an imaginative attempt
to resolve some of the basic aspects of zoning."

We also mailed a copy of the report to each invitee so that people
could study it in advance and not waste valuable conference time
in educating themselves on its contents. (Many a potentially good
conference is ruined by being turned into a question and answer
session because participants don't come adequately prepared for discussion.)

The meeting was held at George Mason College on Saturday, November 18, 1967, with forty-five participants plus seven experts on
land use matters and seven respected authorities on local affairs. The
committee chairman gave highlights of the report. We gave brief instructions for the seven small discussion groups. Then for the next
ninety minutes each of these groups explored one of the following
subjects:

1. Economic and fiscal implications (of the report).
2. Social and esthetic implications.
3. Ethical and political implications.
4. Impact on distribution of authority among appointed and
    elected officials.
5. Impact on landowners in the three zones the report recom-
    mended (holding, developing and developed).
6. Impact on realtors and construction firms.
7. Implications for the planning process, information require-
    ments and how they are to be met.

By this time it was twelve-ten, and we asked each group to use the next twenty minutes before lunch summarizing its exploration.

After lunch, all participants met together, with each group reporting and members of other groups encouraged to ask questions and make comments and suggestions. It was a lively time. By the end of it, we had no doubt that this group of "right people" understood the report and its implications and were ready to see that others would hear of its value and help in the push for action.

There were a number of criticisms of the meeting, of course, on the evaluation sheets. We were grateful to know what people *hadn't* liked and at future conferences worked to overcome such gripes as these given by more than one:

1. Not enough privacy for individual groups, noise level too high, acoustics horrible. [seven people] [Thereafter, whenever possible, we arranged for each group to be in an individual room or at least widely separated from other groups.]

2. Needed more time for development of questions, conclusions and summaries. [five people] [Ever after, we allotted more time.]

3. Meeting too long for a Saturday. Away at two-thirty would be better. [two people] [While we never felt we could wind up an all-day conference on an important matter by two-thirty, we never again kept people past four o'clock.]

On the other hand, so many evaluation sheets praised the conference that we felt very good, indeed. "Likes" expressed by several included:

1. Interchange of ideas; that all these people, many busy and important, were in a dialogue with cross exchange of questions and answers, stimulation of thought, opportunity to clarify misapprehensions. [thirteen]

2. Breaking down the problem into cross-section discussion groups and then synthesizing. [five]

3. Free expression allowed each individual concerning his ideas. Hearing viewpoints of individuals with different backgrounds. [five]

And we were flabbergasted but delighted to read this comment on one sheet: "Being in the urban planning and economic field, we are working up plans for two to three dozen cities. In no other, could or would as high a level of analysis and discussion by citizens and politicians have taken place."

Yet the real test of the conference's effectiveness was what happened afterward. Our purpose had been to prevent the committee's report being filed away and forgotten. Had we succeeded?

Happily, yes. The Fairfax Zoning Procedures Study Committee's ideas have apparently begun to have lasting impact on both thought and action regarding the control of land development in the county and perhaps elsewhere. Later in this chapter, pages 98–103, we discuss the Fairfax County Goals Study and other activities related to the Zoning Procedures Report, and in the Appendix we explain the major thrusts of the report and summarize the subsequent developments.*

Getting Citizen Input for Control of Erosion and Siltation

Fairfax County, one of the first in the country to adopt erosion and sediment control measures and considered a national leader in that field, nevertheless knew more could and should be done. It had spent $3.5 million for the control of siltation and erosion from the 1,200 new site plans approved between 1966 and 1970. Yet siltation from developments still was clogging its lakes, using up water area of streams, eliminating much of their natural ability to purify and losing irreplaceable tons of topsoil.

The county had formulated amendments to its Erosion and Siltation Ordinances in its 1961 code and to its "Policies and Guidelines for the Preparation of Subdivision Plans" and "Site Development Plans Relating to the Control of Erosion and Sedimentation," but had delayed action until we could set up and conduct a conference on the subject.

The policies and guidelines already advocated an annual seminar but the previous year's had been criticized for its failure to include the community at large. The few citizens who had participated had been mostly builders and developers.

We set to work not only to bring a representative range of citizens to this 1970 conference but also to plan a program that would provide the background these citizens would need for educated input.

We invited several organizations and institutions to help plan the conference and to join us and Fairfax County in sponsoring it.†

---

* See Appendix, Chapter 6, "Content and Implementation of the Fairfax Zoning Procedures Study Committee Report."

† Other sponsors:
    Fairfax Area League of Women Voters
    Fairfax County Federation of Citizens Associations
    Homebuilders Association of Suburban Virginia

Citizen groups, conservationists, government people, engineers and builders and developers all had a say in what the conference should cover and how it should be handled.

The planning group wanted the whole range of viewpoints presented at the conference, too. The agenda reflects this. On the day of the conference, October 3, 1970, there were talks on:

1. The problem and need for policies on erosion and siltation control.
2. The economics and technology of siltation control.
   a. A conservation technician's view.
   b. A developer's view.
   c. An engineer's view.
3. Fairfax County administrative procedures for enforcing siltation control.
4. Legal problems in enforcing siltation control.
5. Problems in the formulation of water control standards as to siltation.

The 100-odd participants were certainly exposed to an education in the problem. They already had been sent copies of the proposed amendments. Now they were learning from the talks and from the question and answer period that followed such bits of information as these:

Stricter enforcement and greater control of sedimentation and erosion was going to be expensive to the county, but without them the cost would be many times over.

Suburban development causes erosion and sedimentation many, many times that of agriculture. One estimate of development without control was erosion and sedimentation damage a thousand to one as much damage per acre as farming.

A world can be done to cut down damage:

Restrict builders to using only the land where topography, drainage and soil are favorable.

Allocate for parks and open spaces lands not suited for development.

Stabilize one section before opening another.

Save trees.

Northern Virginia Builders Association
Northern Virginia Conservation Council
Northern Virginia Soil and Water Conservation District
Virginia Society of Professional Engineers
Virginia Polytechnic Institute

Install storm water drainage.

Intercept storm water on critical areas.

Build sediment basins and keep them cleaned out as necessary.

Use permanent vegetation on areas exposed for long.

Seed immediately after rough grading.

Mulch.

Pave as quickly as possible.

Developers aren't the only culprits.

Highway departments are blatant offenders, opening too much territory at a time and being slow to stabilize it. The nation's highway program contributes about 68 million *tons* of sediment annually.

Park administrations are also guilty with their developments on lakes, waterways and critical slopes.

And so on and so on and so on.

Then, from 1:45 to 3:30 P.M., came the discussion period. Participants, with the help of trained facilitators and resource people, explored in small groups their choice of the following questions:

1. What should be the county's role in connection with Erosion and Siltation Control?
2. Should the proposed Erosion and Siltation Ordinances be adopted as now being considered by the Board of Supervisors? If not, should they be strengthened or relaxed and to what extent?
3. Should the proposed changes to the Policies and Guidelines on Erosion and Siltation be adopted as now being considered by the Board of Supervisors? If not, what changes should be made?
4. What standards, thresholds or criteria should be adopted by which to measure erosion or siltation which is detrimental to the public health, safety or welfare?

Again, most of the evaluation sheets praised the conference, rating it excellent or very good. The exchange of ideas, the information given, the calling attention to the problem, the giving of all sides of the picture, were the most repeated of the "likes."

The eight people who criticized the conference included two who wished it had gone more deeply into specific techniques and comparative costs; four who still felt the citizens hadn't been adequately represented because none of the speakers had given the citizen's view; one who would have liked less time for speeches and more for discussion and another who would have liked the opposite.

The county had furnished staff members as recorders for the discussion groups. After the conference, they co-ordinated the flip chart records so the discussion group recommendations could be mailed to the participants for their review.

We found that recommendations for change in the proposed amendments were surprisingly few. In a second meeting, called to get the participants' reactions, they explained that discussions had been mostly supportive instead of critical, but that they had served the very useful purpose of making the discussants think deeply about the problem and explore its implications. From the resulting thought and knowledge had emerged support on the whole for the county's proposal to stiffen erosion and siltation control.

So the list of recommendations for change in the county's proposed amendments was short. Several were for a change in wording. The others were:

1. A review by the county design review agency of the agronomy and engineering practices proposed.
2. Inclusion of professionals representing agronomy in the review committee.
3. Intensifying programs.

Most of these recommendations were accepted by the county and included in the newly revised code and guidelines adopted shortly thereafter. The general public had no objections.

We were happy at this fresh proof of the value of government-citizen co-operation. Sometimes, a local government that courts citizen participation gets badly needed input. Sometimes, when the government already is acting wisely, the input, not being so much needed, is minimal. But the government gets something else equally valuable: citizen understanding and support. Either way, a government that includes its citizens can profit . . . provided, of course, that government has nothing to hide.

Two Local Governments Try Different Ways of Setting Goals

BE IT RESOLVED: That this Board, sensible of the great changes facing Loudoun County, create a Citizens' Advisory Commission to recommend to the people of the County and this Board such improvements in public service, efficiency of operation, methods of financing, and forms of local government as it may find may better serve the wishes and needs of the people of Loudoun County . . .

Following passage of this resolution in February 1970, the Loudoun Supervisors named forty-five citizens to serve as representatives of major areas of interest in the county.

The Supervisors, however, deliberately gave the commission no plan, organization or suggested procedure.

The Resolution itself stated:

BE IT RESOLVED: That the Commission be empowered to elect its own Chairman, adopt its own rules or organization and appoint any additional subcommittees and members thereto as it may see fit.

And when the forty-five met with the Board in March 1970 to receive their commission, the Board vice-chairman restated this hands-off policy in a prepared statement:

Again, we have no wish to tell you how to go about this business or how best to develop the best kind of organization to accomplish it. We only suggest that you give the problem of organization as much thought as you will be giving the problems to investigate. For the success of the Commission and the value of its findings will depend very largely on the methods you, yourself, adopt to do the job.

So the forty-five were on their own. In fact, to punctuate their determination to provide no dictation or interference, the Board left the room.

Commission members quickly organized themselves by forming a pro tem steering committee composed of one representative from each of the magisterial districts, elected by other members of that district meeting in caucus, and one at-large tie-breaker. From this group, members nominated and elected a pro tem chairman.

"Now what?" he said.

Several members who had worked with us on other projects suggested we be called in to conduct a conference with these purposes:

1. To help members get acquainted with one another. (Many had never before met.)
2. To discuss and reach agreement on the topic areas to be covered by the commission. (Suggestions of commission members could be mailed to the pro tem chairman in advance of the meeting.)
3. To demonstrate techniques for effective group work that might be valuable in the months ahead. (Many commission

members had never known any form of procedure except Robert's Rules.)

After debate, the majority was convinced that we could be useful, and a conference date was set for early April.

In preparation, we met for several hours with the pro tem chairman and another steering committee member to study and co-ordinate the sheafs of topic work suggestions that arrived from commission members.

The meeting was in the Carriage House of historic Oatlands mansion south of Leesburg. We arrived early with one trained facilitator for each topic discussion group, flip charts, name tags and box lunches to fortify us before the early afternoon meeting.

We had co-ordinated the suggested problem areas to be studied into six and, using the language given in the suggestions whenever possible, we had this list hanging on a flip chart sheet in front of the room:

1. County government structure and working relations.
2. Financing county government.
3. County development and planning.
4. Education and cultural services.
5. Other people-oriented services.
6. Other county services.

Commission members seated at six tables, each with five to seven people, spent about ten minutes discussing the list with those at their table. Should any problem areas be added? Should any be deleted or co-ordinated?

Then we asked the tables to report to the whole group and two suggestions were made: that the topic "Objectives for Loudoun County—Growth to 1990" be added, and that "Other people-oriented services" and "Other county services" be combined into "Public services." The former suggestion was not agreed upon at that time but later adopted. The latter got an immediate go-ahead.

Next, to create work groups, we asked each commission member to list a first and second choice of topic. Then, while members sipped coffee and chatted, we sorted these into topic discussion groups, finding happily that almost everyone could have first choice.

Now came a long topic discussion period, each group with its own facilitator deciding what work should be done in its problem area. Then each group reported to all the others to work out gaps and overlaps among the problem areas.

The Loudoun County Citizens' Advisory Commission on Community Goals was on its way, its work defined and roughly outlined, its committees even formed, for with the exception of the Objectives Committee instituted later, the topic discussion groups of this conference day became the topic committees which worked until the commission report was delivered eighteen months later.

Two of the committees continued to use the flip chart technique for their meetings, and those members who had studied our methods worked throughout the commission's tenure to get widespread community input into the commission's thinking and its decisions about what recommendations to make. Most committees held public meetings on their subjects; some met with civic and church organizations to explain what they were doing and to receive suggestions; several Committee of 55 meetings were devoted to exploring first one and then other topic area with commission members as panelists. Our Loudoun County representative, working with topic committee chairmen, prepared a comprehensive questionnaire‡ which brought more than 700 replies from the public, answering such questions as:

1. Do you favor assessing real estate devoted to agriculture, horticulture, forest or open space on the basis of use rather than market value? (This question was answered by 656 people with 514 saying "yes." And this response was a strong argument used by the county in its adoption in 1972 of a land use tax.)

2. Should real estate developers be required to bear part or most of the cost of school construction required by subdivisions erected by them? (310 answers said "part"; 305 said "most" and the county had a public opinion poll to support its adoption in 1972 of its Article 12 requiring just such payment by developers.)

3. Do you believe that Loudoun County should co-ordinate its planning with other areas of Northern Virginia by joining regional planning organizations? ("Yes," 477; "no," 129, and the county, the last hold-out in Northern Virginia, has now joined that planning district's commission.)

A number of other recommendations, favored by most of the public according to the questionnaire and recommended by the commission, have been implemented: a sanitary landfill to replace the old county dump; the requirement that developers of large tracts of land set aside adequate land for parks and open space; a consumer utility tax to help pay county bills; increasing the county auto tag fee for the same purpose; separating the county's health district from

‡ See Appendix, Chapter 6, for introduction to questionnaire.

that of adjoining Fauquier County; updating the county's Comprehensive Development Plan; education in drug abuse in the county schools; more special education classes, etc.

Of course, a number of recommendations, endorsed by the public according to the questionnaire, have not been adopted as we go to press. Either they need special legislation from the Virginia General Assembly that would conflict with the interests of other areas that can vote Loudoun down or the Board just doesn't think the recommendation wise (at least yet). The important thing is that the county, thanks largely to the Citizens' Advisory Commission, already had that necessary ingredient, public support, and so could accept many of the recommendations.

We admire Loudoun County's Board for using the Citizens' Advisory Commission. And we admire the commission members for the job they did in educating themselves on vital issues, in spreading that education to the public and in letting the public help them make their decisions.

With all due modesty, we think we got them off to the right start.

Fairfax County also sought citizen participation in the setting of community goals, also with good results. But the method was very different. It was a method which finally gave us the chance to prove the effectiveness of the technique we tried in the Jobs Now project (Chapter 3)—an all-day conference to create continuing groups— which this time achieved the desired results. This time we had the necessary follow-through, the dedicated group leadership (and membership) that held the groups together and kept them moving forward. Also they had some place to go with their findings. Both the county Board and the public were waiting for the report. Quite an incentive.

The background briefly was this: The Fairfax Board, in January 1970, was worried about that county's fast development and its ability to provide needed services. It appointed a committee of seven to advise on economic development and also requested that committee to review the budget proposed for the fiscal year 1971. In April, the committee submitted an interim fiscal report but decided it could not go further without citizen-supported county goals for guidance.

In July of that year, the committee asked thirty-two representative organizations for their views on county goals, but when it tried to co-ordinate these views for its second interim report in October 1970, it concluded:

> The fundamental need is for an orderly and rigorous set of well-defined priorities. . . .

> . . . .

> The selection of such goals should be a County-wide effort. Many individuals and groups have given deep thought to the future of their particular activity or section. All of these activities must be pulled together, compared and analyzed so that out of this process can come a distillation of goals which are economically feasible, highly desirable, and realistic. These need not be permanent, but rather a present statement to be reviewed periodically, since goal-building is a continuing process.

That December, convinced of the need for a countywide effort, the committee asked our help. We set to work with the members to plan a process that would bring countywide participation. At this point, Bert Strauss became an advisor to the committee and worked with it thereafter as a de facto member.

It seemed to us a natural situation for a kickoff meeting that would launch continuing study groups. The Economic Development Study Committee and the Board chairman agreed. We developed a study plan and invited seventy citizen organizations to send representatives to an advance meeting to review it. Fifty people came, and the meeting generated so much enthusiasm there was wild competition for the 200 spaces available at the kickoff session, set for March 12–13.

At the opening session, from 8 to 10 P.M., Friday, March 12, came talks (and time for questions and answers) on facts, forces and alternatives. The subjects were:

Goals: Can We Establish Them and Make Them Effective in Planning and Budgeting?

Growth in Population and Employment

Planning for Housing, Related Services and Environmental Conservation

Planning for Schools

Planning for County Services

The sessions resumed the next morning at nine-fifteen, with two more talks and time for questions and answers on these subjects:

Facts, Forces and Alternatives in Financing Community Development

Data Needed for Intelligent Planning

The group discussions began at ten-fifteen, lasted until twelve-thirty lunch, resumed at one-thirty and continued until three.

Because we wanted each of these groups to become the core of a continuing study group, we had tried to do everything possible in advance to help them. Much, we knew, would depend on these first discussions. If they went well, people would want to carry on.

This time we had given participants their choice of fifteen problem areas:

1. The Environment
2. Education
3. Health
4. Social Services
5. Income, Employment and Manpower
6. Cultural and Leisure Time Programs
7. Justice and Public Safety
8. Planning and Land Use
9. Industrial and Commercial Development
10. Housing
11. Financial Planning and Management
12. Transportation
13. Water and Sewer
14. Performance of Governmental Services—By Jurisdictions (Separate or Joint)
15. Processes of Cost-Benefit Analysis

We had provided each group with a trained facilitator who had agreed to serve not only during the kickoff session but for a session to follow at which the group would organize itself for continuing study.

We had mailed, along with the invitation, a "Seminar and Work Group Plan" which explained that, to the maximum extent possible, the members of each group would represent differing views on the topic (so that no one would expect like-mindedness and be hurt or offended by disagreement), that facilitators would be used, that morning group discussions would cover five points within each subject area:

1. What are the issues?
2. What information do we need about these issues?
3. What basic assumptions do we need?
4. In what concrete terms can we specify goals?
5. How can we determine benefits and costs?

And that: "After lunch each seminar group will complete its morning discussion (if necessary), and prepare to become a continuing work group by determining what additional people are needed to provide information, skills and viewpoints which the seminar members do not have. It will also set a date and place for its next meeting and take whatever actions it wishes toward starting its study (except organizing itself—a step which should be delayed until the group is enlarged)."

Then to emphasize for each participant that this kickoff conference was only the beginning, the plan went on to outline further steps and the timetable for them.

All this careful preparation based on hard experience paid off. The kickoff conference, itself, was all that we had hoped. Participants worked hard and built a base on which to continue. Nineteen study groups were formed that day to explore the fifteen special subjects in detail.

In this study, the Economic Development Study Committee was attempting to achieve, with the help of citizen volunteers and very little money, a result of the caliber of a three-year goals study conducted by the city of Dallas, Texas, at a cost of over $300,000. The work groups, reduced to seventeen when some pairs with the same subjects decided to combine, wrote their own instructions, recruited whatever additional members they needed and selected their own chairmen (three of whom were facilitators we had provided). They were to complete their jobs in two months. Almost all of them met the schedule and did outstanding work for that short time. The very few that didn't gave the committee enough useful material to build on successfully.

The committee looked over the reports with the Board chairman, who had them duplicated and mailed to all the work group members for review and study. In October and November came a series of five feedback meetings, with three related subjects covered at each. Between forty and sixty work group members came to each session —some to propose changes in their own reports, some to suggest changes in others. The committee members listened, asked questions and made notes, but did not attempt to answer any criticisms or comment on suggestions.

At that point a new factor came to the committee's attention. In November 1970, the federal Department of Housing and Urban Affairs had given the county a grant of $125,000 to support a project to design and install a computerized information system appropriate to a unified approach to urban development. By the autumn of 1972, the three-man team working under that grant had completed its analysis and was working to test its hypotheses by developing the data appropriate for the county's fastest-growing area. Its progress had led HUD to encourage a request for an additional grant of $226,000 so the whole county could be covered. The computer team's design included relating the data to whatever goals would eventually be approved.

While the five review sessions were in progress, the committee decided to shift its emphasis from two-, five- and ten-year goals to the computer team's format. That included three levels:

1. The goals themselves, very broad and general.
2. Within each goal, objectives narrower and more specific than the goals, through accomplishment of which the goals could be approached.
3. Within each objective, targets very specific and measurable, so progress toward them could be tested at any time from data produced by the computer. [See Appendix, Chapter 6, "Health Section, Fairfax Goals Report," for an example.]

In early December 1971, and from January 1972 to early July the committee met from four to seven hours a week to change the pattern of the individual reports and incorporate items from the October and November meetings. The members simplified and shortened the reports to make them more readable. One at a time, each subject received concentrated attention.

After a few weeks the county executive loaned the committee a one-person staff: a very capable young woman versed in land use matters who served as writer, advisor and negotiator. At each meeting the committee members went over some of the recommendations and related comments on one of the reports, and then proposed changes. From time to time, as requested, the head of the computer team and the director of the county planning staff joined the discussion.

After each session, Carolyn, our girl Friday, made the revisions the committee proposed and, when we had finished a subject, reviewed them with the county staff members in the interested departments. She then brought the draft back to the committee with the suggested staff changes interlined. The committee accepted, rejected, revised. Carolyn produced a corrected version for the next meeting, had it approved and then sent it to the chairman of the original subgroup for participants' review and comments. When it came back, Carolyn again brought it to the committee with comments interlined.

Some subjects went back again to the staff or subgroup (or both) for a second round. Always, three or four subjects were in the mill and committee members made frequent cross-checks between subjects. Finally, August 31, 1972, slightly less than eighteen months from the kickoff session, the committee sent the report to the county Board.

At a joint session of the Board and the committee in October, Board members raised questions about the report and made largely favorable preliminary comments. After that, two other factors came into the picture: a five-year fiscal plan prepared by the county staff at the Board's instruction and a new development control plan devised by Board members. The Board integrated the recommended goals, objectives and targets, the five-year and development control plans, and the data made available from the computer into the development of a long-range Planning and Land Use system. Meanwhile, a self-generated citizen organization created subgroups to study the health, education, social service, and other components of the county budget and show the county Board how to use the budgets in coming years as stepping-stones toward the recommended goals.

For an example of the value of such outside viewpoints, the people comprising the subcommittee on health were a doctor's wife who was also a member of the county's Health and Hospital Commission and the Comprehensive Health Planning Council of Northern Virginia; a budget analyst of the staff of the federal Office of Management and Budget; and a retired management analyst. They studied the health section of the Goals Report and the 1973 budget proposals, then talked with county staff members and knowledgeable citizens about the county Health Department's problems.

Among other points they found that:

1. The Goals Report called for clarification of the county's organizational structure for health services.
2. The county was considering making some organizational changes.
3. The staff had no health planner, either in its Health or Planning departments.

But the county was requesting two new positions for air pollution follow-up. They recommended that the new positions be dropped for the current year as premature and an overall health planning position be created instead to provide a knowledgeable ball-carrier for a sound, prompt reorganization and a longer-range push toward the other goals. The full committee adopted this proposal, followed by the county Board, and in due course the health planner was hired.

Naturally, we are pleased with the goals program's success. Early signs of a good start were the unusually high level of interest generated by the advance meeting in February 1971, and a Prince William County request for a similar activity. The products of the work groups showed what interested citizens could do in a short period and validated our confidence in the techniques we used to involve them and organize their effort. Since the initiation of the program four members of those groups have been elected to the county Board (one of them defeating a fifth by forty votes), indicating either that we had drawn influential people into it or that the program had made them so.

The Planning and Land Use system pleases us because, beyond its value for Fairfax County, it has the potential of being valuable as a demonstration to other areas.* We also feel good about the self-generated citizen support for the recommended goals and the fact that the out-of-pocket cost of developing them was minuscule: Carolyn's salary for four months plus the reproducing of the work group and committee reports and their mailing to all participants.

For these evidences of a successful program we, and Fairfax County, must thank the then Board chairman, William Hoofnagle, who both initiated and supported it, and all the citizens who participated, but most thanks go to the members of the Economic Development Study Committee for their realization that citizen support would be essential, their ability to provide excellent guidance and their willingness to see the job to its lengthy end.

* Arlington County has begun a program with Community Education Program participation, and the International City Managers Association was so impressed that it distributed to all its members a fourteen-page report on the initial experiment, while the Association's director of research and development took leave to work with a Fairfax County task force in planning the expanded operation.

7

GETTING CITIZEN INPUT ON PROBLEMS OF A PLANNING DISTRICT

Our Northern Virginia area faced a welter of regional problems as the new decade of the seventies began. Everywhere in its four counties and three cities there was citizen and official worry and fragmented effort to "do something" about such critical concerns as growth and environment, financing local government, transportation and delivery of health services.

The Virginia General Assembly had divided the state into potential Planning Districts, hoping regional co-operation would help bring needed solutions, and in our region the Northern Virginia Planning District Commission had been formed with members from six of the seven jurisdictions and several towns.

Our Community Education Program offered its services to the commission, pointing out that we could help to obtain the valuable input of informed citizens, many of whom knew more about specific problem areas than the commission members did, and to educate its widespread public so its suggested solutions would be better understood.

The commission accepted our offer and, in October 1970, adopted a resolution authorizing the Community Education Program "to assist the Commission in obtaining citizen participation in the formulation of District goals and plans."

We suggested fifteen problem areas the commission might want explored and commission members gave top priority to three: Population Growth and Its Implications; Land Use—Environment vs. Development; and Financing Local Government. We proposed a one-day conference on each of these subjects, and the commission chairman appointed two commission members and a commission staff member to work with us in the planning.

Fourteen people gathered for the first planning session, February 22, 1971. We had invited representatives of all jurisdictions of the district to join us and the commission people. However, Alexandria, Fairfax City and Loudoun County were missing. Flip chart records show that three of us agreed to fill the gap, by each taking one jurisdiction and inviting to the next meeting one person who knew that jurisdiction well, to join the group and assist in planning and organizing the first conference. To get this complete representation, we knew, was important in getting all the right people to the conference and in assuring that its content would meet the needs of all the area.

At this first meeting, the group adopted two purposes:

1. To obtain for the Planning District Commission citizen understanding and input on particular problem areas or subjects.
2. When a topic had been selected, to facilitate group activities that would lead to development of goals, formulation of policies and/or solution of problems.

Next, the members considered the three conference topics which PDC members had rated most important to the commission and, after appraising them, selected Population Growth and Its Implications as the topic for the first conference.

Third, we listed the following as purposes for that conference:

1. Provide information for the PDC on:
   a. Key issues, with their problems and implications.
   b. Citizen viewpoints on the issues.
2. Give the PDC clues as to public reaction to plans suggested by the Metropolitan Washington Council of Governments.
3. Help the PDC define its roles and start making plans responsive to citizen needs.
4. Stimulate citizen interest and participation in PDC activities —let citizens know what PDC is all about.
5. Raise level of interest in local governments in PDC.

6. Crystallize policy among the Northern Virginia jurisdictions as to their growth vis-à-vis that of the region.
7. Start a public debate about the issues—provide a basis for intelligent discussion of them.

Fourth, we asked the two members of our planning group who were most knowledgeable about the problem area to bring to the next meeting a list of what they saw as the most important issues to be explored in analyzing the subject.

We were off and running.

While we will briefly describe each of the three conferences that followed, they all had a number of things in common. They were all:

1. Co-sponsored by the Community Education Program and the Northern Virginia Planning District Commission, and all held at George Mason.
2. Carefully planned in a number of preparatory sessions with the planning group enlarged to bring in the necessary participation.
3. Provided the most knowledgeable people available as speakers and resource people to give solid background content for discussion, answer questions and stimulate thinking.
4. Brought together the right people as participants. Much thought was given to each invitation list. It included the state legislators, the elected officials of each jurisdiction, the agencies of each jurisdiction concerned with the topic, the various commissions, councils and organizations concerned with the topic, business, industrial and professional people concerned with the topic, civic leaders.
5. Provided advance reading materials so the process of educating the participants could begin before the conference.
6. Made use of our conference and discussion techniques from the providing of name tags legible across a room (to preclude all the wondering and asking of "who's that?") to the use of flip charts in small groups with trained facilitators.
7. Provided for evaluation of the conference by participants (so we could know what was liked and what wasn't as a basis for repeating the good and eliminating the bad next time around).
8. Provided for summaries of the conferences to be written by

trained people and mailed afterwards not only to participants but to those who planned to be there but hadn't been able to make it.

Population Growth and Its Implications

The invitations prepared by the planning group brought 160 to the one-day session on May 15, 1971. Over half of these represented civic groups; over a quarter, governmental agencies; the remainder, private enterprise.

The subject itself was a natural to generate interest. Northern Virginia's population had increased to 900,000 persons in the 1960s, a 50 per cent gain. Moreover, the experts were projecting that population to double by 1985.

Participants, all meeting together, listened intently to the morning's talks:

"Population and Employment Projections for the Washington Metropolitan Area."

"Comments on These Projections."

"Significance of Economic Forces on Population Distribution."

Next, participants met according to their jurisdictions in small discussion groups with trained facilitators from their own jurisdictions. This was a technique we had not tried before, one especially suited to the subject and generally very well liked by participants.

Each group was asked to discuss and list briefly the factors its members thought generated growth and then the members' concerns about growth. With purely local factors and concerns eliminated, the conference summary lists these:

A.   Factors which Generate Growth.
   1.   Rapid growth in general population.
   2.   Accessibility to transportation facilities.
      a.   Metro (rapid transit).
      b.   Highways.
      c.   National and Dulles airports.
   3.   Physical proximity to the District of Columbia.
   4.   Impact of federal government (largest industry and employer in the region).
   5.   Growth of employment in the private sector.
   6.   Availability of land served by utilities (e.g., water, sewer).

7. Competing tax policies among jurisdictions.
8. Cultural advantages of the area, including higher education.
9. Availability of a wide range of housing at different price levels.
10. Quality of public services.
B. Concerns about Growth Shared by Jurisdictions.
  1. Intensive development of the area will demand more public services and increase the costs to the local jurisdictions. The result of these pressures could be a decline in the quality of public services or bankruptcy for local jurisdictions.
  2. A balanced population established throughout the area according to race, income and age is necessary for stability.
  3. Competitive tax policies and lack of co-ordination of planning between individual jurisdictions are counterproductive for the region as a whole.
  4. As the area develops, the quality of life and amenities will deteriorate (e.g., leisure, health and welfare).
  5. Co-ordination of social service planning with land use and economic planning is necessary for orderly growth.
  6. Strong need for regional decisions on problems such as air, water, sewer and open space is indicated.
  7. Need for better co-operation with the state on the planning of transportation facilities is cited.

The afternoon session opened with three talks on more effective strategies for guiding regional growth:

"Land Use Regulations" as tools for controlling growth.

"Planning and Programming for Capital Spending."

"Revenue Policies, Public Entrepreneurship and Analytical Supports for Decision Making."

Then discussion groups met, each with a facilitator using flip chart sheets. Participants, as usual, had been given their choice of topics and there were several groups each on the three subjects. The conference summary sent later to participants and others who were interested condensed and co-ordinated the flip chart records as follows:

Revenue Policies—The groups on revenue policies discussed the different kinds of taxation and their possible effect on growth. They then made the following recommendations:

1. Change the state law to permit local income tax and real estate transfer tax.
2. Establish a local tax on gasoline with the provision that the revenue can be used for other projects besides roads.
3. Remove restrictions so that localities have the freedom to improve taxes as needed.
4. Remove restrictions in the state constitution which prevent localities from imposing higher tax assessment ratios on commercial rather than residential properties thus preventing localities from imposing differential taxation.

Public Entrepreneurship—These groups submitted the following comments and recommendations:

1. Local governments should operate more like the Board of Directors of a corporation.
2. Develop goals for a local jurisdiction, before developing techniques to govern.
3. Public entrepreneurship is an alternative to private entrepreneurship (e.g., Model Cities Program).
4. Effective long-range planning will not take place under the present system.
5. A technique of public entrepreneurship would be standardization of codes and ordinances on a regional basis.

Analytical Supports for Decision Making—The groups discussed problems associated with obtaining material in its most useful form. These included problems with computerizing information, legal problems of transferring data between jurisdictions, and problems in maintaining confidentiality when sample sizes are small.

Participants' evaluation sheets rated the conference a success, especially as a means to increase communication among local and regional governments and concerned citizens about issues of both regional and local impact. Many emphasized the need to bring such groups together on a continuing basis. Participants also felt that they gained useful technical knowledge on ways to influence growth, and politicians and planners said they were grateful for the collection of information on the desires and concerns of the participants and the kinds of growth desired in individual jurisdictions.

But *we* found the evaluation sheets disappointing. Only 67 per

110 WHAT WE DO

cent rated the conference excellent or good; 26 per cent rated it fair; and 7 per cent, poor or very poor.

The 26 per cent of evaluation sheets downgrading the conference to fair, the 5 per cent calling it poor, and the 2 per cent crushing us with a "very poor" rating reflected a misunderstanding about the purpose of the conference. These participants overlooked its exploratory nature. They had hoped for conclusive action plans to emerge and since this did not happen (in fact was not intended to happen), they felt their suggestions were futile. The truth is that all suggestions were studied carefully by the Planning District Commission and considered in its planning.

As the planning group for the next regional conference set to work, we kept in mind this misunderstanding and sought to overcome it.

Environment and Development

The invitations mailed on October 7, 1971, for this November 6 conference emphasized the use to be made of the conference findings:

In developing its planning program, the Northern Virginia Planning District Commission will use the recommendations of the conference to aid it in focusing on the issues which concern Northern Virginia citizens and organizations.

That, we felt, should make the use perfectly clear.

The invitations also stated that the objectives of the conference would be to consider:

1. How can Northern Virginia accommodate growth and also protect environmental quality?
2. What should be the goals of a regional planning process that seeks to accomplish desired growth and environmental objectives?

We knew our subject of Growth and Environment was vast and many-faceted. All aspects could not be explored in any satisfactory depth in one day by all participants. After much preliminary exploration, we divided the subject into eight discussion topics and formed brief questions for each so participants could begin their thinking before the conference. Then, enclosing the following with the invitation, we asked each participant to mark his first and second choices:

CONFERENCE ON ENVIRONMENT AND DEVELOPMENT

George Mason College
Lecture Hall   *November 6, 1971*

Discussion Topics

1. *Open Space.*
   For what purposes? Where (including types of land that should not be developed because of soil or slope)? How much? How can it be acquired and financed?
2. *Water Supply and Sewage Disposal.*
   Does potable water supply and/or sewage disposal capability limit population growth? What planning and action are needed? How can costs involved be met?
3. *Air and Noise Pollution.*
   How can pollutants be controlled? What is the relationship among transportation planning, development and air pollution? What role does congestion play in pollution? (Traffic, etc.)
4. *Water Pollution.*
   Can our lakes, streams and rivers be made a more valuable asset? For fish and wildlife? For recreation? By prevention of siltation and erosion?
5. *Solid Waste Disposal.*
   What wastes should be recycled? By whom? What should be the capacity of landfill sites, obtained now, for future needs? What provision should be made for heavy debris: automobile bodies, broken concrete, tree stumps?
6. *Alternative Housing Density Patterns.*
   How can housing be distributed on the land (a scarce resource) in patterns that are socially desirable, economically feasible and environmentally acceptable?
7. *Regional Distribution of Development.*
   Where should industrial, commercial and residential development occur? What has and should happen to the "Year 2000 Plan"? How can inter-jurisdictional competition be replaced by co-operation?
8. *Ecological Planning Procedures.*
   How can ecological objectives be integrated into planning?

What environmental data are needed? What part do they have
in the regional planning process?

We also enclosed the agenda with the invitation so that prospective participants could see what format we would follow, a format we
had devised to squeeze all we could of both content and participation out of a one-day meeting. It called for a preliminary general
session with three speakers giving overall background, followed by
concurrent morning topic meetings.

Topic meetings were to open with short talks by one or two resource persons followed by a question and answer period, then
group discussion of:

a. The problems and/or issues.

b. The Northern Virginia situation today.

c. The direction we are going under present policies.

d. The alternative courses available that would better "accommodate growth and protect environmental quality."

e. Impediments to their achievement.

After lunch, the topic groups were to meet again, to complete
their morning explorations, if necessary, and then divide into groups
of eight to fifteen, each smaller group selecting three reporters—one
to report his group's recommendations for national and state action,
one, recommendations for regional and local action, and the third,
recommendations for private enterprise action. These group recommendations were to be made after the group had considered:

a. What goals or objectives should Northern Virginia seek to
achieve?

b. In view of the impediments, which of the alternatives are
most promising?

Next, all the reporters from all the topic discussion groups were
to meet in three different report sessions: national and state action,
regional and local action, private enterprise action. Each was to present his group's recommendations. And another, very skilled reporter for each category of action, was to summarize these and
present them at a closing general session.

It was a highly structured format but we felt it might work. And it
did.

The 125 "right people" attending the conference had a chance to
explore in depth the aspect of environment and growth that most
interested them. Each topic group not only had a chance to recommend action but to hear, in the closing general session, the action
recommended by other topic groups. (And to read the highlights of

other topic groups' discussion in the conference summary mailed later to all participants.)

Moreover, the conference closed with responses to the recommendations by a representative of private industry (the Northern Virginia Board of Realtors), by a state legislator and by the chairman of the Planning District Commission's Regional Planning Committee. Participants at least knew they had been heard by the first two groups and more than heard by the Planning District Commission. Its spokesman assured participants that the input of the conference would be used by the commission in the development of its regional goals and policies plan for a better "quality of life" in Northern Virginia.

So we were back to the purpose of the conference and reassured about it.

We would have taken a week off to celebrate, but the next conference was to be December 11, 1971, only one month and four days away. We already had begun the planning, of course—in fact, the invitations were ready to mail—but there was still much to be done.

Financing Local Government—Who Will Tax Whom and How?

A whole new bag of worms, one that was plaguing our area, areas all across the nation. The local budget squeeze was painful. Jurisdictions were saying they must either increase the local tax bill or cut services. There was talk of reforming the property tax, of redistribution of fiscal responsibility (especially for schools), of rethinking of price mechanisms for public services. No one questioned that local government was in crisis and *something* had to be done.

We had timed the conference for the month before our state legislators went to Richmond for the 1972 session of the Virginia General Assembly. The conference, hopefully, would send them off fully aware of the financial problems on the home front and the ways the home front hoped the General Assembly would help. Several likely solutions to local financing could come about only through enabling legislation. To provide participants with some advance education, we mailed them a sheaf of reading matter.*

* The "Summary of Proposals for Property Tax Reform Adopted by the Governor's Committee on State-Local Cooperation" (August 1971); "The Bendheim Commission and Local Government" by Dr. John L. Knapp (September 1971), presenting highlights of the revenue picture for Virginia state and local government as seen by the staff of that commission; "Comparative Fiscal Facts: Virginia and Adjoining States," a

Our planning group decided the conference would have two purposes:

1. To consider the revenue dilemmas which faced the 1972 session of the General Assembly;

2. To explore ways of improving relationships among the state government, local governments, regional bodies and private industry, and ways of best controlling and distributing the mounting costs and responsibilities needed to meet urban problems.

Again, the question was how to break the total subject down so participants could explore more deeply the aspects that most interested or concerned them. We decided on three morning and three afternoon discussion groups, each participant to choose his group in advance and each group to have knowledgeable speakers and resource people, time for questions, answers and discussion and a reporter to summarize the findings for other groups when all met together.

These were the morning topics:

1. Should the state assume basic responsibility for elementary and secondary education?

2. How should the costs of highways, mass transportation and pollution abatement be shared among governments, landowners, users and polluters?

3. What are the implications of the state takeover of welfare (rigidity vs. flexibility—state standards vs. local)?

The afternoon topics:

1. Reform of the property tax.

2. Modernizing the income and sales taxes.

3. Potentialities and problems of user charges.

The planners suggested these questions for the afternoon discussions of all three groups: How to provide for taxpayer equity? How to provide for disadvantaged taxpayers? Local control vs. more equitable statewide tax systems. Mobility of taxpayers. Administrative problems. Governmental entrepreneurship. Differential land and improvement tax.

Then, to be sure our state legislators were there to get the benefit of all this, we set to work to get them on the program, using them liberally as speakers or resource people.

---

table put together by Dr. L. Ecker-Racz, a well-known fiscal authority; and an article from *Psychology Today*, "The City as a Distorted Price System," by Dr. Wilbur L. Thompson.

The plan worked well, drawing 141 participants with an especially high ratio of General Assembly members and elected and appointed officials. Our evaluation sheets were back to normal. About 80 per cent rated the conference excellent or very good and the rest called it fair. No poor or very poor rating.

"What do you think were the strong points of these sessions, if any?" the evaluation sheet asked. Some answers:

1. Bringing together of resource persons, legislators and interest groups.
2. The opportunity for elected officials to discuss these topics in a non-political setting with knowledgeable persons.
3. Able speakers. Recaps of other sessions.
4. Diversity of viewpoints represented.
5. Provided an opportunity for the airing of divergent opinions.
6. Innovative ideas.
7. Small sessions provided better discussions and more time for questions.
8. Sending out reading materials in advance.
9. Good organization, time scheduling and facilitating.
10. Communication and education.
11. Indication of probable trends.
12. Good breakdown of topics.
13. Good way to communicate with state legislators.
14. That participants had enough time to ask questions and discuss problems.
15. The issues became clearly defined.
16. Rich background of many participants.
17. The very fact that it was given and well attended.

"What do you think were the weak points, if any?" was the second evaluation question. Some responses and our comments:

1. Size of topic sessions should be smaller. [We are always in favor of small discussion groups. Our fellow planners, however, had wanted to try larger sessions.]
2. Some participants hadn't done their homework. [We had provided the homework but couldn't stand over people with a whip.]
3. Not enough time to discuss the many problems. [At our next conference, on transportation, we allowed two days.]
4. Elected officials given priority. [Intentional this time, as we've explained. They were the ones in position to act.]
5. Parts a little too technical for ready understanding. [If they

> hadn't been, we would have been criticized for not getting down to the nitty-gritty.]

6. Should have been a lay person or just a taxpayer or recipient of services on panels. [These people were in all the discussion groups. When it comes to speeches, most people want experts.]

7. No real final result—e.g., a report to someone. [This person should have waited a minute. Reports were mailed soon after the conference to all participants, including the legislators and local officials.]

8. Should have been more people here. [We invited more but couldn't hijack them for the day.]

9. Inadequate identification of precise issues before legislators. [We expected the participants to do that.]

10. Too much speaking; not enough dialogue. [More dialogue and others would have said, "Not enough speaking." We tried to hit a happy medium.]

11. Too much time on reiterating the problem and not enough time on constructive suggestions. [Maybe so, but you can only guide speakers and participants. Those who want to reiterate will.]

12. Editorialized reports from some reporters. [True, though we had asked them *not* to do this.]

13. The day was too beautiful outside for us to want to be inside. [But nobody had the excuse of lousy weather for not coming.]

On the whole, we were pleased with the conference. We were especially pleased when our state legislators and local jurisdictions began to take hard looks at new ways to raise money (and a significant number of their citizens revealed knowledge of the need and support for innovation). One jurisdiction came up with a formula for assessing new development for services that development would engender. Authority for a land transfer tax nearly passed in the General Assembly. There was action for local piggyback income taxes, local cigarette taxes. User charges, utility taxes, assessments, license fees were re-examined. Two jurisdictions hard pressed for school facilities adopted a twelve-month school plan to make greater use of existing facilities. In fact, the whole area was looking at new ways of raising needed revenue and stretching what it had.

We think our conference did a lot to give needed background and start thinking on a level sophisticated enough to cope.

Transportation

In January of 1972, the Community Education Program and the Planning District Commission brought together an advisory committee of legislators, officials and citizen leaders representing the jurisdictions of our area. Our purpose was to ask them, what next? What should be the subjects of regional conferences in the coming year and in what priority order? They picked transportation to come first and health services† second.

So, having again consulted a representative cross section of the power structure of our area (instead of deciding ourselves), we got busy on plans for a transportation conference. This time we drew into our planning two agencies vitally concerned with the subject: the Northern Virginia Transportation Commission and the Metropolitan Washington Council of Governments.

One of the first decisions was to allot two days to the conference instead of the usual one because of the complexity of the problems and its crisis proportions.

Crisis, indeed. Area "expressways" had become crawlways at rush hours, bridges across the Potomac were clogged, bus companies were going broke and providing very poor service at ever higher prices. The Metro system construction was just beginning and there were grave doubts it would ease congestion much even when finished. Topping it all, the Washington area had suffered days of dangerous auto-engendered air pollution.

We set the conference for two Saturdays in May—May 6 and May 20. The May 6 sessions, we decided, would be problem-oriented with emphasis on exploration of the present transportation predicament and the shortcomings of traditional approaches to transportation problems. On May 20, speakers and participants would move on to discuss specific alternatives and how the best of these might be made part of a balanced transportation system.

We named our subject "Economics and Politics of Balanced Transportation for Northern Virginia"; then planned the two-day agenda, booked the best available speakers and resource people, selected and reproduced background materials to provide information and stimulate thinking and mailed out invitations.

Because it was taking two probably beautiful Saturdays, getting facilitators and participants was a whale of a job, but worth it. Al-

† Because we made use of educational TV for this conference, we give it its own brief chapter, Chapter 8.

though only a total of 120 attended on May 6 and ninety on May 20, they were "right people"—decision makers or decision influencers, elected officials, representatives of agencies responsible for transportation planning, leading citizens.

On May 6, the morning focus, "Perspectives on Our Transportation System, was given in three talks:

"Understanding Transportation as a System: The Problem of Keeping Pace with Demand."

"The Transit Predicament and Its Implications."

"The Urban Freeway Predicament and Its Implications."

A question-answer-comment period followed each talk. Afternoon focus was on "Some Shortcomings of Currently Fashionable Plans, Policies and Mechanisms for Coping with Transportation Problems." In order to bring all participants the maximum content and, at the same time, the chance to ask questions in the more relaxed atmosphere of a smaller group than an all-conference assembly, we tried a new format and got good results. We divided participants alphabetically into three groups. Each group met in a separate room and was visited in turn by three sets of speakers. Each set of speakers talked and answered questions on one of three topics:

"The Economics of Transportation."

"Politics: The Problem of Institutions and Interest Groups."

"The Need for More and Better Attention by Planners to Land Use-Transportation Interrelationships."

The heads and notes of participants were packed with facts, figures and ideas to mull over in the two weeks before the next session.

On May 20, the morning focus was "Reappraising Metropolitan Transportation Planning."

Participants met in general session for a talk on that subject. They then formed eight small groups for discussion of their topic of preference. Three groups discussed *shaping urban development*. Topics of the other five groups were: *reducing peak hour traffic, improving service/better marketing, changing the regulatory environment, subsidy of bus operations and innovations in financing*. Each group, of course, had a trained facilitator to lead discussion. Each group, too, had a knowledgeable member who started the thinking with a brief talk and then served as its resource person.

Whew! Even though this was a two-day conference, time was too limited for a report-back session on these discussions. We included highlights of the flip chart records, however, in the summary mailed later.

We also included a summary of the afternoon's small group discussions of free transit versus transit pricing governed by supply and demand, with subsidies given directly to low income users. The summary combined the flip chart highlights of the various groups in order to avoid repetition:

On Subsidizing Transit

The level of transportation desired by most will not pay for itself and subsidies are needed. However, there also should be user charges to pay a realistic share of the cost and some way found to counteract these principal objections to subsidization:

1. It discourages the improvement of services, stifles creativity and encourages status quo.
2. Money spent on transportation subsidies is money not spent on other social needs.
3. Government funds for operations would mean government control, and day-to-day decisions about services and routes should not be made via the slow government route.
4. If there is a public service and people come to rely on it, an alternative service must be provided if the initial service is discontinued due to public policy decision.
5. Free transit or very low fares would increase vandalism.

Transportation for the Poor

1. Some form of direct subsidy aid to low income people who need help in buying transportation. Perhaps the poor could buy special tokens for a low fare or the poor could be given tokens or direct cash payments to be used for transportation.
2. Suburban employers might pay for bus pools to take low income ghetto residents to the suburbs for jobs.
3. Charge people who benefit through higher land values to pay for transportation for poor people.
4. Put transit stations where the poor live and where they need to go for employment.

To solve transportation problems, various modes must be used. Taxes, user charges, subsidies, land use planning all must play a part. Metro, buses of all sizes, jitneys, taxis and the private car all will be needed to move people around. There must be co-ordination among agencies and local and regional co-operation. We must work against over-regulation. Plans must be politically and administratively feasible. Certainly, thought should be given to:

1. Reducing use of automobile.
   a. Overcome the mystique of the automobile.
   b. Advertise the true costs of cars, and, via peak hour user charges for congested highways, make the true costs visible to the car owner.
   c. Place toll gates at entrances to congested areas.
   d. Improve other forms of transportation (Metro and buses), provide jitneys, etc.
   e. Reduce the need for long trips through land use planning that brings homes closer to employment, recreation and other services.
   f. Reduce peak hour traffic volume through car-pooling.
   g. Perhaps the Highway Trust Fund should be converted to a Transportation Fund.

2. Encouraging use of mass transit by improving it.
   a. Air conditioning.
   b. Convenience to homes; walking distance.
   c. Different sizes of buses.
   d. Keeping on schedule; reliability.
   e. Frequency of runs.
   f. Routes where needed.
   g. Public information about service.
   h. Transfer co-ordination.
   i. Bus stops protected from weather and crime; Metro stations protected from crime.
   j. Billing once a month or use of passes or credit cards.
   k. Provide incentives such as reserved bus lanes, priority in traffic signals.
   l. Provide for stops in site and development plans of new construction.
   m. Assign buses to employment areas.
   n. Franchise total transportation service, not only buses and Metro, but jitneys, dial-a-bus, etc.

3. Using new communication techniques to reduce transportation

needs. Present technology has not really been tapped in this area. Why should all employees go to one central point for eight hours every day?

4. Land use planning.
   a. Give incentives to industry to come to the suburbs and require in turn that industry give a transportation subsidy for employees such as bus tokens or contract bus service.
   b. Encourage compact development of communities.
   c. Provide incentives to improve housing and environment in the central city.
   d. Some types of employment could be and should be located near or actually within residential areas or residential buildings.
   e. Work to overcome the adverse effects of Metro, i.e., the density and pollution it will create around stations.

A general session talk on "The Need for Administrative and Institutional Changes" followed the small group discussions and closed the conference.

People filled out their evaluation sheets and, still talking transportation, walked down the steps of George Mason's red brick lecture hall and up the winding walk to the parking lot.

Again, we felt good. A balanced free-flowing transportation system hadn't miraculously appeared, of course, but the kind of people who could bring it about had been stimulated into some pretty deep thinking, some pretty concentrated exchanging of information and ideas.

The summary had this to say: "It seemed evident, after the two days, that providing balanced transportation must rest on many factors. Present systems must be made ever more effective as innovative new systems are tried. Planners must be less bemused by long-term planning and work on steps to take in the next year, two years, three years if the long-range goals are to be reached. Administrative machinery must be made more efficient. Above all, transportation planning should never be undertaken as a thing apart. It should be undertaken within the framework of total planning and solutions often should be sought through better use of existing facilities and reshaping land use rather than through the traditional methods of merely expanding transportation facilities."

8

MAKING USE OF EDUCATIONAL TV TO REACH MORE PEOPLE

Our advisory committee for 1972 (see Chapter 7) had recommended that a regional conference on health care follow the conference on transportation.

The result was probably the most exciting conference we'd ever helped plan and conduct. It was held in the studios of Northern Virginia's educational television station, WNTV/Channel 53, and broadcast live to our whole area, the first such regionwide activity to have such coverage.

Some of us worried about the innovation, fearing people would turn into actors rather than participants and that, instead of a conference, we would have a performance. Not so at all. If anything, the knowledge they were on TV seemed to bring out the best conference behavior in both speakers and discussants. As they went about the serious business of the conference, they seemed on the one hand especially inspired, alert and productive, and, on the other hand, virtually unaware of the cameras.

Credit for this must go first of all to the high caliber of the participants. Being leaders in their various fields, they already were used to thinking and talking in the spotlight. Moreover, that Saturday of

December 9, 1972, their primary concern was not to turn in a good "show" but to listen and learn, think and contribute and, thinking together, help explore "Health Care in Northern Virginia: Whose Business?"

Much credit must go also to the director, producer and cameramen of Channel 53. From the beginning of our joint undertaking, they understood what we were trying to do and worked closely with us to help achieve the desired results. They graciously gave advance briefings for conference principals, helped with timing and offered advice on what would be most effective from the TV standpoint, but, throughout, it remained *our* conference.

Planning began in much the usual way. Nine months before, in March 1972, an initial planning group met with us and two representatives of the Northern Virginia Planning District Commission.*

We decided that the purposes of the conference should be:
1. To explore the health needs of the Planning District.
2. To improve communication among professionals in the health field, legislators and local officials (later we added "citizens active in the health care field").
3. To lay the groundwork for a health program in the District.
4. To open the way for a 1973 conference to determine priorities.

The Comprehensive Health Planning Council of Northern Virginia agreed to join George Mason and the Planning District Commission in sponsoring the conference. Now, as planning sessions continued, came careful planning of the agenda, booking of speakers, resource people and facilitators, and preparation of the invitation and list of invitees. (See Appendix, Chapter 8.)

We chose the conference date with care. The General Assembly would convene in January for its 1973 session. Since the conference would raise health issues pending before the legislature and provide a forum for legislators, health providers and citizens to discuss them, we wanted a time as close to January as possible without running into crowded holiday schedules. December 9 seemed ideal.

* The group included representatives of the state Comprehensive Health Planning Council and the Mental Health Services Board; the Northern Virginia Medical Council; the Fairfax Hospital Association; the Arlington Medical Council and Health and Welfare Council; the Prince William County Hospital Board; and the directors of the Fairfax and Loudoun County Health Departments, a legislator, an elected local official and the president of the Eighth District Nurses Association.

After deciding the morning should be devoted to talks and audience comments on ambulatory care, the role of the public health agency in health care and long-term care, we chose questions to be answered in two of these talks and booked our speakers:

"Ambulatory Care—Alternative Delivery Systems"
In the delivery of ambulatory care what should be the roles of:
1. Private physicians?
2. Health maintenance organizations?

How can preventive care be used to reduce acute or other more intensive care?

What should be the distinction between walk-in clinic and emergency room services?

"The Role of the Public Health Agency in Health Care"
"Long-Term Care"
In the delivery of long-term care, what should be the roles of proprietary, private non-profit, and public institutions?

Is a balance needed between skilled and moderate care facilities? If so, how can it be developed?

We planned the afternoon to begin with small group sessions. Each group would discuss one of three subjects (ambulatory, home or long-term care) to raise and put in priority order questions for the morning's speakers. Depending upon participants' choices, there would be as many groups on each subject as necessary for good discussion. One of the groups would be televised.

The afternoon would continue with a general session at which each group's facilitator would ask that group's questions of the panel. We settled on the facilitators to be sure the questions would be stated briefly and as the groups wished. A member of the Virginia legislature, active in health planning, would close the conference with her reactions to it.

Working with Channel 53, we then planned special events to be on camera during breaks in the conference. We described these special events on the agenda so participants could co-operate:

Special Events

During the morning coffee break, 10:20–10:50, a group of legislators, newsmen and citizens will interview the first three speakers on television. During this period, conference participants are asked to remain out of the broadcast studio. Those wishing to watch the interview can do so on monitoring sets in the Press Room and in Studio B.

During the luncheon break, Channel 53 will air programs related to health care.

From 2:15 to 2:45 P.M., while participants are reassembling in the studios after the small group discussions, Mr. William O'Neill, the chairman of the subsequent panel, will interview on television the heads of the three organizations sponsoring the conference: The Hon. Jimmie H. Singleton, chairman, Northern Virginia Planning District Commission; Mr. Pierre S. Palmer, chairman, Comprehensive Health Planning Council of Northern Virginia, and Dr. Barnard Joy, director, Community Education Program of George Mason University. During this period, please return to the studio quietly so you do not interfere with the broadcast.

Meanwhile, extra care had to be given to conference timing. We prepared a script with the necessary introductory remarks and explanations to be given by the various chairmen and announcers, then invited these people to a studio briefing so the TV people could check their rate of speaking and acquaint them with timing signals. The briefing served also to make these conference leaders feel at home in the studio so that at the actual conference they could do a better job of serving as hosts for the speakers and other participants.

For this occasion, we divided the facilitator's role in the small discussion group to be televised, calling the discussion leader the facilitator and a person at the flip chart the recorder. These two people† also attended the studio briefing to help decide where to set the flip chart, where to hang the filled flip sheets and where the facilitator should sit in the circle of chairs, as well as to become acquainted with the studio and timing signals.

We had made other preparations to help the televised small group feel at ease. Its members all had agreed in advance to be on camera. Plans called for them to meet in a special room the morning of the conference to be introduced to one another and, later, to be excused from the morning session a little early so they could lunch together before taking their places in the circle of chairs before the cameras.

Every seat in Channel 53's main studio was filled that balmy but

† We appointed ourselves for the simple reason that we had more experience than anyone else.

wet morning. The director's hand went down, the camera at the back of the room and the two side cameras began whirring softly and the chairman of the Planning District Commission began his introductory remarks.

At first, some audience members looked at the cameras or gazed through the glass panels of the control room at the monitoring rows of TV pictures inside. But soon they forgot cameras and monitors and both speakers and questioners were acting as they always have at our conferences—only a little better because they were on stage.

The morning sessions went smoothly, enthusiastically and on time. Then the special small group to be televised met for their early lunch on schedule. Two members of the group revealed in their talk at lunch that they would have plenty to say later—almost too much, we feared. They quickly established dominance, then spent most of the mealtime giving information unrelated to the morning subject matter and answering questions from the others.

We let it go for a while, then announced pleasantly but firmly that the group had been doing all the wrong things in this informal rehearsal, that on camera we were to limit ourselves to *group* discussion of the morning talks, to *group* formulating of questions for the morning's speakers, and then to a *group* setting of priorities for the questions. To do all this in the time allowed, we would have to forgo giving new information and interviewing one another unless it was directly pertinent to the questions we were listing for the speakers.

There were blushes, sheepish grins and apologies from several members who had worked with us before, knew our discussion techniques and realized they had done little or nothing to keep the warm-up talk on focus.

We pushed back our chairs and hurried to the main studio, where the scene was set and waiting—just enough chairs for group members forming a crescent, with the crescent closed by the flip chart and enough empty wall space to hang flip chart sheets as they were filled. Microphones stood in the center and television cameras behind the circle on either side.

All took chairs except for the recorder, who stood by the flip chart. The men adjusted ties and trouser legs. The women smoothed skirts, fluffed hair. Then the hand signal and the announcer (director of community development for the Planning District Commission and interim director of the Comprehensive Health Planning Council of Northern Virginia) introduced himself and said from the script: "I would like to welcome you to this discussion group for our Conference, 'Health Care: Whose Business?' This is one of several discussion groups of about ten to twelve people meeting during this hour and fifteen minutes to discuss the issues raised by this morning's speakers and to develop questions to ask the panel of speakers later this afternoon." Then he introduced our group resource person and us as facilitator and recorder. He did not introduce the others because we preferred using a subtitle of identification for each discussant when he or she was on camera.

The televised group discussion was very different from the lunchtime warm-up. Although one of the two who had dominated then, several times began to dominate again in the televised session, it was obvious he did it out of habit rather than defiance, and he accepted with good cheer tactful interruption and re-steering of the discussion both from us and other group members. Now, held in check and on course, this really brilliant and well-intentioned person had much to contribute to the group. All its members proved good discussants. The give and take flowed smoothly, the flip chart sheets filled up with questions, priorities were established and by the time the signal came to close the discussion period, we were ready with our priority questions.

We felt our session could stand as a good demonstration of the potential of TV for group discussion. There were, of course, shortcomings, but none that couldn't be overcome the next time around. The tearing of the flip chart sheets from the pad, for instance, was noisy and distracting. This would be simple to remedy by having them pre-torn and merely affixed to the pad with masking tape. In studying the tape later, we saw that our lettering was not legible enough for the viewer. Either our lettering should have been larger or we should have thought to tell the cameramen to use their zoom lenses. Also the camera did not focus enough on the records to keep viewers reminded of the reason participants kept staring so much in that direction. All little things that could be easily fixed.

At the same time as our televised discussion, of course, other small groups were meeting off camera—eleven others in all, each with its own resource person and facilitator to ask that group's priority questions on camera when the whole conference met again. We later compiled and reproduced the questions of all the groups to mail to participants. Not all the questions could be asked and answered by the speakers in the closing general session, but each group had a chance to ask at least the top one. Answers to the others were included in the conference report which all participants received later.

Members of the planning group felt that the conference achieved all four of its objectives. Also, in our opinion, the opinion of participants, sponsors and Channel 53, the conference proved the desirability as well as the feasibility of live coverage of future conferences. Unfortunately, Channel 53, new and with small resources, had not developed means of measuring how many people at home were watching all or part of it. We are certain we reached a number not at the conference—people especially interested in health matters, families and friends of at least part of the participants. In one way or another, we have heard from such as these. But how about the great anonymous mass of others? We can only wonder.

Next time, for one thing, we will build in an audience response mechanism by which watchers on TV as well as actual participants at the conference can submit questions. We will have a switchboard to accept calls and a messenger service to relay them. We will also seek to organize group TV participation, with small groups meeting in homes or offices to watch proceedings, then engage in their own group discussions following the same guidelines as the actual conferees. We don't expect our televised conferences ever to win high mass audience ratings, but if via TV we can bring 5,000 to 10,000 concerned citizens of our area to a conference instead of 150 or so, participatory democracy in Northern Virginia will have taken a giant step.

9

FOR BETTER LOCAL
GOVERNMENT

A County Unmuzzles Its Key Officials

It is human for leaders of organizations or bosses in government or industry to be enthusiastic about full group participation when that participation supports their own views or intended actions or positions. Then, fortified by the support of the group, singing the praises of participation, they can happily go about creating the changes or keeping the status quo they wanted. On the other hand, if the unshackled group comes up with views or suggestions critical of or unpopular with the leadership, it's human for these people to downgrade the whole business and try to pretend the findings were somehow manipulated or misinterpreted in the record, or inconclusive, and so of no real consequence.

Our experience in one jurisdiction in 1966 is an example. We were just beginning our activities in the area, getting acquainted with the citizen and official leadership and anxious to test our techniques.

The jurisdictional representative of our then pilot project convinced a local government official that a "community relations workshop" for their staff people would improve communication and teach techniques that would help in problem solving.

In the spring of 1966, the pilot project director conducted the workshop, outlining the needs which make people behave in groups as they do and periodically breaking the total group into three divisions which identified a number of governmental problems the participants wanted to solve. The jurisdictional executive did not participate in the workshop but gave it his blessing.

Afterwards, the originating official and other participants were enthusiastic about the intra-group communications which developed when the participants were divided into subgroups and expressed the desire for follow-up sessions.

We were pleased to conduct these sessions. The various departments named people to participate. We met in small groups for three afternoons, the originator again very much with us, but his boss, the executive, again otherwise occupied.

Although the flip chart records contained a lot of repetition and a certain amount of elementary stuff, the implications of much that was said were pretty damning. One of the principal problems facing the county officials obviously was the executive himself:

1. *Opening problems.*
   a. With chief executive
      —Difficulty of communicating.
      —Difficulty of getting action.
   b. Intra-departmental
      —Communication between employees.
      —Co-operation between employees.
      —Personality conflicts.
   c. Inter-departmental
      —Lack policy statements.
      —Natural inclination to pass the buck.
      —No one has authority to call or chair a meeting.
   d. Communication with the public.
   e. Communication between the government and the school system.
   f. Communication between the executive branch and the elected officials.
2. *Need for conferences.*
   a. Lack of policy statements.
   b. Passing the buck.
   c. Conferences between department heads at management level.
   d. Conferences between people in agencies with common interests.

e. Getting wider circulation of information within a department.

f. Helping people to understand that each cog in the machine is important.

g. How to instill pride, sense of responsibility and recognition in employees.

3. *Possible benefits of conferences.*

a. Advance notice to enable an agency to plan work better (avoid crash programs).

b. Eliminate duplication of work.

c. Create better understanding.

d. Help in disseminating information to public (better public relations).

e. Having all viewpoints on a problem discussed in one group.

f. Attack such problems as lack of policy statements.

g. Reduce number of problems created by one department head not conferring with enough others.

h. Bring out differences in points of view.

i. Improve operation and, as a result, public relations.

j. Get better understanding of other departments' problems and problems that concern them.

k. Help define problems.

l. Help eliminate duplication.

m. Reduce number of directives necessary.

n. Would provide a forum to develop policies where needed, to explain policies which are not understood and to assure a Regulation Book which is up to date and adequately indexed and distributed.

o. Would be takeoff for problems which involve only some departments.

4. *Subjects which might profitably be discussed in interdepartmental meetings.*

a. Health.
    Environment.
    Air pollution control.

b. Welfare.

c. Juvenile Court.

d. Schools (have school system represented).

e. Chief executive's office.

f. Zoning.

    g. Sanitation.

    h. Planning.

    i. Have each department head explain its work to the others in a series of meetings.

    j. Current events meetings.

    k. Problem discussion meetings initiated at request of a department head or the chief executive.

    l. Outline policies and procedures for governing construction of buildings.

    m. What to do because of dead-end streets created by throughway.

    n. Problems created by a street washout.

5. *Miscellaneous comments on meetings.*

    a. Department manuals would reduce need for meetings or give points of reference.

    b. Manual on meetings would clear way for them—a page in administrative manual.

    c. Meetings would permit exchange of information.

    d. Mail distribution center needed.

    e. Training needed for people who answer phones.

    f. Properly equipped conference room, including coffee urn.

    g. In meetings include someone with authority to make decisions, or summarize viewpoints when decision must be by co-operation.

    h. Put emphasis on avoiding problems—not laying blame for past failures.

Altogether, the sessions were very revealing. The officials of this populous and rich jurisdiction were operating under an archaic system of top control. Conferences and the group approach to problems were new to them. They liked the idea and enthusiastically listed needs and advantages, subjects and suggestions. But the one who could follow through hadn't chosen to participate. And since he had been told that our purpose was to provide training in problem solving not problem solving itself, he had an out. Apparently, he took it, filing our findings away somewhere. We hope it wasn't the nearest trash basket. Life in that government continued very much as of yore.

Insofar as creating change was concerned, the sessions failed. If the governing body had ordered the meetings and the executive's participation, it could have been different. Or if he himself had wanted the sessions in order to improve communication with his staff and get their ideas and constructive criticism, all would have been well. But not so. We had erred in not having this very essential "right person" either with us or really for us. He had permitted the sessions, even paid lip service to the idea, but that was about all. We hadn't known we would open a Pandora's box for him but we did, and, not liking the contents, he ignored them.

We consoled ourselves that, at least, we had proved that our techniques could combine problem solving with training of local government officials. We also had met some very fine people, several of whom participated later in other projects of ours and demonstrated that our lessons had rubbed off.

Happily, in our work with local governments, the future was to be brighter. We cite four examples of teaching key officials of local governments in our area how to apply principles most of them knew to some extent in theory but too often ignored in practice.

Making the Supervisor Easier to Work with and More Effective

In 1970, Fairfax County asked us to conduct a course in supervision for a number of its department heads and top assistants. The city of Alexandria decided to join it, too.

This, we knew, was a natural for training by problem solving. Since 1965, Bert Strauss had been doing just that while teaching a course called "Introduction to Supervision and Management" twice a year for the Graduate School of the United States Department of Agriculture. When he took over the course, he converted it into training by problem solving and it had been beautifully received ever since.

So with considerable confidence, we approached our June 1–5, 1970, workshop on Applying the Principles of Supervision. Alexandria and Fairfax County listed these goals:

1. To provide an educational experience to supervisory personnel which is designed to assist them in understanding and performing their respective roles.
2. To promote interaction, dialogue and co-operation between the supervisory personnel of each of the two governments and the school system, ancillary agencies and non-profit associations in its jurisdiction.
3. To provide a means by which local government services can be performed with increasing efficiency.
4. To determine the feasibility of George Mason College offer-

ing this course and similar urban affairs courses to other
Northern Virginia jurisdictions and graduate students.

The two jurisdictions assigned people they wanted to attend. All
of them were directors or deputy directors of departments or heads
of major departmental components. All were confronted daily with
problems of supervision. All had to interact with subordinates, su-
periors, peers, other agencies, outside agencies and the citizens of
their jurisdictions. While all of them had been well trained in their
trade or profession, few had been to any school but that of hard
knocks and on-the-job experience when it came to the skills of supervision. They needed to be able to define, analyze, act and evaluate
in order to solve the problems confronting them. And, most importantly, they needed to be able to get the co-operation of others
in finding and implementing solutions.

We planned to teach them useful principles of supervision, train
them as facilitators, so they could use those skills in tapping the resources of their subordinates, and introduce them to problem-solving
patterns they could use in their jobs. At the same time, our techniques would give them a chance to apply all they were learning to
problems of special concern to them at the time.

The course was set for five mornings in a large George Mason
classroom. We sent each participant a copy of *The Human Organization* by Dr. Rensis Lickert as advance reading to supply background
on the principles of supervision and made an advance written assignment. This assignment was an easy one—provided the participant
had read and understood the book. Its purpose was to assure that
the advance reading was done and to let us know whether all participants had grasped the basic background concepts.

We began the workshop by emphasizing that the book was only
background, not a text, and that now we would move on to acquaint
them with supervisory skills useful in applying the principles in the
book and to assist them to begin to acquire these skills. This would
be done through short talks by us and practice discussions by them.*

Throughout, we kept our lecturing to a minimum in order to let
participants learn by doing, each group reinforcing its learning by
making guided evaluations of its own discussions.

And we had mimeographed several aids for participants:

1.   How Good a Discussant Are You? [See Chapter 14.]

* For example, see talk on "The Informal Organization," and, also,
"What Motivates People," Appendix, Chapter 9.

2. Suggestions for Discussants. [See Appendix, Chapter 14.]
3. A Pattern for Problem Solving. [See Appendix, Chapter 13.]
4. Application of Factors Which Make a Group. [See Appendix, Chapter 9.]
5. Suggestions for Self-Improvement. [See Appendix, Chapter 9.]
6. Some Criteria for Noting Improved Personal Ability. [See Appendix, Chapter 9.]

All other subjects were explored by the participants themselves in their learn-by-doing discussions.

The first two mornings the four small group training discussions were on subjects we had introduced. Staff members facilitated the first two sessions on:

1. Objectives of supervision and steps toward accomplishing them.
2. Delegation of authority.
   a. What constitutes delegations of authority.
   b. Reasons for delegating authority.
   c. Reasons for not delegating authority.
   d. Conditions under which supervisor will be willing to delegate authority.
   e. Factors involved in deciding what to delegate.
   f. Steps in deciding.
   g. How can a supervisor assure himself that authority he delegated is being properly carried out?
   h. How to get those above to delegate authority.

Then four participant facilitators began to try their skills, with a staff member as guide in each small group. Each of the groups now discussed:

The Ideal Supervisor
1. How an ideal supervisor would conduct himself.
2. Obstacles to becoming an ideal supervisor.
3. Making ourselves ideal supervisors.

When the participant-facilitator had finished putting the group's thinking on the flip chart sheets, our staff member became facilitator again in order to let the group evaluate its work. Then each group reported to the others. As we listened, we were impressed by the thinking that had been done and reminded of similar thinking by federal employees during our Department of Agriculture course. Yes, the problems of a supervisor and the ways to become a better one are pretty much the same anywhere—in business, in industry, in all levels of government.

Co-ordinating the points made by all groups and eliminating obvious repetitions, this is what our Alexandria and Fairfax County people had to say:

A. How an ideal supervisor would conduct himself:
1. With care (TLC).
2. With confidence.
3. With authority.
4. Set example.
5. Recognize achievement.
6. Be polite, courteous.
7. Sense of humor.
8. Be firm, but fair and consistent.
9. Be willing to follow as well as issue orders.
10. Develop trust and confidence in employees.
11. Keep communication open.
12. Ability to motivate.
13. Be motivated himself.
14. Ability to delegate authority.
15. Show respect to subordinates.
17. Be a good listener.
18. Show personal interest in employee.
19. Have competence.
20. Have character.
21. Be consistent in behavior and standards.
22. Be ready to recognize leadership in employees.
23. Keep employees informed.
24. Be willing to assist the employee in his problems.

B. Obstacles to becoming an ideal supervisor:
1. Not given support by superior.
2. Lack of technical knowledge and/or supervisory techniques.
3. Subordinates who aren't qualified for their work.
4. Poor working conditions and lack of equipment.
5. Personality and character shortcomings.
6. Impossible task.
7. Budget limit.
8. Lack of motivation (supervisor, subordinate).
9. Lack of one or more basic traits mentioned previously.

    10. Prejudices:
- a. Within himself.
- b. Within the organization.
- c. From without.

    11. Failure to delegate properly.

    12. Past personal association with fellow employees.

    13. Lack of support of top management.

    14. Communication barriers within the organization.

    15. Resentment—if promoted from ranks be able to prove yourself.

C. Making ourselves ideal supervisors:

    1. Consult subordinates before making decisions.

    2. Be prepared and knowledgeable in organizational goals.

    3. Be motivated.

    4. Take training courses (technical, supervisory).

    5. Establish high goals.

    6. Develop self-confidence.

    7. Learn to delegate authority.

    8. Develop and train subordinates, show them respect.

    9. Keep yourself aware of the qualifications of a good supervisor and check yourself against a qualifications list.

    10. Accept responsibility.

    11. Promote the worthy.

    12. Be loyal to top management but at same time consider feelings and needs of subordinates.

    13. Be ready and willing to go the extra mile.

The second morning, with other participant-facilitators now having a chance to practice, the discussion subject in the four small groups was Ideal Subordinates. Again, after our staff members had led group evaluation sessions, there was a report-back by each group to the others. We have consolidated the flip chart records:

Ideal Subordinates

A. How an ideal subordinate would conduct himself:

    1. Show respect.

    2. Support his supervisor, be loyal, co-operative.

    3. Recognize supervisor-subordinate relationship and accept supervisor's decisions.

    4. Ask questions when he needs answers.

    5. Be willing to make suggestions.

    6. Keep supervisor informed.

7. Be honest.
8. Anticipate.
9. Be willing to accept responsibility.
10. Follow good example of supervisor.
11. Understand scope of his responsibility.
12. Learn how to perform his assignment (job knowledge).
13. Conform to ethical standards.
14. Seek additional responsibility commensurate with ability.
15. Carry his part of the load.
16. Be willing to accept new ideas.
17. Be willing to go beyond normal work load.
18. Teamwork assistance—work well with others.
19. Take pride in the organization.

B. Obstacles to bringing subordinates to top performance:
1. Lack of motivation.
2. Poor working conditions.
3. Low salary, insufficient fringe benefits, etc.
4. Superior lacks authority.
5. Lack of training.
6. Communication difficulties.
7. Inflexible organization.
8. Negative approach by subordinate and/or supervisor.
9. Laziness of subordinates.
10. Outside influences.
11. Favoritism.
12. Lack of opportunities for advancement.
13. Increasing work load without increasing personnel.
14. Lack of materials and up-to-date equipment.

C. Bringing subordinates to top performance:
1. Communicate (up—down—peers).
2. Give recognition.
3. Delegate responsibility—give employee chance to prove ability.
4. Job training, including advanced training.
5. Group approach to problem solving.
6. Make employee feel needed.
7. Eliminate or minimize obstacles.
8. Set good example.
9. Provided an equitable work load.
10. Be watchful for a good performer and compensate him properly.

11. Build up subordinate's ego.
12. Correct:
     Insufficient salaries.
     Poor working conditions.
     Increasing work load without increasing personnel.
13. Provide sufficient materials and up-to-date equipment.
14. Provide opportunities for advancement.

Again we nodded our respect for the depth of the thinking and thought of the universality of the subject. Federal government people in Agriculture's supervision course had come up with many of these points.

We closed the second morning's session by asking the whole group to name problems of supervision that especially concerned them. These problems, we explained, would be the subjects of our small group practice discussions the rest of the week. Our students, by this time, were caught up in the course and obviously anxious to get the maximum help from it. Straight from on-the-job worry, resentment, frustration and conflict came the suggestions of problems to explore:

1. How to criticize constructively and acceptably.
2. How to improve a subordinate's attitude toward his job.
3. How to overcome frustration created by a supervisor.
4. How can a younger supervisor prove to an older employee that he is capable of supervising?
5. How to clarify a situation with overlapping responsibilities between two organizations.
6. How to get across to an employee that he is not as good an employee as he thinks he is.
7. How to overcome professional versus non-professional jealousy.
8. How to get people to accept your different ideas.
9. How to keep a promoted supervisor from over-supervising his previous responsibility.
10. What to do when a citizen will not accept a correct explanation (or a fact) or a government procedure.
11. How to avoid political involvement in day-to-day problem solving.
12. How to get subordinates who should be a group to work as a group.
13. How to get supervisors to work as a group.
14. How to find time to give needed support to subordinates.
15. When does delegation of authority become abandonment?

Participants filled out cards listing their first four subject choices and which they would like to facilitate. That afternoon our staff arranged the schedule of the last three mornings so each participant would facilitate a one- to two-hour problem exploration and be a discussant in four others. The arrangement allowed each person to spend most of his time in groups exploring the problems he had chosen from the list.

Then came three lively mornings with the training going ever more smoothly as each participant began to perfect his skills as facilitator or helpful discussant. Interest was intense, for now we were talking about where these people lived, their actual on-the-job problems. While we can't claim that all these were miraculously solved as a result, certainly those who posed them were given a chance to think them through in an orderly fashion with their peers and take back to their offices suggested courses of action that were likely to ease if not completely erase their difficulties. Only once was the suggestion made to "learn to live with the situation," and this advice was to be followed only if all of four other suggestions failed.

Working with these problems gave us a good chance to demonstrate the value of role playing, especially when suggested courses of action involved trying to persuade another person to make a change of some sort. In these instances, we had the person who would have to do the persuading assume the character of whatever ogre (or nincompoop) he would have to face. This made him think through the likely arguments and attitudes he would encounter and, while in the other person's shoes, he would also in effect see and hear himself. (See Chapter 16 for more about role playing.)

Just before we closed the workshop, people from Alexandria met in one group and those from Fairfax in another to exchange ideas about applying what they had learned to job situations in their jurisdictions.

We were pleased that all but one of our students said he found the workshop highly useful—especially since we discovered that only one participant actually had asked to take the course. All the others had been assigned.

A good week.

Introducing Better Budget Procedures

It is always a lot of work to plan a conference of several days.†
Somehow, though, it is always worth it, and our workshop of

† See Part Three for details of how we do it.

March 23 to 25, 1970, for local officials and staff people involved in the budgetary process was no exception.

There was a real need for study, exchange of ideas and pooled thinking by those concerned with local jurisdiction budgeting and those concerned with local jurisdiction planning. Too often some of these people had prepared a plan and others had prepared a budget with so little co-ordination that the twain could not possibly meet.

We mailed prospective participants this summary paragraph explaining the objectives of the workshop:

> The budgetary process is the central element of the local jurisdiction planning effort. It is the point where objectives are translated into programs—and the resources needed to implement programs are spelled out. There has been a major revolution in public budgeting techniques in recent years. This workshop seeks to provide the conceptual background of these recent changes while, concurrently, presenting the pragmatic techniques which are used to develop a realistic budget. Special emphasis will be placed on the techniques applicable to rapidly urbanizing areas.

In the same folder, we also mailed the agenda. Introductory talks and panel discussions (each with question-answer-comment periods) would take all the first day and until 2:30 P.M. the second day:

"The Planning-Budgeting Process"
"The Budgetary Process—Revenue Estimating"
"The Budgetary Process—Executive Review of Agency Estimates"
"The Capital Budgeting Process"
"Legislative and Citizen Participation": demonstration of a review of a typical local jurisdiction budget by a group of citizens and the deputy county executive
"The Relationship of Budgetary and Tax Policies"
"Budgeting at the State Level"

Then, finally, would come small group discussions, with our trained facilitators at their flip charts. The small groups would discuss Improvement of Executive Budgeting Procedures. We say "finally" this would happen because we had argued for small group discussions after each speaker or panel had finished. Other planners, however, had voted us down.

The conference, deliberately limited to no more than fifty participants, drew a nice range of "right people" not only from our own

Northern Virginia region but from other parts of Virginia sharing similar problems of planning, programming and budgeting.‡

The setting was a large, pleasant, well-appointed conference room in a motel just off the Capital Beltway, where all participants could come and go with ease and out-of-towners could be lodged comfortably. Participants sat at small tables facing a head table for speakers and panelists. Everyone moved to a private dining room for meals.

It was a stimulating and informative two and a half days, although we still think it would have been better if the participants had been given more time and the speakers and panelists less.

By the time we got to group discussions at two-thirty on the second day, people were showing signs of fatigue and confusion from so much undiluted information being thrown at them for so long. Had the information been discussed in small groups along the way, it would have been fresh in the participants' far fresher minds and they could have built up a background of discussion from which they could move to more definite conclusions.

Even so, the participants pulled themselves together and did some pretty good thinking about the need for adopting budgetary procedures that would:

1. Provide greater co-ordination of planning, programming and budgeting.
2. Enable the public to be heard *before* budgets are prepared instead of after.
3. Enable public, officials and staff to work together to set goals, objectives, priorities and timetables.
4. Make budgeting a continuous process.

At the end of that second afternoon, we asked the remaining participants to suggest problems for the next morning's discussion. The next day, following their suggestions, we formed three discussion groups, one on the roles of a governing body and its staff, and two on how to involve middle management in the budget process.

The most interesting material produced came from the groups on involving middle management: they suggested that professionals such as teachers, social workers, young upcoming personnel, as-

‡ Participants: county and city planners, public school budgeting officers, city and county budgeting people, local elected officials who had to make final decisions, representatives of the public segment such as realtors, the construction industry, the Chamber of Commerce, the League of Women Voters, school boards.

sessors, accountants, librarians, etc., should identify problem areas. Department heads and staff could then formulate programs to meet those problems and co-ordinate them into a preliminary budget.

At this point, top and middle management would share in setting priorities and prepare a revised budget proposal for the governing body's approval.

During this entire process, middle management should acquaint the community with proposals being considered, seeking invitations from public groups to present budgetary items and obtain public reaction.

So the workshop ended. And in spite of our criticisms of it, we noted some dividends. Afterwards, the people from our area who had attended it were speaking and acting on a new level. Several formed a group to push Fairfax County into revising its budget procedure to give citizens a voice early in the process. Those who also came to our next workshop on local financing and our regional conference on the same subject made reference to the budgeting procedures background gained in this workshop and seemed to be thinking from it. Moreover, there began to be action in local jurisdictions that showed considerable effect—involving citizens in the setting of goals and priorities, for instance (Chapter 6), and more continuous planning not only of programs but of sources of revenue to finance them.

When some change comes about, it usually is hard to credit any single source for it. Various influences have worked together, and even those people intimately involved in creating the change seldom can trace exactly where they got the idea. Usually they think it sprang full-blown and unaided from their own clever minds.

Where Will the Money Come From?

Our next workshop completely eliminated small group discussions, we think to its detriment. The planners argued that our first priority was to provide needed information and that to cover the necessary topics with time for full-group question-answer-comment periods would take the full three days of the workshop. Available to us as faculty were some of the very best people in the field.* This op-

---

* Dr. L. L. Ecker-Racz, former director, U. S. Treasury Advisory Staff and author of *The Politics and Economics of State-Local Finance,* had agreed to direct the workshop and speak on several aspects of financing in which he had pioneered the thinking. Other speakers would include the director, Office of Tax Analysis, U. S. Department of the Treas-

portunity for state, regional, district, county, city and town officials (our prospective participants) to hear the latest from the best must take precedence. Give them the information now. Let small groups discuss how to use it at some other time.

We must admit that the faculty was impressive and the need great for education in the content they could bring. The summary of course objectives we mailed to prospective participants throughout the state described this need and what the workshop would offer:

> After two decades of record growth in spending, Virginia local governments' still unmet needs confront a period of severe revenue stringency. The sources that financed much of past expenditure increases are contracting: tax increases, new taxes, state and federal aid, and bond financing. The workshop will explore the opportunities for new revenue from more effective use of existing sources and from politically least objectionable new sources. State and federal support will also be examined.

The agenda was so crowded with the presentation of pertinent information that it provided for talks even at lunch. These were the subjects for the three days:

Wednesday, April 22
    Local Finances: Out of the 1960s and into the 1970s
    Virginia Economic and Social Trends
    Property Tax: Structural and Administrative Repairs
    Property Tax: Raising Its Level of Tolerance: Senior Citizens, Farmers, Business, Planners and Developers

Thursday, April 23
    Consumer Taxation
    Income Taxation
    Tax Issues at the State Level
    State Support of Local Finance
    Federal Support of Local Finance

Friday, April 24
    Financing Capital Improvements: Faring Better in the Bond Market
    Alternatives to Tax Exemption of Municipal Bonds—Industrial Development Financing

---

ury; the assessment standards specialist, District of Columbia Department of Finance and Revenue; and two assistant directors, U. S. Advisory Commission on Intergovernmental Relations.

The workshop was held a month after the Budget Procedures workshop, in late April 1970. Place: the same motel just off the Capital Beltway again providing easy accessibility for all and lodging for out-of-town people. Also limited to fifty participants, it attracted a statewide sprinkling of supervisors, county executives, city managers, finance directors and regional economists. It also drew an impressive list of state officials, principally from the Division of Planning but including an assistant attorney general. The remainder of participants, of course, were our Northern Virginia people most involved with local government financing.

There is no question the workshop was useful in educating those who attended it. They left with a comprehensive view of the problem and a background in new and innovative approaches to financing they could think about and, perhaps, try. We were sorry they didn't have a chance to explore the subject together in small groups, but that came in our conference of December 1971, on "Financing Local Government—Who Shall Tax Whom and How?" (See Chapter 7.)

Local Officials View Citizen Participation in Planning

Citizen participation in local government is going on in all Northern Virginia jurisdictions. Advisory and planning groups are helping to make democracy meaningful in our communities. Some have been officially named, others just encouraged. Some have legal authorities and responsibilities and others are merely pressure groups.

Citizen participation can make major and unique contributions, and is essential if we are to preserve the democratic ideal as local government attempts to cope with the expanding urban and industrial problems. Citizen participation, however, is fraught with risks and dangers. It is easily perverted and easily destroyed. It can generate explosive and controversial situations. It often confuses sources of authority and responsibility.

George Mason College offers an opportunity to local officials in Northern Virginia to exchange experience and explore together the implications of this growing citizen involvement and the techniques needed to make full use of this important resource.

So we described the problem and purpose of a two-day seminar on "Citizen Participation in Planning for More Effective Use of Resources" we conducted in September 1971 for a small, carefully selected group of key government staff people, elected officials and citizens serving on advisory commissions in our Northern Virginia area.

In preparation, the Community Education Program staff conferred with city and county executives to be sure the seminar would deal with real and pressing problems. Then we prepared a tentative agenda designed to bring out to the fullest extent the problems and experience of participants.

TENTATIVE AGENDA

September 15, 1971:

9:00–12:30   What is the experience of executives of local and regional government agencies in using citizen groups?

What advantages have they found? What difficulties and problems have they encountered?

Why were such groups established? What responsibilities do they have?

Resource people: city, county, and regional executives.

1:30–5:00   What do elected officials think about advisory and pressure groups of citizens?

Are they useful in pushing programs of elected officials? Or is it best to keep them at arm's length?

What problems do elected officials encounter in dealing with organized citizen groups?

How many relations and functions be improved? Resource people: board members.

September 16, 1971:

9:00–12:30   What do citizens themselves think of advisory and other citizen groups? What do they think are advantages and problems?

Resource people: citizens who are active in such groups.

1:30–5:00   What have we learned from listening to and discussing these problems with other participants about citizen participation in local government?

Are there some principles to be distilled as to the role citizen groups should play? To what

> extent should those affected by programs control policy and decision making? To what extent can such decision making be decentralized to the neighborhood level?
>
> How should citizen groups be organized and trained?
>
> What are the useful roles such groups can play?
>
> What problems can we anticipate? What are the ways to minimize difficulties?

Response to our invitation was good, just the range of representation we wanted so all pertinent information could be shared and all participants see the problem from all major viewpoints.†

Above all, the people were the right ones and very interested in the subject. Obviously, they all realized they were among understanding peers and could skip the flowery praise of citizen participation they would have used in public. Instead, they posed penetrating questions about its value, the difficulty of making it both really useful and practical, the problems it raised. In the two days the discussion ranged over a variety of points. We list a few of them as examples:

1. What are the real purposes of creating citizen groups?
    a. Response to alleviate pressure, appease the public.
    b. Gather facts and make recommendations.
    c. Open up channels of communication with the public.
    d. Gain citizen help and support.
    e. Serve as a sounding board for political viewpoints.
    f. Get rid of ardent enemies by naming them to commission.
    g. Provide a form of patronage for political friends.
2. How do decisions get made and implemented?
    a. Others besides citizens actually make the decisions.
    —What happens when citizen recommendations don't dovetail with those of staff or elected officials?

† Participants: members of city councils and county Boards of Supervisors, city and county chief administrators, planning directors, school board members, school superintendents, public school directors of research, Health and Welfare Council members, Citizen Advisory Commission members, directors of housing and community development, Department of Social Services members, Community Action Program officials, a public information director, the superintendent of the Department of Public Welfare, and co-ordinators of volunteer services and of juvenile and domestic relations courts.

—Should there be government representation on citizen commissions to keep them "practical," "within limitations"?

b. Some reports die on vine because commission during work didn't consider and study impact.

c. Time element important in considering recommendations.
—Should they come before elections so candidates can say which they will support? It would be practical.
—Should they come before budget preparation so plans can be included to pay for recommendations? It would be practical.

3. For whom do citizen groups speak?

a. Appointed commissions and committees vs. volunteer civic organizations.
—Which reflect citizen views more accurately?
—Should their work be co-ordinated?

b. Same faces seen again and again.
—Same names repeated on committees, commissions, etc.
—Only 4 to 5 per cent of citizens used.
—Volunteer is an "amateur professional."

4. What citizens should participate in government decision making?

a. Representatives of groups.

b. Those knowledgeable in subject matter.

c. Those representative of jurisdictional interests.

d. Do we need great numbers of participants or only good representation of public?

e. Is it cricket to create a crisis?
—Is achieving participation just for participation's sake a worthy thing?
—A crisis can test ideas and get citizen feedback.
—A crisis pulls county, city or town together.

5. How involve more citizens?

a. Many citizens have useful talents, skills and information, but too many can't work in groups.
—Some dictate. [Our techniques can control them.]
—Some are shy. [Our techniques can help bring them out.]
—Some just plain don't like group activity. They may take job because of status it brings, but then they either skip meetings and responsibilities or put down the efforts of

others. [Our techniques either bring out the best in this group, too, or encourage the others to think good riddance and go on effectively without them.]

b. How help the economic and educational minority become better able to participate?
—Like anyone else they can learn skills but majority must be supportive and encouraging.

c. Move toward neighborhood service and neighborhood government encourages greater citizen participation.

d. Be on lookout for new talent and encourage it.

e. There can be citizen committees to study almost all county or city problems.

6. How can citizen participants be persuaded to be more practical?

a. The more citizen participation the greater the proliferation of goals.

b. Special committees or commissions and civic organizations tend to recommend programs costing money.
—At the same time, government faces continued public pressure for an acceptable tax rate.
—Public is two-faced, wanting both programs and lower taxes.
—It is very difficult to sell the idea of spending money now to save money later.
—Without sufficient revenue to implement citizen recommendations, they have to be ignored.

c. Suggestions:
—Assign staff members to groups to make sure they know fiscal limitations.
—Ask groups to recommend not just what they want but how to get it.
—Ask groups to include study of impact of recommendations before making them.
—Ask groups to sell public on paying for suggested improvements.
—Ask group to set time-phased objectives as well as broad long-range goals.

7. What are the advantages of citizen participation?

a. It helps educate citizens.

b. Government tends to operate after the fact; citizens can help it look ahead and predetermine policies.

    c.   Government gains citizen support.

    d.   Citizens can provide valuable input of fact and thought.

    e.   It is economically sound. Government gets a lot of good, intelligent, hard-working help for nothing.

The conference closed with a pretty firm consensus on the advantages of citizen participation. Although, at times, there had been cynicism expressed, the emphasis had been on practicalities. No one had played a soft violin for the volunteer, but everyone was convinced of the value of his participation. These people weren't stupid. Maybe citizen participation brings problems, but look at those persuasive plus factors under number seven again. No smart local government would want to do away with all that.

10

INFORMING STATE LEGISLATORS

In February of 1969 the Virginia General Assembly was to meet in special session to consider updating the constitution of the commonwealth. It was a much needed updating. In its long history, Virginia previously had overhauled its constitution every thirty years on the average. But now more than forty years had elapsed since the last major revision and these had been the years of the most rapid change in Virginia history.

A blue-ribbon Commission on Constitutional Revision had gone through the constitution section by section, comma by comma, and recommended changes, including some forward-looking proposals concerned with local government, taxation and finance, education and other matters of vital concern. Some of these recommended changes were extremely controversial. All of them required thorough study on the part of legislators. Did they go far enough? Or perhaps too far? What would be the effect on the localities the legislators represented?

Several members of the General Assembly from our Northern Virginia area asked our Community Education Program to conduct a conference on the proposed constitutional revisions in order to help send our delegation members to the special General Assembly session with their homework done. The conference would provide a structure for them to explore together the major recommendations for change and, if we included the chairmen of our local governing bodies, their chief executives, commonwealth's attorneys and circuit court judges, the legislators would also go to Richmond with the counsel of these important local people.

Readily agreeing that such a conference would be useful, we enlisted as fellow planners the legislators who had suggested the conference, and, working with them and a county manager, set the date for January 17, 1969, at George Mason (with many prayers, of course, that we wouldn't have one of the crippling snowstorms our area sometimes suffers).

Since all the desired participants were very busy people, we decided to begin the conference at 2:30 P.M. This way, with enough warning for advance scheduling, participants could finish the major part of their regular day's work before heading for the conference. Then, rather than ask them to come back another day, we planned a buffet dinner in George Mason's cafeteria with sessions to follow until 10 P.M.

The real puzzler was how to tackle the report of the Constitutional Revision Commission in part of one afternoon and an evening. It was a thick volume. Obviously, we couldn't go through it point by point in so short a time. We could, however, send copies to all participants asking them to study it in advance. Then, for the conference, we could limit exploration to the major issues.

After the planners, including ourselves, had carefully studied the report, we picked what seemed to be the six most controversial issues:

1.   Bill of Rights, Franchise and Qualifications for Office.
2.   Division of Powers, Legislature and Executive.
3.   Judiciary and Corporations.
4.   Local Government.
5.   Taxation and Finance.
6.   Education, Conservation and Future Changes.

We arranged for staff members of the Constitutional Revision Commission and other experts to serve as resource people and planned an agenda that would give each participant a chance to discuss in small groups (seven to nine people) whichever two of the above issues most concerned him or her. The agenda called for these two small group discussion periods before dinner, with resource people and facilitators. After dinner, we planned a general session for the small groups to report the gist of their discussions to all and then for the resource people, sitting as a panel, to respond to questions from the floor. After this, and closing the conference, participants would meet by jurisdictions to decide whether they wished to plan for public discussions in their localities.

We thought it a rather good plan and it worked well.

It did not snow. Turn-out was excellent. County executives, state senators and members of the House of Delegates, judges, resource people, commonwealth's attorneys, city managers, facilitators and chairmen of Boards of Supervisors, each with a name tag, filled their coffee cups, bent one another's ears for a while, then after a brief welcoming address, moved into the classrooms off the Lecture Hall lobby to sit around tables for their first assigned discussion.

We had sent each of the facilitators a copy of the Constitutional Revision Commission's report and a fifteen-page summary of it, a list of the persons invited to participate and a letter which said, in part:

"Our thinking is NOT that you should become an authority on the report. Instead, we suggest that you learn enough to follow what your group members are talking about so the questions you ask them can be pertinent . . .

"A suggested discussion pattern:
1. Explain briefly the process you and the group will be using. (It's given in the subsequent paragraphs.)
2. Ask the group to identify, and you list, the controversial proposals in, and omissions from, the sections the group is discussing. (Try to do this quickly but be sure not to overlook the omissions.)
3. Ask the group to provide a reporter. (He or she can use the points you put on flip chart sheets to pick out the highlights for the five-minute report, so put down whatever seems worth noting.)
4. Ask the group members to discuss the proposals and omissions in any order they wish but to help you see that some time is kept available for each. In discussing each one, if its significance, ramifications and potential impact come first, they will provide good points against which to check the pros and cons.
5. Near the end of the discussion time, ask the group if it wishes to pick the highlights to be reported or prefers to go on discussing to the end and let the reporter pick them."

We did some table-hopping that afternoon to satisfy ourselves that discussions were going as they should and to observe the effectiveness of our facilitators (some of whom were getting their first experience after training).

Most discussions were, indeed, going as they should. At one table as we took an empty chair, participants were in animated discussion of the attorney general. Why should he/she be elected? Did the electorate really know his/her qualifications? People were contributing well as the reasons for election came out: Voters should make it their business to know his qualifications. The attorney general was third in line of succession and *could* become governor. Besides (the facilitator was getting the points down nicely):

—Attorney general doesn't just represent the governor.
—Attorney general sits in judgment on the governor and the General Assembly (so neither should appoint him).
—Problem of top leadership is great, and election of attorney general gives exposure.

Satisfied, we moved on to another table, another discussion. Participants there were talking about the proposed annual versus the traditional biennial sessions of the legislature. They were rapidly reaching consensus in favor of annual sessions, and the smiling, alert facilitator was catching all their reasons on the flip chart sheet:

Arguments for Annual Sessions

1. At present, losing man's talents second year.
2. Present rush at end of session.
3. Difficulty in planning biennial budgets—annual meeting can have better format.
4. Committees not so rushed with work, better organized.
5. Biennial sessions—more power to executive.

Again reassured, we moved on. At the next table, all was not going so well. The facilitator, a new one, seemed overwhelmed. The discussion was off track; one participant was engaged in a long monologue; a couple of participants had stopped listening to him and started talking to each other; the facilitator begged for help; no one paid attention except the man nearest her, who began telling her what to write on the flip chart; what he suggested had nothing to do with what anyone else was saying. We stayed on, becoming a member of the group, helping (as any group member can) to get the facilitator over the hump and the group back on the right track. (See Part Three, "How We Do It.") All was soon well, and, hoping it would stay that way, we visited another table. Points of view on gubernatorial succession were coming thick and fast, but everyone was being heard and the competent facilitator was helping everyone stay on subject as the flip chart sheet filled with the gist of their talk:

Gubernatorial Succession

1. All ex-governors felt one term o.k.
2. Explore possibility of change—should be treated from fresh point of view rather than tradition as was done in the past.
3. Would governor be more responsive running on his record?
4. Commission heard no strong sentiment for governor to have more than one term.
5. Why not keep good talent? Carry out full program.
   —Governor is powerful now. More terms, too much power.
   —Leadership deteriorates second half of term.

The first small group discussion period ended after an hour and twenty-five minutes. People, still discussing their topics, headed for coffee, then formed new small groups at which each participant could discuss his second priority issue. Again we table-hopped. This time the facilitator who had been having trouble on the first round seemed to be doing better. In fact, all seemed fine at every table. People were thinking through these controversial issues. The discussions were forcing this, forcing also the listening to other views and the experience or factual information that had led to those positions.

The after-dinner sessions were good, too. The general session provided a chance for everyone present to consider, at least briefly, the controversial issues explored by the smaller groups, hear the highlights of the thinking in those groups and question the experts on the panel. The final meeting with their fellow officials from their own jurisdictions then helped them make any plans they wanted to make.

Friends in the legislature told us later that our Northern Virginia delegation showed the effects when the General Assembly met. Most other legislators hadn't done their homework or had struggled with it in isolation. Ours was the only group which made any impact of consequence. We felt good about that. We felt good, too, knowing that our local officials were informed and had had a chance to make their views known to the legislators before they had to act or take positions.

In fact, all concerned were so pleased about it that we began laying the groundwork for another pre-legislative conference the following year.

Our Second Pre-legislative Conference

So much about the first conference had been successful that we followed a similar format for the second, setting it for early January of 1970 before our Northern Virginia delegation went to Richmond, scheduling it for 2:30 P.M. to 10 P.M., holding it at George Mason, where the facilities were excellent, planning discussion groups of seven to nine people each with a knowledgeable resource person and with discussions led by a facilitator.

This time, however, our planners arranged for three small group discussion periods, instead of two, giving each participant a chance to be in on the explorations of three subjects. The agenda called for two of these periods before dinner with highlights reported during a longer dinner hour. For these afternoon discussions, we chose four major categories and divided them into subordinate topics. Thus, when participants received their invitation, they received also a registration form (see Appendix, Chapter 10) asking them to list four topics in priority order. Although they would only discuss two, we needed third or fourth choices if we found it necessary to equalize groups in numbers and viewpoint. Actually almost everyone could be given his first and second choices, but the few who graciously accepted assignment to third or fourth preference groups helped us provide the balance so needed for good discussion.

We offered no choice for the evening small group discussions. All groups had the same subject: Revenue Sources. No one complained. All agreed that providing the needed money was probably the greatest problem the 1970 legislature would face.

Two paragraphs in our invitation mailed nearly a month in advance explained who was being invited (a somewhat expanded group this time) and the conference's purpose:

We are calling this meeting after checking with ranking members of both parties of the legislative delegations and the local governments of four of the seven Northern Virginia jurisdictions. Invitees are limited to the members of the delegation, the members of the county boards of supervisors and city councils, the chief executive officers of the jurisdictions, school superintendents and one member of each school board, the county and city attorneys, one representative of each county or city chamber of commerce, each civic federation and each League of Women Voters, resource people specially selected for their knowledge of the problems to be explored and people trained to facilitate small group discussions.

The purpose of the exploration will be to provide an opportunity for legislators, local government officials and civic leaders to obtain information and exchange ideas on problems on which legislators have indicated that such an airing would be most useful . . .

It was bitterly cold on the day of the conference. Many secondary roads were blocked and schools closed. However, all major roads were open and in most of our region traffic was whizzing along. Attendance was very good, and people stopped talking about the weather as soon as they gathered in their pre-assigned afternoon discussion groups.

From the seventeen topic choices we had offered, participants had given priority to nine. Especially popular had been:

1. Zoning Procedures and Housing
2. Metropolitan Transportation
3. Schools—State Aid Distribution Formula

We formed two discussion groups on each of those subjects and one group each on:

1. Development of Higher Education in Northern Virginia
2. Election Laws
3. Overlapping State and Local Responsibilities
4. Potomac River Compact
5. Legislative Processes
6. Disposal of Solid Wastes

The result was that six different small group discussions could be under way during each of the three discussion sessions (two in the afternoon and one in the evening).

This time we had assigned two legislators to each discussion group, one of them responsible for a short opening presentation of background information and issues likely to be before the General Assembly. The facilitator's first task was to list on a flip chart sheet the points the legislator brought out. Thus, in every small group, the facilitator's magic marker was moving rapidly. Typical was this listing for the Election Laws group:

1. Central registrar.

2.   State computerized registration list.
3.   Electoral board selection.
4.   Order on ballot.
5.   Use of voting machines.
6.   Strengthening State Board of Elections.
7.   Absentee ballots.
8.   Campaign contributions.
9.   Primary date.
10.   What constitutes residence?

And this for the group on Overlapping State and Local Responsibilities:

1.   Definition of overlap.
2.   Greater division between local and state.
3.   Conflict in authority and decision.
4.   Mandatory formula shares without local consultation.
5.   State administrative "layers" in localities.
6.   Confusion in enforcement responsibilities.
7.   Enlarged staffs due to overlap.
8.   State funding formulas versus increased urban programs.

The resource people finished their presentations, then in all the small groups the facilitators asked their group members to pick the points they wanted to discuss. In most cases they wanted to discuss them all and began with a vengeance—significance, ramifications, potential impact. Toward the end of the period, a couple of groups were even ready to draft recommendations. These, for instance, from the group on overlapping responsibilities:

1.   More local input in state study commissions.
2.   Consider overlap when new programs are adopted.
3.   Should be commission to study what should be shared, ways of sharing, areas of responsibility.
4.   People should be educated on problem.
5.   Should be regional commissions for regional matters (e.g., pollution).
6.   Decisions should go through discussion and debate.

And this paragraph from the group discussing Development of Higher Education in Northern Virginia:

We recognize this is a tight budget year (and what year isn't?) but the importance of receiving this approximately $20 million cannot be overemphasized. The purpose of the higher education plan of 1966 would be defeated if enrollments are curtailed and programs set back. There has been a dramatic shift in attitude in Northern Virginia toward George Mason and Northern Virginia Community College in recent years. No one wants to reverse that. Emphasize particularly the need for:

1. The Eastern Campus of Northern Virginia Community College.
2. An additional building at George Mason.
3. The state legislature to plan building for a number of years.

The same pattern was followed for the second round of afternoon small group discussions and for the evening discussions on revenue sources. Interest remained high and attrition was very low. At ten o'clock, as the legislators, local officials and civic leaders went out into the frigid night, they were still talking about their latest subject, the problems of financing.

We eavesdropped on one group of three delegates to the General Assembly.

"When people demand services they should have to tell us what new taxes they want to finance those services," one said.

"There must be some source of revenue we aren't tapping," said another.

"I'm not sure corporations are paying what they should," said a third. "Or what about higher tuition for higher education with payment after graduation? Or what about pari-mutuel betting? Maybe Maryland's thirteen million and West Virginia's nine million last year was less than expected but it was a hell of a lot more than nothing."

"Oh, no," said the first, "I'd never vote for pari-mutuel betting."

We smiled as we wearily collected flip chart sheets and other materials. At least, we had them thinking and starting the debate.

"Swell conference," said a county executive as he passed us buttoning his storm coat. "Have one every year. Damn useful."

We rather thought so ourselves, but instead of conducting more conferences specifically called pre-legislative, each of our regional conferences co-sponsored by the Northern Virginia Planning District Commission (Chapter 7) has zeroed in on problems to be faced in the General Assembly and always with our legislators not only in mind but very much present.

11

TRAINING FOR COMMUNITY ACTION AGENCIES

Like many millions of others, we were excited (and optimistic) about the concepts of the "war on poverty." Helping the poor to help themselves! Communities organizing to reverse the generation after generation repetition of unemployment or underemployment, squalor, ignorance, malnutrition, welfare dependency, despair! What better expenditure of public funds, we asked ourselves, than to provide the direction needed to reverse the fate of the disadvantaged across the land: the migrants, the Indians, the people of Appalachia, the blacks in ghettos or rural areas?

With real enthusiasm, we readily accepted requests to use our techniques to try to help this nationwide effort. We already have described some of our work—the Jobs Now project (Chapter 3), the series of job fairs (Chapter 4), volunteer aid training and helping a staff and board of a day care association to better understanding (Chapter 5).

In addition, we conducted workshops which brought considerable community input to the board and staff of the Loudoun Community Action Program but came too late to achieve their two major purposes: to bring considerable participation of those to be served, and to end the strife between warring factions on the board and staff. We also helped plan and conduct successful evaluation sessions for the Loudoun Headstart program and successful training of Head-start parents in working together as a group to achieve their goals.

In one book, of course, we can't describe all our recent work, and we mention these Loudoun County activities only because our experience with them can add to the evidence of how difficult it is to conduct a war on poverty.

The disgruntled ask why, after such vast expenditures of money and effort, have so many of the results been disappointing? We readily concede that there are many complex reasons but we submit that one major reason, not at all complex, is that too many people haven't known the basic techniques for thinking, planning and working together.

Consider on the one hand, the volunteers, all too often of the Lord and Lady Bountiful stripe, confident in their inherited or acquired position in the world, full of talk about "the practicalities," cocooned in what they have been taught is proper procedure (usually Robert's Rules), partly motivated by their genuinely bleedings hearts but also likely to be concerned with their own egos, their own motions, their own plans of what to do.

Consider, on the other hand, the professionals, also secure in their position, for they have studied sociology and methodology in school and worked with these problems on the job and can even speak a special jargon in discussing them. They, too, are partly motivated by genuine concern but they, too, have plenty of self-interest: how the thing will look on their reports, how they will triumph over other professionals, how such and such an action will help or hurt their careers.

Then consider the people to be helped, often resentful of the position and confidence of both volunteers and professionals; uncomfortable in the presence of the others, usually inarticulate; sometimes, really or defiantly, wanting just to be left in their accustomed life-styles, where, at least, they do not feel pushed around.

It takes a lot of basic training in the best group techniques for these segments to learn to pull together, and in too many areas, this training hasn't been given. Or effective techniques have been introduced too late to do much good.

When the conditions have been right, the people concerned united in their purpose, their campaigns intelligently planned and diligently carried out, battles have been won. Our success with the job fairs is an example. Other efforts have brought worthy, although limited, results—the better understanding created in the Fauquier-Loudoun Day Care Association, for instance.

Also, the evaluation sessions for Loudoun Headstart and the training of Headstart parents were both triumphs—for what they were. However, they were never intended to be more than small parts of a major campaign. The major campaign was the countywide Community Action Program, and it was doomed for the simple reason that most of the people involved in it didn't know effective group methods and, without them, they were pulling in all directions instead of together.

We were called in too late to do much. In fact, by the time Loudoun County friends serving on the Community Action Board asked our help and arranged for us to give it in the winter of 1967–68, the war was no longer really against poverty but between individuals and factions of board and staff. Meanwhile those to be served were all but forgotten—except that everyone else was worrying because they weren't participating as they should.

We learned that the Board had never "wasted time" adopting goals. Each individual had his own goals for the program and these might or might not agree with any other member's. Board meetings had been called infrequently and primarily for the purpose of giving formal approval to decisions already made by the executive committee. The result, naturally, was very poor attendance, particularly by members representing the intended beneficiaries. The few of these who did appear sat uncomfortably on the hard wooden seats in the Board of Supervisors' antiquated meeting room, where the sessions were held. They were virtually ignored by most of the others. We wondered that any of them ever bothered to come.

Adding to the unhappy picture was the fact that several active Board members wanted to disregard regulations and guidelines issued by the national office of the Office of Economic Opportunity (but continue receiving OEO funds). They didn't feel the regulations and guidelines were right for the local situation. Other active Board members were horrified at the idea of taking the money and not the rules. The paid Community Action director was on one side. Most of the rest of the paid staff was on the other. Lines were rigidly drawn and emotions high. What's more, this division had spread to the concerned part of the community, where sides also were being taken.

About all we can say is that we tried. Had our approach been used from the beginning and our principles of group planning and action been followed throughout, we think the situation would have been very different. Our approach would have taught all concerned the importance of their own and everyone else's participation. By teaching all these people ways to work together constructively, it would have helped prevent the fracturing into factions and steely viewpoints.

Now there was still hope—provided everyone involved really wanted to forget their differences, find their points of agreement and work together on these. On this slim chance, we planned and conducted three workshops. One was to be exclusively for Board members and staff, with a special effort to get out the participating poor. The other two were to include all the concerned citizens of the community who wanted to attend. At all three, people working together in small groups were to set goals in these important categories:

1. Jobs
2. Shelter
3. Food/clothing
4. Involvement—Participation of Other Citizens
5. Education
6. Discrimination

The primary purposes of the meeting exclusively for Board and staff were:

1. To show the warring factions they had more in common than, perhaps, they realized, that they could agree on many goals and, once having set them, could, if they would, co-operate on the action steps necessary to reach those goals.
2. To give non-participating members a chance to participate and prove to those who had virtually ignored them their worth as fellow workers in the cause.

The purpose of including concerned citizens was to provide community input, encourage more co-operation and support from the community at large and help the also divided community come to agreement with Board and staff on Community Action goals and how to achieve them.

The meetings were held on three winter evenings in the large social hall of a modern, attractive church in Purcellville. Physical arrangements were fine—right-sized tables, name tags, good lighting, wall space for flip charts, etc. Attendance was good, too—at least in numbers. However, conspicuously absent were most of the participating poor on the Board, and the concerned citizens attending were all from the minority of the public who already supported the concept of community action in the county. No one from the skeptical majority of the community bothered to come.

Even so, we worked hard to try to make the sessions useful, and to be sure of flip chart sheets filled with worthy goals. The problem was in the already glued-in attitudes. We watched a couple of Board members sit in stiff silence, contributing nothing except contempt at what they obviously considered a waste of time. We watched other Board and staff members dutifully put on a show of co-operation but we sensed that it was only a temporary truce, like that of people who really dislike each other being "civilized" long enough not to spoil the party and dutifully playing the game suggested by the hosts (us). So, despite the enthusiasm of a few Board and staff members who apparently really wanted to break down old barriers and accomplish something, most seemed to consider the sessions only a stalling tactic keeping them from their "real work" of fighting each other.

Our written summary (struggling hard for optimism) pointed out that the sessions, at least, had made a wide range of suggestions available. Those could, we said, be used in determining priorities.

We also made these suggestions for obtaining more adequate representation of intended beneficiaries:

A. One possibility would be to hold well-advertised meetings in each of the areas where intended beneficiaries are concentrated. Such meetings might be conducted in various ways:

1. A series of traditional general meetings in which officials invite residents to state their views. We do not recommend this because in such meetings a few verbal people usually do all the talking and it is very difficult to know how representative their views are.

2. A series of workshops in which participants might be asked first to spend thirty minutes putting the categories of Jobs, Shelter, Food/Clothing, etc., into priority order. When these had been reported and the high categories determined, the groups might be asked to take each of the two or three highest categories and put the suggestions within those categories in priority order. The results of this process in several communities should be very informative.

3. The Board might prepare a proposed program and, after submitting copies of it in advance to the families in each community, hold a series of community meetings in

which small groups expressed their reactions to it. Here again the accumulation of results in the various communities should provide valuable guidance.

B. For a longer-range situation one or all of the following might be useful:

1. Repeat annually whatever process of community meetings worked out well.

2. Have the communities replace Board members who find themselves unable to attend meetings and participate in them.

3. Give the total Board more decisions to make, so attendance would be more rewarding.

It was all too late. The Loudoun *Times-Mirror* splashed this five-column headline across its front page:

New Split Hits Poverty Unit In Clash Over Policy Aims

The quarrel now was over the policy and operation of Headstart, the only Community Action activity that had widespread local public support. Naturally enough, the fresh dissension was based on the old business of whether to follow OEO guidelines. The same people said emphatically yes. The same other people said the guidelines were no good "in the local situation." Our workshop had not succeeded in persuading anyone to back down on his or her previously announced stand.

We were not surprised. Once people publicly take positions, they rarely disavow them. That is why it is so important to involve people in working out group solutions before they have made pronouncements as individuals or factions. In the beginning, they can act with open-mindedness. Without losing face, they can rub the edges off their differences before any real polarization of views occurs.

Soon afterwards, the OEO national office made an investigation: the Headstart director was fired, and the Board of Supervisors took over the Loudoun Community Action Program. The Board continued Headstart and later supported the day care activity undertaken by private citizens. However, Board members were so disillusioned by the recent in-fighting that they let most of the rest of the Community Action concept die.

That segment of the citizenry who cared undertook separate actions that partially filled the gap. One group began the day care effort mentioned above and formed a Day Care Association with neighboring Fauquier County (see Chapter 5 for our work with it). Another group (with some overlap) helped us organize job fairs (Chapter 4). But the chance had passed for the overall comprehensive attack on poverty that a successful Community Action Program might have provided.

A Better Start in Appalachia

Sometime earlier, Strauss had a chance to give training to poverty fighters when that training could do the most good—at the beginning of the effort.

In August of 1967, he went to southeastern Kentucky to conduct a training course for three levels of people about to intensify a Community Action Program in an area where extreme poverty and deprivation were the rule, not the exception as in Loudoun.

It was strictly moonshiners' country—wooded hills, picturesque but pathetic log cabins and unpainted houses hidden up or down narrow, twisting roads, a couple of hogs here, a couple of cows there, a few chickens, lean mongrel dogs on sagging porches.

The four counties of the area, Leslie, Knott, Letcher and Perry, gave it the name of LKLP.

The previous year, Strauss had set up a successful training program in another Kentucky county, Jackson. He, the director and assistant director had worked out a plan to train residents right out of the hills to work with their own people. He had directed the first three days of the course, enabling him to train the two directors in facilitating discussions and conducting role playing as the course began. Now LKLP wanted him to train not only the local people who were to run community centers in three of the four counties but also the men who were to co-ordinate the work of the centers in each of those counties and the training director of the four-county area.

Although this was not part of either the Northern Virginia Pilot Project or the Community Education Program, we include it as a successful example of:

1. Providing training through problem solving for three different levels of an organization in the same series of meetings, with people who were to work together helping to train each other.
2. Training people of the upper two levels to train others later, when, according to the LKLP plan, the program would be extended.
3. Demonstrating what people at even the lowest level of edu-

cation and income can contribute when they are encouraged to participate.

The people who actually were to run the community centers came from those old cabins and unpainted houses of the area, with a range in education from the third to eighth grades in mountain schools. They were products of the unique Appalachian subculture. Appalachian experts (at least so-called) warned us not to expect any work ethic in these people. We were told that they had developed no mechanism for resolving conflict except violence and that too many social change artists had gotten to them, telling them they had been exploited and nothing about their condition was really their fault. The experts also said that dictatorial direction was all Appalachian people could understand, that they were only interested in personal concerns, not social change or community betterment.

Having worked with similar people in Jackson County, Strauss didn't take these "experts" too seriously. With optimism, he, the LKLP director and training director began the three-day course by setting these objectives:

1. To orient the individuals who had been selected as Community Information Depot operators so they would:
    a. Understand what their job as CID operators was.
    b. Be able to explain it satisfactorily to others.
    c. Realize the major difficulties they would probably meet in performing their work.
    d. Recognize the opportunities that some of the difficulties would present.
    e. Develop a better degree of confidence in their ability to do the job.
    f. Have a realistic plan for starting their work.
2. To improve the county co-ordinators' skills in training and working with subordinates so:
    a. Each county group would leave the training session as a working team (with a great deal still to learn from experience but with a good foundation for working together on which to build).
    b. The co-ordinators would be able to give the training director the assistance he would need to plan and conduct subsequent operator training courses successfully without outside help.
3. To improve the training director's skills so he would:

a. Have the ability and confidence to plan and conduct future training courses successfully.

b. Have improved ability to develop the county co-ordinators' skills as planners, trainers, supervisors, missionaries, negotiators, and members of his own advisory team.

The first day's session did not include the fifteen local people who were to run the community centers, five in each of the three counties chosen for the program. Instead, this first session was devoted to some advance training of the training director and the three men who would co-ordinate the work of the community centers in the three counties. Also participating were the county developers (the title LKLP used for people more often called county directors) of the three counties and the "big boss," the director of the LKLP Community Action Council.

This advance training for the three county co-ordinators, the three developers and the training director followed much the same pattern we now use in training facilitators (see Chapter 14). Strauss had them practice leading discussions so they could serve as facilitators for small group discussions on the two days to follow.

These practice discussions also served to define the purposes of the community centers, called Community Information Depots (CIDs):

1. To provide services and information about resources in the community and outside it which would help the community and its people.

2. To promote organization of the Community Information Depot community to help people change their attitudes so they would use their resources better for a higher standard of living.

3. To promote whatever new activities in the community the people of the community might decide they needed.

The next day, with the fifteen local people who would run the Community Information Depots present, the director of the LKLP Community Action Council opened their training with a short talk which was part welcome and part explanation of the techniques Strauss would use in running the course. The training director followed with a brief explanation of the purposes of the community centers decided the previous day.

Then, using each county co-ordinator as facilitator for his group of five depot operators, the small group discussions began. These were interrupted only by a few short periods for answering questions and a number of role-playing sessions in which the local trainees practiced their approaches to various expected problems and problem people.

In their first discussions, the local people training to run the CIDs listed the kinds of information and services the people of their communities needed. They were anything but tight-mouthed and uncooperative. A long and helpful list was soon on the flip charts:

Kinds of services and information needed in the community

1. Transportation to see doctors.
2. Help with clothing, mending and laundry.
3. Help in preparing food in the home.
4. Information on what medical care covers.
5. Information about social security, public assistance, and other existing problems.
6. Filling out income tax forms.
7. Information about organizing little league teams.
8. Information on starting girl scout and boy scout troops.
9. What to do about people without income.
10. Information about community improvement programs.
11. Sewing group and a place to meet.
12. Information about finding jobs.
13. Information about improving roads.
14. Help for elderly people in their homes.
15. Help in getting second-hand clothing and home furnishings.
16. Help in getting vitamins for community.
17. Information from Health Department on use of vitamins.
18. Information and aid from Health Department about diabetes.
19. Information and service from mobile x-ray.
20. Tell community about what Health Department offers them.
21. Information on well water testing.
22. How to make sure your water supply is safe.
23. Information and service on raising money for community services.
24. Information and service on helping leaders attract industry.
25. Information on what skills are needed to get jobs.
26. Information about business schools and vocational schools.
27. Information about credit.
28. Helping to encourage people to try again.
29. Helping to bring people together.
30. Help bring people to the community to tell about getting sewer system or water system.
31. Information about how to get jobs after a person gets training.

32. Information to encourage people to stay in school, showing films and to reach the parents.
33. Information about making money to go to school or college.
34. Service on improving housing and repairs.
35. Information on planning a budget.
36. Information about credit unions and how to start them.
37. Information about starting a co-op store.
38. Service of providing after-school skill training and practice in the community.
39. Information about hot-lunch program.
40. Give information to PTA about school conditions—make sure that information is correct.
41. Help parents and teachers understand each other better.
42. Help community work to get better allowances for large low income families.
43. Help to improve projects so that they don't hurt people's pride.
44. Give information as to what other communities are doing.

Next Strauss asked them to decide what they needed to know in order to provide the services and kinds of information they had listed. They got right to work on that assignment, too, each group coming up with a long series of questions. The training director answered some factual questions immediately:

1. Do we have anyone in CID to give legal advice?
2. What is LKLP?
3. What is the purpose of CID program?
4. What is the difference between OEO and CID?
5. How much help can we expect in terms of money, manpower, material, etc.?
6. Background of supervisors.
7. How do we go about getting film for movies?
8. What is the maximum income in excess of our CID salary?
9. Will the government help the communities sell products they make?
10. Can we get instructors on community projects?
11. How much of utilities will be paid by CID and how much will be paid by the community?
12. How will the Nelson Amendment Program help CID?
13. Who furnishes office equipment?
14. Do the communities have to furnish equipment for sewing, woodwork, etc.?

15. What does the LKLP have to offer the people?
16. What are our legal holidays?
17. The "can do's" and "can't do's" of an operator.
    a. The operator's working hours are from eight to five with one hour off for lunch.
    b. Telephone calls from the CID phone will be the responsibility of the CID operator.
    c. Don't always be THE LEADER. If you do:
        1. You will find yourself doing all the work.
        2. You won't be able to do your job of helping others to help themselves.
        3. The organization will not get stronger.
    d. Do your best to help. DON'T MAKE PROMISES.
18. A problem-solving method:
    Get an agreement on:
    a. What the group wants to accomplish.
    b. The difficulties.
    c. A general plan to reach the goals the group agreed on.
    d. The steps needed to make the plan work.
    e. A step-by-step plan to let the group know as we go along how well we are doing.

Some called for answers that couldn't be given on the spot. They included policy decisions not yet available, the functions and operating methods of public and private agencies with which the operators needed to work and facts the training director could not supply offhand. These, too, were listed so answers could be supplied as soon as possible:

1. Where do we get information concerning free hot-lunch programs?
2. Who should we contact to get information on sewing clubs?
3. What are the limitations for the operators concerning transportation?
4. What does the mobile operator's job cover?
5. Information on existing public agencies. (How can we get information?)
6. What agencies have to offer and the limitations of these agencies.
7. Can the operator serve as an election officer?
8. Need to have a copy of business transacted during all LKLP meetings.

Still other questions were naturals for examination later through discussions and role playing:

1. Why do people organize?
2. What help does our county co-ordinator give us?
3. How do we get clothing for needy members of our community?
4. What activities can we have to raise money for our communities?
5. How could we bring jobs in our community?
6. What is the relationship between the operator and the county co-ordinator?
7. How do we attract public interest in CID?
8. How do we go about obtaining recreation equipment?
9. How do we help low income families on school problems?
10. How do we go about getting better roads?
11. When operator is gone from center, should he get someone to stay at center until he returns?
12. How can we help people not eligible for public assistance?
13. How do we get information about attracting new industry?
14. We need to know the facts about the problems. (Are the parties involved AWARE that a problem exists?)
15. Generally, what will our job be?

Next, these people out of the hills, hopeless according to some "experts," went on to list attitudes of their neighbors which needed to be changed so the people of their area could make better use of their resources for a higher standard of living:

1. Don't want to help themselves, but want help from others.
2. Fear of changes in community.
3. Better not to work than to work.
4. There is no use trying to change laws or government.
5. Lack of concern for each other.
6. Lack of self-respect and respect for the community.
7. Loss of hope for a better life and higher standard of living.
8. Lack of concern about the health of the family.
9. Treat the man no better than he treats you.
10. Lack of concern for the community and its programs.

They moved on, still with the three county co-ordinators serving as facilitators of their own groups, to discuss ways of changing these attitudes and countering critics:

How to find out what people want enough to work for it

1. Talk to them in their homes.
2. Call a meeting and talk to them there.

3. Go to friends who know people in the community and ask them to contact their friends.
4. The leader stands back and lets the people have their way.
5. Talk to the person who is against the idea or have his friend talk to him.
6. Let the people know that you really want their opinions and not that we are a know-it-all ourselves.
7. Have programs for all income groups and ages in the community.
8. Start the story at the mouth of the creek.
9. Telephone people and have them call their neighbors.
10. Have a get-together with food, music, to talk about what the community might do.
11. Suggestion box for community projects or even complaints.
12. Don't make or imply promises.
13. If the person doesn't know you, say who you are.

Suggestions for countering critics
1. Ignore them—let your success pull them in.
2. Build them up and draw them into your project.
3. Turn the other cheek.
4. If you plan to approach him or have someone else do it, find out all you can about him first.
5. Find out what advantage would mean something to him.
6. Don't talk about changing attitudes, things he might consider a personal affair.
7. A friendly approach has a good chance of getting a friendly response.
8. Don't over-emphasize the government part.
9. People of different ages and different income groups will respond to different things.
10. Don't lead people to believe you want them to give even a little money (money—no; help—yes).

Before the course ended, the local people had their turn practicing facilitating with practice discussions on:
1. How will we operators get furniture for our offices?
2. How will we operators get people interested in the Community Information Depots?

And everyone had a chance at role playing. Participants sought answers to two especially knotty questions in these little projected real life dramas:
1. How do the operators find out what their communities want

badly enough to work to get it? Who do they talk to? And
how? There were several role playings of this for the whole
group with different people each time.

2. How do we operators explain our jobs to people who ask
    about them? Groups of three or four acted out this one until
    each person once or twice had taken each of the three roles—
    community depot operator, person wanting to know about the
    depot and evaluator of the probable accuracy and effectiveness
    of the performance.

County groups discussed "What support can the operators expect
from the co-ordinators?" and "How do we start on our jobs?"

All the steps in the course helped participants explore potential
problems in the work ahead and accept useful new concepts that
could aid them in meeting these problems. Opening talks, question
and answer periods and discussions helped the participants unfreeze
their pre-training attitudes. The later activities and discussions gave
them practice at working within the new concepts and began to provide them with the support they would need to carry out these concepts.

An evaluation of the course by participants closed the sessions.
The questions and answers follow:

Evaluation

1. How many of you feel ready to do your job? Feel fairly
    ready? Feel not ready?

    In one county group all five members took the safe course
    of saying they were fairly ready. In the other two groups five
    reported themselves ready and four fairly ready.

2. What should you know about your job that you do not know?
    a. Need more experience.
    b. Need to know more about our community.
    c. Under what conditions could we be dismissed?

3. How has this training session helped me to do my job?
    a. Help to understand how to get my community organized.
    b. Broadened my viewpoint.
    c. This program can be very important if we can get the
        community to operate.
    d. Getting to know other operators and county co-ordinators.
    e. Gave me an idea of what my relationship with the com-
        munity is.
    f. Gave me ideas and information that I can use on my job.

g. Gave me an idea of how to approach the community and my job.

h. Gave me confidence of my ability to go out and get the job done.

i. Gave me the feeling that I am not alone in my job and have people feel ready and willing to help me with any problems I need help with.

j. Ready to do the job? Fairly ready!

4. How has this training session helped you?

a. Taught me how to approach the community.

b. Have better understood the structure of OEO.

c. Learned how better to deal with people.

d. Learned how systematically to solve problems.

e. Role playing has shown us that some people may be hard to deal with.

f. Learned that if we try hard, we will reach our goal.

g. Have made friends here.

h. Learned how a community can get bigger and better things done by working together.

i. Taught us more about our supervisors, their roles and background.

j. Taught us how to better settle differences of opinions in community.

k. Taught us that the communities should be more active.

l. Learned not to make promises.

5. How we would change the session:

a. Have more role playing.

b. Show film on someone organizing a community.

c. Have the leader ask more questions of the more silent members of the group.

In a report to the director of the four-county LKLP Community Action Council, Strauss wrote this appraisal of the participants:

The training director was a very apt pupil and I have no doubt of his ability, with the assistance of the co-ordinators, to plan and direct subsequent training courses for operators. My only suggestion is that, since he has not yet directed role playing, it would be useful for him to practice doing so before the next course begins. He could do this in staff meetings with the co-ordinators and they could develop their skill in it at the same time.

Of the co-ordinators, I expect performance of very high quality from one and of good quality from another. The third has excellent capability but I think the degree of his success will depend on the training director's skill to help him understand that, bright as he is, there is still much that he can (and needs to) learn.

The operators will, of course, perform at different levels within a wide range, but I think that range will be of a quality which will surprise many people. The thinking that came out of the discussions (as shown by the flip sheet items listed) was sound and broad-gauged. A number of operators demonstrated good organizing knowledge. They didn't realize, of course, how difficult their jobs will be but they took off with excellent spirit and I think two co-ordinators (and perhaps the third) will give them the support that will enable most of them to accomplish much of what you hope.

Strauss's assignment completed, he returned to the Northern Virginia area. He often wondered, however, how the Community Information Depots (and the operators he had trained) were faring. About a year later, he received a copy of an OEO evaluation of LKLP dated June 1968. The part of the report dealing with the Community Information Depots had a number of cheerful things to say. For instance:

1. The referral aspect of the CID program appears to be operating very well. The operators have a good understanding of their role in the referral process and perform this service in a superior manner. They are cognizant of the local agencies which can be of assistance and know where to direct the people concerned.

2. The operators spend approximately twenty hours a week out in the communities delivering meeting announcements, visiting, arranging transportation and otherwise assisting people.

3. The medical transportation provided by the Community Information Depot program is filling a major service gap and was credited by a number of people for having actually saved lives.

4. The procurement of a physical structure in which to meet brought about a community effort of significance in an area which is unaccustomed to communal interchange.

5. In a number of communities, people worked very hard in raising funds for the construction of new facilities or the renovation of existing buildings. The buildings provide a visible improvement in the community. The center represents a living symbol of something happening for the good of the community. People are generally pleased that they have some place

to go and hold meetings, exchange ideas and work on hand-crafts and the like.

6. In Perry County, another group is working to have tele-phone lines installed for a section of the county. The poor are actively participating in the effort to come to an agreement with the telephone company.

The principal shortcoming of the program, according to the evalu-ation, was that the tackling of any major issues which would sub-stantially affect poverty had not yet occurred. "The main thrusts of LKLP are programs and jobs, not community organization," the re-port stated. It went on: "The operators perceive their major re-sponsibility as referrals rather than community organization. They spoke of community organization but lacked any understanding of what they were organizing for or what was to be done once the group was established."

We think that if Strauss had been called back to work with the operators strictly on that point, the difficulty could have been over-come. He certainly could have introduced the operators to techniques of community organization and helped them develop an organiza-tional plan that they, knowing their people, would have judged feasi-ble. However, the invitation did not come.

Not entirely content with the OEO evaluation and anxious to see for himself what progress had been made, Strauss revisited the area in 1970. He found a lot to hearten him.

The Community Information Depots may not have looked im-pressive to the city-oriented. Most of them were located in such quarters as the room above the combination grocery store and gas station at a crossroads and bore such names as Frank's Creek, Beef-hide, Blair Branch, Millstone, Blackey, Joshua, Sassafras, Rock Fork, Red Fox, Thousandsticks, Grapevine, or Buck Horn. But appearances were deceptive. People quickly began flooding him with accounts of accomplishment.*

Although not all the Community Information Depots had contin-ued, they had sparked sixty-five active community organizations and more were planned. Local people had repaired 2,000 old people's houses, the government paying for materials but volunteers providing the labor. Volunteers also had built more than 1,600 suspension bridges across creeks so that families living on the other side could

* See Appendix, Chapter 11, for a sample page from the Community Achievement Report, March 1969.

get across to the road. The Teen Corps of America had sent in high school and college kids to help build 125 of these bridges and two community centers and had spent $25,000 in one county. On and on: a community-owned sawmill and an arts and crafts workshop both providing local employment in Perry County; cable TV and community and roadside parks in Leslie County; a school for the mentally retarded in Letcher County; cottage industry in Knott County—to name just a few of the accomplishments.

Strauss talked with the then head of the LKLP staff, who had been one of the co-ordinators at the time of the training course, and with several center operators who had taken the course. Had the training been of any value? he asked. Definitely, they assured him. It had worked out what depot operators should do and how. It had given them confidence and they came up with the slogan "We'll always try again." They credited the course with getting the program off to a right start, for teaching them to work with others and to realize that people together could do what no one alone could hope to do. From the beginning, they said, they had worked *with* local officials and local staff (especially health and welfare), not in competition.

Maybe the sort of community organization the OEO had sought had not been achieved and there had not been enough attention to eliminating the basic causes of poverty in the area. But certainly there had been a great deal of the kind of community organization that could relieve symptoms, and to those who had found relief, the program seemed effective, indeed. No doubt they had felt that relieving symptoms should come before doing research on the disease for the sociologists back in Washington. A natural enough decision. When people are hurting, their first interest is in doing something to make themselves feel better. This these local people certainly did, and we think they have every reason to be proud of themselves for it.

Perhaps one of the troubles with the poverty war was that too often those in charge, whether paid workers or volunteers, didn't really want the participating poor to have any ideas of their own about the priorities. Too often the approach was Big Brother knows best, Big Brother spouting love and understanding and a lot of sociological gibberish out of one side of his mouth and a lot of rigid, dictatorial directions out of the other. To the poor, it didn't make much sense and when it got too bad, they dropped out.

When they had a chance to decide for themselves from the beginning what they needed and how to get it, most of them were surprisingly effective.

Helping Another CAP Staff Work Together

Loudoun County could best have been described as exurban when we tried to help the Community Action Program there. The LKLP area of Kentucky, of course, was Appalachia.

We also conducted training sessions for the Alexandria Community Action staff and include a brief summary of the experience not only because so much of the poverty war was concentrated in urban black ghettos such as Alexandria's but because the experience also supports our contention that a major difficulty in the poverty war was the inability of too many people to work together to obtain a clear picture of their goals and how to overcome the obstacles that lay in the paths to those goals.

In the spring of 1969, our old friend Joe Killeen (Chapters 2 and 5) was sure this was the case with the Alexandria CAP program. He recently had taken the job of Community Outreach director, to learn that the previous policy had been to take a predetermined program to the people to be served. Joe wanted to change that so that the people to be served could decide their own program. He also found that the CAP staff had little concept of how to work together themselves. He wanted to change that, too.

He asked us to conduct some sessions that would teach group techniques to the staff so they could use them not only in future planning with each other but with the people they were supposed to help.

We suggested a series of facilitator training sessions with the practice discussions to concentrate on whatever work-related subjects the staff chose. Six training sessions in five weeks followed. These sessions were conducted in the morning on office time, of course, for two and a half to three hours.

At first, we encountered more than a little hostility. Of the twelve staff members on the rolls, only eight came to the first session. The others just couldn't take the time. Even those who came seemed to think what we were trying to do rather silly. "How do we take flip charts into the community?" they asked.

One supervisor with a staff of five, in charge of a whole downtown area, began with a big chip on each shoulder. "What's this got to do with Community Action?" he asked. So many people cannot see the importance of method, of learning how to be more effective. Their sole concern is with content and they don't see that learning how to approach that content is a big share of the battle. At least, they don't see at first. Before the sessions were over, this supervisor was an enthusiastic convert. "All of a sudden, it hit me," he said. "I could see how useful this was, what a help it could be."

The others, too, gradually changed their minds about the usefulness of the sessions and persuaded missing staff members to join the course.

The practice discussions with different staff members serving as facilitators brought out some good group thinking. On May 6, 1969, for instance, the group suggested three possible topics to discuss:

1. Goals for this year and change of direction.
2. Better job opportunities for heads of households.
3. Organize single voices into one voice.

Then they decided to work first on their goals for the year and went on to list problems:

1. Image hang-ups.
2. Staff hang-ups.
    a. Communication between offices.
    b. Chain of command.
    c. Communication between staff/commission.
3. Program in its entirety.
    a. Purpose not clearly defined.
    b. Structure not the best.
    c. How program was formed (the poor not represented initially).
    d. Effectiveness not felt in community.
4. Problems with agencies.
    a. Gaps with and between agencies.
    b. Poor attitudes of agency personnel toward poor (should work with the total person).
5. Attitudes of public officials who are lawmakers toward the poor—lack of communication between policy makers and the poor—local and national.
6. Lack of funds.
7. Attitudes of the poor.
    a. Lack of faith.
    b. Defeatist attitude.
8. Unable to see clearly what we can and cannot do.

With staff members still taking turns at the flip charts while the others practiced good discussion techniques (facilitator training), they set as their first goal for the year:

Better program:

a. Develop job opportunities (to include those under sixteen).

b. Develop opportunities or more low rent and low cost housing.

c. Stimulate more interest in/for better education for children and adults.

    (1) Make people aware of existing education opportunities.

    (2) Make education more convenient in terms of cost and time.

    (3) Make education more relevant.

d. Create a realistic emergency assistance program.

e. Start a "close the gap" campaign with agencies toward the poor.

f. Work directly with the Outreach and Headstart programs to make them more effective—programs already funded (working with what we have to maximum use).

The next morning concentration was still on a better program. The flip chart records highlighted the discussion:

Program: Work on attitudes and get the people together.

1. Talk to people, listen to what they're saying and not saying.

2. Find out what the people think is most important.

3. Gain their confidence.

    a. Dispel false images.

    b. Be honest.

    c. Don't make promises that you can't fulfill—what you *do* is more important than what you say.

    d. Don't give advice.

4. Tell people about existing information from agencies and people in the community.

5. Look for leaders of all forces in the community (of the poor) and bring them together.

    a. Suggest value of meeting.

    b. Help them plan their own meetings.

    c. Encourage the leadership to communicate in the community.

    d. Neighborhood worker keep close contact on both ends (swap referrals).

    e. Addressed information will be delivered or mailed.

Hostility was pretty much overcome by now and the staff members, whether taking a turn as facilitators or discussants, were doing an ever better job. On May 8, the training session discussion was focused on how the community worker should relate to the ongoing project, including how to evaluate progress.

On May 16, staff members put their activities in priority order:

1. Emergencies
2. Outreach
3. Referrals to agencies and jobs
4. Organization in community
5. Neighborhood Youth Corps
6. Co-operation with other agencies
7. Volunteer transportation
8. Training
9. Meeting
   a. Staff
   b. Commission meetings

Then the training sessions concentrated on the priorities. For instance:

Community Organization

1. Make staff aware of information that exists.
2. Work out staff hang-ups.
3. Goals: a. Long-range—co-op in Cameron Valley.
            b. Immediate—buying club.
4. Plan of action:
   a. Make the people aware of *what* a buying club is and how it *might* benefit them.
   b. Make the Housing Authority aware of the plan and seek their co-operation.
   c. Keep other key people informed, interested and involved.
   d. Get consensus of sponsoring group (meet with them first).
   e. Bring community and sponsoring groups together (including key people if possible).
5. Organization.

Plan of action—How?

a. Making people aware.
   (1) Door-to-door visitation.
   (2) Printed information.
   (3) Telephone heads of different organizations and groups and influential members and follow up with letter where necessary.
   (4) Correspondence.

      (5)   Audio-visual aids.

      (6)   Speaking engagements.

b.   Co-operation of Housing Authority.

      (1)   Telephone head of Housing Authority.

      (2)   Make him aware of program.

      (3)   Discuss our plan of action.

      (4)   Inquire about his views.

      (5)   Obtain his commitment.

          His staff.

          Himself.

          His facilities for this project.

          His time and knowledge.

          His encouragement to expand into other projects (if successful).

          This to be a pilot project for other housing developments.

          Possible use of his facilities for other programs.

c.   Other key people.

      (1)   Telephone.

      (2)   Meeting with them.

      (3)   Written matter.

d.   Consensus of sponsoring groups.

      (1)   Get all information together.

      (2)   Call a meeting with them.

      (3)   Let them decide if this is the plan they want as a project and if they can work with it.

      (4)   Obtain a definite commitment.

e.   Bringing community and sponsoring groups together.

Organization—How?

1.   Keep sponsoring group involved and interested.

2.   Bring in other forces in community.

3.   When the community shows enthusiasm, get the sponsoring group and the community together.

      a.   Get acquainted.

      b.   Discussion.

      c.   Work out program—and assignment of responsibilities.

      d.   Let's roll!!

Notes to keep in mind:

1.   Beware of any agency take-over.

2.   Try to make this kind of program available to others who need it.

3. Keep looking for key people—never close it to a few.
4. Amen.

As we ended the training sessions, the people involved seemed enthusiastic not only about the plans they had made but the method of discussion, of thinking together in an orderly fashion, that had produced the plans. We were pleased to receive a letter from the acting director a couple of weeks later. It said:

> "Thank you very much for offering to our staff the sessions in facilitation. The training came at a very appropriate time, as we were going through a process of self-evaluation in preparation for a change in outlook and direction. In the facilitation sessions the staff also had a chance to focus on some of its operational problems.
>
> "We had an opportunity to put our training in practice in goal-setting prior to a recent training assessment by VACAT. Now the flip chart and magic marker are very important tools in our regular staff meetings, and each member of the staff has a chance to be a facilitator.
>
> "On behalf of the staff, may I express our gratitude to you for helping us to acquire this skill."

Part Two

WHY IT WORKS

12

GETTING PARTICIPATION

All the forgoing stories illustrate how we use a group-centered, non-directive approach to problem solving. For a change, look with us at this recent experience of a civic leader in a suburban county when the increasing use of drugs among his county's high school students disturbed him.

He knew drug abuse is a national problem and it worried him. He felt helpless about changing the national situation, but a local attack was something else. Locally, he had a lot of ideas about what could be done. Each area clean up its own back yard. Put all the areas together and presto! Who knew? Maybe his county could set an example that could be repeated all over the nation. In any event, he was going to *do* something instead of just worrying about it and saying, What a mess.

Fine—so far. Enough successful local attacks on many of our national problems and they would, indeed, be solved. Local examples often serve as guides and inspiration to other areas. And someone had to take the initiative in his county. If only he had called in several other civic leaders and a few key officials to help him plan . . .

Instead, all by himself, he sent out invitations to a hundred other leaders for a meeting on the subject. In this case, there was so much concern about drugs in the high schools that half the people on his invitation list came. But had there been more sponsors lending their influence and know-how to getting out the crowd, the meeting would have been better planned, more representative—and vastly more likely to launch a successful effort. It always is. The participation of others in the planning of this first meeting would already have engendered their enthusiasm, their support and, very importantly, their ideas for making the whole endeavor go.

Even so, all was by no means lost when the fifty gathered in a school cafeteria on the appointed night. The room was buzzing with enthusiasm. Obviously, everyone present wanted to help change the situation. Everyone present had ideas. They were exchanging them eagerly before the call to order. If only the leader had utilized techniques that would have taken full advantage of the resources of the people in the room . . .

What happened? Well, in brief, he muffed the opportunity for everyone. Having called the meeting, he felt that he was in charge. Having decided in advance what should be done, he proceeded to outline his plans and to make assignments to carry out his ideas. He didn't ask the others what they thought. He told them how it was going to be. When a few tried to make suggestions, he was chairman and he squelched them. The crowd listened in ever more apparent frustration as he talked on and on. A few rather grimly accepted the assignments he gave them but more found excuses and went home determined not to come to the next meeting *he* set.

There were only twelve at his next meeting and five at the third and last, when the leader disbanded the group, muttering about public apathy and callousness.

This is an extreme example. Yet how often, disturbed about some problem and willing to throw a piece of our living selves—mind, time, energy—into some effort to change an undesirable situation for the better, have we given up a lunch hour, a morning, afternoon, evening (or many of them) and gone forth only to find our minds ignored, our time wasted, our energy unused, our only purpose apparently to follow servilely the ego, the high-handed domination of some so-called leader or ruling clique or committee? How often, as a result, have we crawled back into ourselves, thwarted and frustrated if not embittered?

And those of us who call ourselves leaders—how often have we ignored the minds, wasted the time and failed to use the human resources that were available for worthy causes? How many times have we cursed the apathy of others when we, ourselves, have done much to create that apathy by shutting them out in one way or another?

The Need for Participation

Social scientists have long known (and research continues to emphasize) that only participation will release the untapped supply of energy and ideas that are available in any group concerned with tackling any problem. Industries long ago discovered that participation in decision making results in greater production. It also cuts down on absenteeism, and provides a real incentive to better the product or process, whatever it may be. In any organization, at any conference, the situation is comparable. When the members are allowed to build with those at the top, the whole enterprise picks up new energy. It makes little difference whether these members are paid for their services or are volunteering; whether one talks in terms of man-hours or mind-hours. The salvaging of time and energy is the same.

Unfortunately, this non-directive approach is not widely used. Here and there it has been accepted by this or that volunteer group, this or that agency—with results that prove its superiority. Yet, for many of us, it represents a big switch. Traditionally, as a nation, we are accustomed to the directive approach. We divide our groups into the shepherds and the sheep. Robert's Rules of Order are the Authority, more or less rigidly followed. The leaders see themselves as keeping control and leading the group to conclusions they usually have predetermined. Normally, in a community meeting, only the most vocal—or the most desperate—rise to address the chair. People express their ideas largely in terms of motions made without prior problem analysis and resulting in either apathetic "ayes" or heated debate—and polarization of views. Decisions result from majority vote, with minority reactions ranging from resigned acceptance through frustration to departure or sabotage. The majority of group members rarely join actively either in planning or execution.

While the directive approach is useful when it is necessary to give explanations, instructions or decisions already made, it severely handicaps any group facing a problem that must be solved, for it ignores most of the group's resources. It bottles up the vast supply of good thinking which the whole group can provide and which was never more urgently needed across our nation. Moreover, it cuts off the great potential of enthusiasm and support needed for truly effective solutions. When people find their intelligence, knowledge and opinions ignored, they naturally lose interest in the work to be done. After all, the decisions, whatever they are, are not *their* decisions.

The Early Studies

The research on which this understanding of group behavior is based began in the late 1920s. Western Electric Co., a subsidiary of AT&T, hired a group of Harvard social scientists headed by Elton Mayo and F. J. Roethlisberger to determine the working conditions which would enable workers in the company's plant at Hawthorne, Illinois, to reach and maintain the highest possible levels of production.

The researchers began with a study of small groups of women making parts for radios. Some groups they called "experimental" and others "control." From time to time during several months, they changed working conditions in the "experimental" groups, never in the ones labeled "control." The "experimental" groups were treated to such inducements as lengthened rest periods and shortened working hours. They also received improved tools and better placing of the materials they used. With each change, production went up. But oddly production increased not only in the "experimental" groups, where the change had been made, but also in the "control" groups, where it had not.

Puzzled, the researchers cut back working conditions in the "experimental" groups to exactly what they had been at the start. Production went up again in both types of groups! Eventually, the study led to the finding that it wasn't the working conditions that increased production. What really mattered to both groups of workers and brought out their best efforts was that for the first time in their lives they felt important. Other people knew what they were doing and cared about the results.

Research of the Hawthorne type was very limited during the depression of the 1930s, when companies had little money for such "frills." The next landmark in the series came in 1938, when Drs. Ronald Lippitt and Ralph White, then graduate students at the University of Iowa, decided to study group behavior for their Ph.D. theses, working with the brilliant Viennese social psychologist Dr. Kurt Lewin.

In an initial experiment with four boys' clubs, each under a different kind of leader, they studied the effects of different types of leadership. They used the benevolent authority type, the laissez-faire or non-interfering type and the democratic type.

The attitude of the benevolent authority type was, "These are fine boys. I must direct them in the very best way I can." The laissez-faire leader thought, "These boys are like beautiful plants. My job is to nurture them carefully without interfering with their growth." The democratic leader is best represented by a typical greeting: "Hi, gang. What are we going to do today?"

The groups of eleven-year-olds were matched as well as possible in interests, intelligence, background, skills and so forth. Each club met in the same place as the others but at a different time. From time to time, leaders were interchanged. On other occasions, a leader left the room for a time and a janitor or some other outsider walked in instead, looked at the boys' work, pointed out mistakes and made himself as disagreeable as he could.

The outsider walking in on the group with the benevolent authority type leader created complete group breakdown. The group went to pieces and the boys were unable to complete their work. Faced with the outsider's criticism, most of the group turned on one of their fellows and attempted to make a scapegoat of him.

Group members under the loose hand of the laissez-faire leader showed good individual development in knowledge since they had to work things out for themselves. However, they were behind the first group in accomplishment and rarely worked as a team—except when their leader left the room. They would team up then all right —not for work, but for a game of cops and robbers. When the obnoxious outsider entered and pointed out mistakes, they, like the first group, attempted to blame a victim.

Boys in the democratic leader's group went right on working when he wasn't there. They felt it was *their* group, not his. They did not pick on one another. When the unpleasant stranger came in, they showed their anger not by turning on anyone of their group but by such safety valves as smashing plywood stacked nearby for their use. This group, in which the democratic leader had encouraged maximum participation in decision making, showed the least dependence on him. The boys could continue their effectiveness in his absence, maintain respect for all members and act as a group against outside threats.

During World War II, when preferred cuts of meat were in short supply because of shipments to the armed forces, the United States Department of Agriculture launched a campaign to promote use of less popular cuts such as hearts and kidneys. The department used the usual methods of publicity and also sent home economists to speak to groups of housewives, explaining the need to use less popular cuts. Most successful of the meetings were those in which the housewives then talked over the difficulties of getting their families to eat such cuts and finally, having expressed their anticipated problems, agreed to make the attempt.

Subsequent research indicated that when the ladies had committed themselves to using the cuts, they usually followed through on their agreement. It had become their decision, not the Department of Agriculture's.

Shortly after World War II, a significant experiment occurred at a pajama factory in Marion, Virginia. Every time the management introduced new styles requiring changes in the manufacturing process and in piece rates paid workers, the very groups which had produced most highly before the change became the poorest producers afterwards. Why was this? The perplexed management decided to introduce the next change in three ways. To some groups, the management simply issued the new instructions and rates as always. And, as always, production fell with these groups. In fact, it never reached a satisfactory level and trailed production by entirely new employees. Trying a second method with other groups, a management representative met with work group representatives to discuss the changes. In those groups, subsequent production was satisfactory, though not outstanding. The third method proved by far the best. A management representative met with each work group, and in these groups subsequent production approximated its previous high.

The principle of participation explains this phenomenon. The groups with the highest production before the change were those in which cohesiveness was highest. When members were dissatisfied with the arbitrary way they were handed their new work assignments and piece rates, they showed their resentment by reducing their production. The more cohesive the group, the better they stuck together in keeping production down. Having one of their members represent them in talks with management helped their morale enough to make their production satisfactory in spite of the changes. But when all members of a cohesive group had the opportunity to discuss ways to work out the new system, full understanding and high morale combined with the cohesiveness to spur the workers to the highest level of production.

Extensive research and experience since these early examples, including the experiences we record in this book, have continued to demonstrate the value of using the whole group. Isn't it time, then, that we, as a nation, make maximum use of this discovery in attempting to solve our overwhelming problems?

The Facilitator

A turn to the group-centered, non-directive approach emphatically does not mean a turn to chaos, everyone talking at once, everyone disagreeing, nothing decided. Leadership is still needed, but a new kind of leadership, the kind that frees the resources of the group while maintaining order and providing direction.

Because the old word, leader, has so many connotations of performer or tyrant or both, we call the kind of leader that our work has proved most valuable a "facilitator." His job, as mentioned in earlier chapters, is to facilitate the discussion and decision making, to help the group be as effective as possible. He makes it easier for each member to give his best to the whole group. He does not rule or direct. He puts his faith in the participants' interest in and knowledge of the problem and their ability, with his aid, to think it through rationally and reach a solution which they will join in carrying out. To do this, he uses proven skills and techniques discussed in later chapters.

These skills and techniques are all designed not to aggrandize him but to:

1. Help the participants explore a problem and improve their understanding of it.

2. Help them integrate their thinking and work together to reach a decision on which they can agree and which they will carry out with zeal.

3. Help them plan and organize the process for carrying it out, including the assignment of responsibilities to individuals.

4. Help them plan evaluation of progress, review the findings, replan and reassign responsibilities as necessary.

Part Three

HOW WE DO IT

13

WHAT WE DO WITH A REQUEST FOR HELP

Explore the Situation Thoroughly

When we are asked to help get a problem aired or a difficult situation explored, our first step is to talk to the people who want our help. What are you trying to accomplish? we ask. Why? What obstacles—including people—are in your way? If we decide to participate, we ask them to bring together from five to ten other persons who are or should be concerned about the situation. This bringing together becomes planning session number one.

Include All Viewpoints

Often a basic difficulty seems to be apathy, inadequate co-operation or lack of information, and we ask that this initial group include members whose thinking represents all the important viewpoints about the situation. We do this because, for a solution to be truly workable, it must have widespread support. The earlier we include proponents of all viewpoints in the planning, the likelier we are to come up with a plan that all can consider "ours," not "theirs." This helps provide built-in co-operation. For instance, in organizing the Committee of 55 (Chapter 1), we made sure the founders included representatives of most of the diverse segments of Loudoun County. In planning for the successful job fairs (Chapter 4), we included *as planners* not only the people who initiated the action (could see that it was needed), but representatives of those to be helped (people needing jobs) and those who could help them (corporations such as Westinghouse and IBM, the Virginia Employment Commission and the Chambers of Commerce.)

Even Enlist "The Enemy"

Very often, when the requesters are aware at the very beginning of actual or potential resistance to what they have in mind, we insert an extra step, asking them first to bring together only representatives of the groups they think *favor* their purpose. This is to give those groups an opportunity to reach agreement on their thinking and to decide jointly how to involve the opposition most effectively. The second decision can be difficult to reach since it requires a use of imagination and a projection of thinking, to which many people are not accustomed. This is one of the situations in which role playing, discussed in Chapter 16, can be useful.

There are times when planning groups hesitate at this point. Inviting resisters to join them in the planning seems suicidal. But if the objective cannot be reached without the co-operation of these resisters, the sooner they become involved the better. This is the point at which the requesters and their friends decide whether they want to create a solution which all parties will carry out, or try to impose their own predetermined ideas without regard for the needs of people with other viewpoints. The latter choice is infrequent since most people working in community activities have seen the inadequacy of too many imposed solutions. Upon occasion, however, the "to-hell-with-them" decision is made. If so, we explain that our techniques don't fit such an approach and bow out. Usually, however, the decision is to enlist the opposition and change it from opposition to support.

Be Prepared to Give Time—and Patience

Before the group is as widely representative as it should be, several meetings may have to be held, each one going over essentially the same ground: the situation as it looks to the people discussing it, their objectives and the barriers they see en route, and, always the question, "Are all necessary viewpoints included in this planning?" Some important viewpoint may be overlooked for a long while. You may recall, for example, that in planning the School Volunteer Aide Conference, Chapter 5, the planning group did not think of the need to involve the teachers' associations until it began a thoughtful examination of the potential barriers—in that case, teacher resistance.

Each time people representing new viewpoints join the planning group and the same ground is covered, there are, of course, fresh differences of opinion to be reconciled. This may sound repetitious, boring or unnecessarily time-consuming. It isn't. Each time the group looks at the problem from a different viewpoint, it sees elements that were missing before. Each time it works out misunderstandings or disagreements at an early stage, it saves much time and many headaches later—the best assurance of a successful beginning that the group can have. Also, the members learn quickly that important changes in their thinking can emerge when they think through the import of a different viewpoint—and that these changes are normally very useful.

Reach Agreement on a Specific Problem and Specific Goals

When all viewpoints are at last represented and the planning group at its second, third or even fourth meeting has agreed on the essentials of what it wants to change, the situation it would like to have exist (its goal) and the barriers on the way, the members have eliminated major areas of potential trouble. They know what they want and that agreement is both a big step forward and a control on future discussions and plans. The more specifically they can state their problem and their goals, the better their chances of success.

Always Use a Facilitator

Another of our techniques is what makes this process feasible. Our discussion leader, whom we call a facilitator because that word correctly expresses his role, records the pertinent points of the discussion on a flip chart as he hears them. Any member who disagrees with a point that is put into this visible record can state his disagreement, discussion ensues and the facilitator changes the point to meet the group's satisfaction. When a flip chart sheet is filled, the facilitator hangs it in a readily visible spot and by the time the meeting ends the story of the group's thinking that day is hanging all around the room. Usually it has been reviewed and changed several times in the process. If at the next meeting new members are present, the sheets are rehung and the new members have the opportunity to go through the essentials of the thinking at the previous session, to raise questions and to make suggestions which frequently lead to changes.

The facilitator's conduct of the discussion is important in other ways, too. Essentially, his job is to create an atmosphere in which everyone feels free to participate, and to help the group bring out and organize its thinking as members build on each other's contributions. He does this by listening intently and asking questions when it seems necessary to:

1. Clarify an unclear point.
2. Bring out a viewpoint which is being overlooked.
3. Pull the discussion back on course.
4. Push it off dead center.
5. Test for consensus.

He usually addresses his questions to the whole group because this gives every member an invitation to respond. If, instead, he asks one member, he can create several difficulties. That member may be embarrassed by not being ready to answer. Other members, who may wish to do so, cannot. By thus interfering with free exchange of member ideas, the facilitator would prevent the discussants having valuable interplay of thought and building on each other's thinking.

When the facilitator does ask a question of an individual he does it for one of three reasons. The question may be a follow-up on a person's previous comments or may elicit particular information needed at the moment. The other occasion is when the facilitator believes that the ongoing discussion is no longer useful. By intervening he assumes control and, through one or more directed questions, puts it on another course. Knowing when to do this is one of a facilitator's important skills.

The facilitator rarely makes a positive statement and never takes sides, though his questions may often be intended to induce one side to analyze, more carefully than it yet has, what the other is saying. He even puts his summaries and tests for consensus as questions, "Is this what we are saying . . . ?" "Do we agree that . . . ?" His open attitude tells all the members that their thinking is being respected. Since respect is one of the responses each of us wants most strongly from our fellows, this recognition encourages the discussants to keep cool more easily, and consider others' thinking more reasonably, than under the traditional rules of discussion to which most of us are accustomed. (The training of facilitators, the use of the flip chart and other practices we discuss later.)

Answer Some Important Questions

When the planning group members have agreed on what they want to achieve and the barriers in the way, the focus of their questions changes. They now raise such points as these: What people feel the change is needed? Who will give understanding and support? Which people do we need to provide necessary skills, knowledge and prestige? Who can accomplish the changes we want, or are in position to persuade others who can? Who must be persuaded?

When they have answered the "who?" questions they go on to the "hows?" Is a conference or a series of meetings a useful way to reach them? What can we accomplish that way? Are there other ways that might be better? Can our organizations do it or do we need to involve others? Or start a new one?

Now . . . If It's to Be a Conference . . .

At this point, obviously, the planning can go in one of several directions. Let's start with the most frequent decision: to have a one-day conference of from about fifteen discussants to three hundred, using small discussion groups. The conference may involve members of several organizations or local governments, perhaps a mixture of both plus citizens who are interested but not connected with any organization (our conference on the use of volunteers in the schools, Chapter 5, is a good example). Or it may focus on bringing together people from components of an organization, such as the local branches of one that is countywide or county branches of a statewide one.

If the conference involves several organizations (or governments or components) and the previous meetings have succeeded in including all viewpoints, influential members of these organizations are already in the planning committee. If they are not, better get them in quickly (as we did with the teachers' federations in the school volunteer example). When all are in, some will have to go back to the official decision-making groups of their organizations before they can assure the organizations' support. For those not sure of being able to get that endorsement, a bit of role playing (Chapter 16) may help in thinking through how to go about getting it successfully.

Plan for Interested, Knowledgeable Discussion Groups

If the problem is a complex one, the planners usually can identify several points of greatest controversy. To get the best discussion and also assure each participant a chance to tackle his pet difficulty, our invitations list those controversial points and ask the registrants to number their discussion choices in order. We then set up groups accordingly. For example, at a 3 P.M. to 10 P.M. conference of about seventy state legislators and local officials to explore proposed changes in the Virginia Constitution (Chapter 10) the planners provided for two sets of discussions in the afternoon (so each participant could join in exploring two subjects). Each group included a resource person who had helped prepare the recommendations or was highly knowledgeable on the subject. After a buffet supper, the resource people sat as a panel to discuss questions that had been raised, but not completely clarified, during the afternoon.

Do You Want Orderly Discussion, Well Used Time and Useful Conclusions?

If you do, a planned discussion pattern is essential. Without one each group wanders until it develops its own design, which may be never. At best, this takes what should be valuable time, leaves the facilitators without an important tool and reaches a wide range of results rarely pleasing to either planners or participants. Form 1 (see Appendix, Chapter 13) carries a pattern we usually introduce if the planning group has no starting point of its own.

Normally, we do not have to point out that the pattern on Form 1 is that which the planning group has been using. Frequently the next reaction is, "We can't possibly do all that in a two-hour session." We agree, but indicate that:

1. If the planners wish discussion in depth they may have to provide more than two hours for it.
2. Something like the following, Form 1, steps 1 through 3, are essential to analyze a problem.
   a. Agreement on the essential problem requires the group members to consider the causes of the symptoms and gets them all on the same beam.
   b. Agreement on goals is a meeting of minds which gives everyone a common purpose and an invaluable control on the group's future activities.
   c. Listing the barriers and using them to test the feasibility of suggested solutions opens the way to a depth of analysis which is the best assurance the group can have that it is headed in the right direction.
3. Some conferences can stop at the end of step 4, on Form 1, Agree on recommendations, but steps 5, Agree on an action

plan, and 6, Agree on an evaluation plan, are necessary to reaching a desired action goal.

If this pattern does not fit the situation well we use modifications or other approaches. For example, the most important barrier may appear to be a person or a particular group. In that case, when the barriers are listed we ask such questions as, "Who can reach these people?" "To whom do they listen?" When we know who those intermediate people are we raise the same questions about them—and continue the process until the members create a chain they believe feasible to use between themselves and the barrier group or person.

Having found a way the planners think will reach the barrier group, the next question is, "What kind of appeal will interest them?" The planners may think they can answer that question or that they need more information first. In either event, sooner or later they will outline an approach. At that point, role playing can be useful to test the feasibility of their plan.

Initially, each planning group member takes one of three roles: a member of the selling team, a member of the barrier group or an observer. The persons playing barrier group members do their best to think themselves into those people's situations and attitudes so they can respond as they believe the actual people would. After the role playing we lead an analysis of what developed during it, including making sure that we are not drawing conclusions from unrealistic moments.

If the participants feel that the play has been useful enough, they review their plans for approaching the real barrier group in the light of their findings. If they think it has not been an adequate test, they change roles and repeat the process until they are satisfied with the results. (For more complete guidance in role playing see Chapter 16, "Continuing Groups".)

We also use a third approach to problem solving. In this method, the planners determine key questions for the participant groups to answer before they attempt to make recommendations or determine courses of action. For example, in the six-month program to propose goals for Fairfax County (Chapter 6, "Tackling Problems of Community Growth"), the instructions for the first day's sessions were as follows:

The morning group discussions will cover five points within each subject area:
1. What are the issues?

2. What information do we need about these issues?
3. What basic assumptions do we need?
4. In what concrete terms can we specify goals?
5. How can we determine benefits and costs?

After lunch each seminar group will complete its morning discussion (if necessary), and prepare to become a continuing work group by determining what additional people are needed to provide information, skills and viewpoints which the seminar members do not have. It will also set a date and place for its next meeting and take whatever further actions it wishes toward starting its study (except organizing itself—a step which should be delayed until the group is enlarged).

The facilitators we provided led those two sessions and the ensuing one, at which each group created its own organization and laid out its study plans. At that point each facilitator either retired from his group or became a continuing volunteer member, depending on his interest in the group's subject area.

The planning group uses one of these patterns or works out whatever design fits its purposes. Sometimes the group stays with a brief conference. Usually this happens when its goals are limited. It may only want to get a good airing of a subject or to open communication by throwing together groups of people with a variety of viewpoints on a problem. These are valid purposes and a one-day conference can accomplish them. The same is true if the planning group believes in spontaneity above all, or just wants to get people together because "something useful is bound to develop" or "such interesting ideas come out of unstructured discussion." Conversely, if the planners are trying to initiate a change they usually stay with (or shift to) a longer-range, more completely defined plan.

Whatever the planning group's purpose, we always find ourselves fighting to give the discussion groups enough time to get into their problems in depth. Sponsors press for more speakers—and the speaker who keeps to his allotted time is a blessed exception. Also, at the end of the day, time is required for a closing general session. The best answer we have found so far for a one-day conference on a tough problem is to have the groups continue with the same subjects after lunch (or dinner if the conference is in the afternoon and evening) as before. Usually, the early phase is completely exploratory, Form 1, steps 1 through 3 or 4 if the groups are following our discussion pattern, with all decision making left to the later session.

This requires that if resource people are needed they be available for both sessions.

Decide About Speakers and Resource People

Usually, by this time some of the planners have been wanting to talk about speakers and have been more or less politely persuaded to wait until the more basic questions were settled. After some preliminary questions, now is the time. The questions are: What people do we need to give us information that most of our participants won't have? What different kinds of information? How many such authoritative people? Do we want them to make speeches or sit with discussion groups as resource people? Or both?

The answer to that last question is almost always, "Both," so we try to find speakers who can be resource people too. Normally we share with the sponsors the responsibility for locating those paragons. In doing this we follow two criteria. First, we try to find a modest person who knows the subject well rather than a speechmaker with a big name (or ego) and superficial understanding. Second, we emphasize the desirability, in the limited discussion time our groups usually have, of a local expert who knows the situation at first hand and also can approach it with a minimum of bias, over an outsider who may be better versed in theory or principles but must take the discussants' time to learn the immediate problems. Since resource people must know their subjects well, getting the right number for each discussion topic can be a problem. To assure that we have enough, when the registrations come in, we try to find standbys among the discussants or, when that isn't feasible, to recruit knowledgeable local people who will be willing to help if we need them.

Answer Questions of Funding

Suddenly, and usually for the first time, a new problem comes into play: money. Will our authorities give us their time or want honorariums? If the latter, how much? And what other costs will we have to meet? We of the planning group can't answer that last one until we've made some other decisions. How long should our conference be? If it's to be more than a half day, who pays for the meals? And if overnight, for the rooms? Those answers will depend not only on the content of the conference but also on what participants the planners want to have attend, how much time they will be willing to spare for this conference and how much, if anything, they'll be willing (or can afford) to pay. If they can't be expected to pay, or won't, what sources of funds can we tap? And for how many participants do we need them?

Plan for Materials

Then there are the questions about advance mailings and handout materials. What ones are needed? Are they available or must they be produced? Who can we get to prepare them? How quickly can we get them? What will they cost? If we send them out in advance as we receive reservations (which can be expensive), will people read them? If we give them out at the conference, when can we do it so people will have time to read them before the discussions but not take their attention from the speakers?

Arrange for Facilitators

This is the time, too, to start arranging for discussion facilitators. The key questions are: How many do we need? Can we get that many experienced ones or will we have to train some? Who is to do the training? (This is not a question when one of us is involved; we do it after the members recruit trainees.)

Set the Time and Place

When the planners have answered these questions the time is ripe to decide when and where to hold the conference. We recommend that it be at least eight, and preferably ten to twelve, weeks away. Many groups tend to make these decisions before they have covered the basic ground we have just been over—but if they do so before they know how much time they need for all their preparations and what space they should have, they may handicap themselves seriously, perhaps so seriously they'll defeat their purpose. If the main body of desired participants are to come as citizens or representatives of citizen groups, we find a Saturday the most feasible day. A midweek 3 P.M. to 10 P.M. session is normally more satisfactory to governmental officials.

Assign the Jobs to Be Done

At this point there is plenty of work to do. The planning group members give themselves assignments: some to line up resource people, some to work on funding, some to find or develop handout materials, others to line up facilitators, someone to find a suitable meeting place available on the selected date, one or two (if necessary) to make initial contacts with other organizations—and at the next meeting they find out who are the workers and who are the drones.

Be Sure Duties Are Fulfilled

Now come meetings, usually two or three, when the members report progress on their assignments. Inevitably, there is some replanning. A desired resource person is not available, an expected source of funds falls through, no appropriate location is available on the date set. One member is absent and another knows that he (or she) hasn't begun to work. Should another member take that assignment? A difficult question, with the answer usually postponed until after one or more conversations with the presumed delinquent.

Settle the Matter of Mailings and Publicity

As soon as the necessary information is known come the decisions about publicity. Is it only sending announcements to a selected list of people and organizations? Or does the planning group want newspaper and radio coverage too? This is the time, weeks in advance, for the planners to arrange with those media for whatever coverage they wish. Timing mailings is important too. If the budget can stand two mailings, a good combination is a preliminary one about three weeks ahead, giving only the subject, time, place and sponsorship of the conference, and a second, more complete, ten days later. If only one mailing is feasible, a time two to three weeks in advance is usually good, particularly if it is followed by supporting radio and newspaper stories.

Make Final Arrangements

Two or three weeks before the conference is also the time to assign responsibilities for the jobs necessary to carry it out successfully. These include arranging for:
1. Food and coffee breaks (if pertinent).
2. Audio-visual equipment (if pertinent).
3. Getting reports reproduced and to participants quickly (if pertinent).
4. Getting rooms set up as the planners want them (with flip sheets on stands or hung with masking tape, markers and extra masking tape, if pertinent).
5. Registering participants as they arrive and giving them name cards (with the names printed in large, bold letters visible fifteen or twenty feet away).

6.   Acquainting participants, resource people, recorders and facilitators with their discussion group and room assignments.

7.   Distributing, at appropriate time, handouts not previously mailed, including guidelines for discussants and resource people, if pertinent, and refresher summaries for facilitators and recorders.

8.   Having people available to do such things as make changes in group assignments, run unexpected errands, get audio or visual equipment to function properly, get room temperatures adjusted and take care of whatever was forgotten. (If the conference has two or more registrars, one can double in this role after the initial wave of participants has arrived.)

Line Up Facilitators

This is the period, too, for training facilitators, when that is necessary. But we find this of such importance that we treat it separately in Chapter 14.

The number of facilitators needed depends, of course, on the number of participants the planning group expects and the size of the individual group. We find that when the participants are intensely interested in the problem and well informed, they want to talk and that a group of five, plus a facilitator and a resource person, is the largest that gives everyone a good opportunity. When the interest is less intense, or the participants less well informed, more can be included, but even then about ten is the maximum for real discussion. Another important factor is that, for the best discussion, each group should include representatives of the whole range of viewpoints.

The discussion group size often requires a choice between having too many for the best discussion or leaving out one or more viewpoints. In that case, we prefer the larger group (but not more than about eight participants, resource person and facilitator). Alas, if many more or many fewer discussants than expected actually appear at the conference, the best planning is meaningless and last-minute combining or splitting of groups may be necessary. The only way to prepare for the latter contingency is to have a few extra facilitators and resource people available if it seems a possibility.

Give Thought to Reporters

Although the facilitator records the highlights of the discussion on his flip chart, some planning groups want a more complete record. This requires the recruiting of a number of reporters equal to that of facilitators—a potential problem in two ways: 1) There is a general but erroneous assumption that anyone can record capably. Actually, good recording requires intent listening, quick understanding and the ability to separate meaningful remarks from the all too frequent chaff. Enough people with these abilities can be difficult to find. 2) Whenever a reporter yields to the frequent temptation to participate in the discussion, the record will be incomplete until he remembers his role and returns to listening long enough to become aware of where the discussion is now. If he has sufficient poise he, of course, admits his lapse as soon as he realizes it and asks the group to fill in the gap for him—but neither most reporters nor most groups relish this interruption. So training reporters can sometimes be important (see Chapter 14).

Plan a Warm-up Session

Finally, there are small, related items that can make a contribution out of all proportion to the time and trouble they require. One of these is the practice of the Arlington Committee of 100 and the Loudoun Committee of 55 of having a warm-up luncheon at which the speaker or speakers discuss the conference problems with a group of interested people who represent the range of viewpoints regarding it. Besides enabling the speakers to know what the issues are so they can limit their remarks and co-ordinate them on what is desired, this assures holders of each viewpoint an opportunity to present their views for consideration. The dual benefits are that the speakers are more likely than otherwise to talk to points of interest to the discussants and that they, having heard that this procedure has been followed, are more likely to come ready to listen with open minds.

Give Guidelines to Resource People

Another practice refers to resource people, whether they come as speakers or not. The role of the resource person in a discussion group is not well understood by many people, so we like to have an orientation session with them, or if that isn't possible, give them a brief set of guidelines on paper, Form 2 (Appendix, Chapter 13).

Explain the Facilitator to Discussants—and Seek Evaluation

We also like to give the discussants a brief note about the facilitator's role, since it is new to many of them, and to give them a chance to tell the planning committee what they think of the meeting. Samples of the note to discussants, Form 3, and those types of reaction sheets, Forms 4, 5 and 6, are in the Appendix, Chapter 13.

If the Conference Is to Be Only the Beginning . . .

Let's suppose now that the planning group decides that something more than a one- or two-day conference is needed: perhaps the conference is to be used as a jump-off for a set of continuing groups, as in our Jobs Now project (Chapter 3) or the Fairfax County goals project (Chapter 6). In that case, be sure that the facilitators and participants are intensely interested in their groups' subjects and understand that continuing action is expected. Otherwise, those who find that more is wanted from them than they intended to give will fade away—and some groups will fade with them. If you can't find or adequately train intensely interested facilitators, you may want to adopt the technique used in the Fairfax goals project: using facilitators for the early, pattern-setting group sessions and then having the groups organize themselves under the leadership of their most interested members.

The moving spirit in the planning group must be prepared to ride herd (in a nice way, as a good facilitator should) on all of the work groups as they progress toward their interlocking objectives. We realize that this may be dropping casual mountains on the heads of some planners and facilitators but there is no alternative. The chances of success of a project or an organization without a vigorous, understanding head compare unfavorably with those of the proverbial snowball in hell. (Again see Chapter 3, "A Meeting on Jobs—and Where It Led".)

Some of these groups may grow into new need-solving organizations, as did the Northern Virginia Day Care Association (Chapter 3). Some may turn to experimenting with needed new processes, as did our job coaching group (Chapter 3). Some may serve a recurring need as have our legislative conferences (Chapter 10) and job fairs (Chapter 4). Whatever turn they may take, the attitudes and techniques we have found useful, and reported in this book, can open the way for them to reach their goals successfully.

If Only a New Organization Can Cope . . .

These attitudes and techniques can also apply effectively in case the planning group decides that the situation requires a new organization. We started the Loudoun County Committee of 55 (Chapter 1), with three well-placed persons who represented the viewpoints of the county's largest industry, the League of Women Voters and people interested in youth. Using our pattern, they added three members to the planning group to bring in viewpoints the three of them did not represent. That group of six invited fifty-five influential citizens of all viewpoints to an evening meeting. The thirty who came determined, first in small groups and later as a totality, what they considered the county's most important problems. They then agreed that a new organization which could serve as a focal point for unbiased citizen exploration of each problem was needed. In two subsequent meetings, using small groups and total discussion as appropriate, they created that very successful committee which has become the sounding board for both citizens and county officials as the county moves into a highly volatile period of change, from being completely rural to absorbing the impact of people, businesses and institutions flowing out from nearby Washington, D.C.

In another jurisdiction, the story was different. Lulled by the Loudoun success and having little knowledge of the jurisdiction, we did not recognize important differences between the two counties' social structures, or that the original three citizens were not as representative as in Loudoun, or that their invitees failed to include some important points of view. The organizing process went well but citizens with unrepresented viewpoints saw the resulting organization as another pressure group and invaded its third and fourth meetings with enough verbal violence to prevent its serving its intended purpose. No further meetings were held.

"But My Conference Is Different!"

Many conferences, of course, are not as complex as the ones we have written about in this chapter. We have taken these examples because they gave us the opportunity to mention all of the aspects we believe significant. But, though those which are less complex require less effort in some ways, the degree of care and thought we have outlined are still important if the activities are to be successful.

We use a simpler format, for example, when the purpose is to enable professional people to exchange information and clarify it by discussion, or to prepare officials to take effective roles in later meetings where citizen involvement is important. Such a conference may be a one-day affair or it may consist of four to six sessions during two or two and a half days with all participants in residence at a nearby woodsy retreat.

At such a conference, the usually twenty-five to thirty-five discussants may sit in conventional meeting style along both sides of tables arranged as three sides of a rectangle. The resource people address them, singly or in panels, from a head table which makes the fourth side. After each speaker or panel the discussants raise questions which generally lead to a combination of answers by resource persons and general discussion.

In groups of this size reticent people have a relatively slim chance of entering the discussion but in the longer conferences, since all the participants are staying in the same place and eating together at small tables, much small group discussion takes place outside the conference room.

An alternative seating pattern can make discussion easier without reducing the focus on the head table. This design places the discussants in semi-facing rows, either with or without tables in front of them, as shown below. As also shown there, the head table becomes the third side of a triangle.

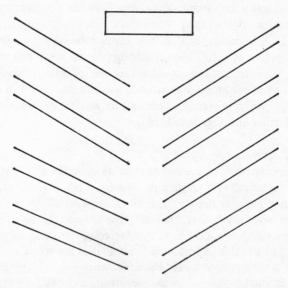

In this pattern, the discussants can easily swing from facing the head table to whatever participant is speaking. No one has to lean out over a long table, with ten or twelve people on a side, to observe a speaker. Also the pattern permits seating people more closely and in a smaller space.

In either long or short conferences, one way to give all participants an opportunity to get in their questions is to use the buzz group technique when each speaker concludes his remarks. Instead of taking questions from individuals, the chairman asks the audience members to form small groups, usually of five or six, and each group lists in priority order the questions its members think are worth raising. The chairman then takes each group's first question in turn, follows with the second questions, and so on. General discussion can develop at any time. This process has the advantage of eliminating queries which are self-serving, foolish or unimportant and, since some questions raised by one group are also raised by others, does not take as much time as it sounds. After the group questions have been answered, others can be taken from individuals and general discussion can ensue on points on which discussants are not yet satisfied.

For larger groups than thirty-five, a conference of this type usually opens with a general session to explain its purpose and pattern. Then topic groups of twenty-five to thirty-five discussants, each with resource people versed in its topic, go to separate rooms for the scheduled number of sessions. When appropriate, we split each topic group into subgroups for buzz sessions. The closing general session usually follows one of the same patterns as those described elsewhere in this chapter for conferences using small discussion groups.

For even this simple format, the same care is necessary as in conferences using small groups and facilitators. Our planning committee is just as representative and goes through the same steps explained earlier in this chapter (except for those related to using facilitators and assuring that discussion groups have a representative variety of viewpoints). The planners take particular care in selecting discussion topics and resource people because the conference depends on them more completely than when small groups permit the discussants to make major contributions and even, when they wish, to modify a topic or the approach to it. Similarly, the same kind of attention to detail is needed in taking the preparatory steps for the conference and making the plan work (Chapter 15), although when the group is small some of those activities are easier to perform.

Conferences of this type which involve a large number of citizens as well as professionals rarely last more than one day. The citizen discussants know a lot about the problem (though often they could well know more). Taking two or two and a half days from their own concerns and paying their expenses is not very appealing.

Some Guidelines for Conferences to Create Community Change

If the sponsors' purpose is to create change in the community, here is a summary of the important considerations for the planning phase:

1. Set clear goals and check against them frequently.
2. Involve people with all the viewpoints needed to reach the goals, including:

   —Participants, who can push action to reduce the barriers.

   —Opponents, who must be converted.

   —Resource people, who can supply the needed information and skills.

   —Facilitators, who can conduct discussions which help people thinking together.

   —People who can provide needed prestige.

   —People who can provide sympathy and support.

3. Provide enough specific information to avoid stumbling over facts.
4. Allow enough discussion time to permit the study groups to dig into their problems thoroughly.

14

TRAINING THE PEOPLE WHO MAKE THE CONFERENCE GO

Training Facilitators

We usually train facilitators in groups of five or six, providing a trainer for each group. This gives us enough people for a good discussion and with this number we can complete the training in three two-and-a-half-hour sessions. We favor two-and-a-half-hour sessions because we can keep groups together that long without a break and most people can find that much time in a morning, afternoon or evening.

Orientation

When we are training groups simultaneously, the opening session begins with everyone together for a brief explanation of how facilitators differ from usual discussion leaders and why we use them. We also explain that, since facilitating is a skill, the course contains two aspects: demonstration and skill practice. In the first session there is something of a balance between them—(the later ones are almost all practice). We then distribute copies of the following form "How Good a Discussant Are You?" and ask the trainees to look first at items 24 through 34, which obviously are activities that defeat accomplishment in any discussion but unfortunately occur with great frequency in most.

George Mason College Community Education Program

Subject Discussed: _____ 19__

HOW GOOD A DISCUSSANT ARE YOU?
HOW OFTEN DO YOU—

To Facilitate Progress of the Discussion:
    1. Question what a statement means
    2. Ask about an overlooked viewpoint
    3. Question the course of the discussion
    4. Summarize
    5. Test for consensus

To Make Discussion More Penetrating:
    6. Ask a pertinent question
    7. Initiate thinking
    8. Use logic in attempting to find a solution
    9. Try to separate facts from opinions and assumptions
    10. Try to integrate separate ideas

To Improve Both Discussion and Group Solidarity:
    11. Listen
    12. Draw others into the discussion
    13. Build on others' contributions
    14. Bring discussion out of chaos
    15. Support others, give others recognition
    16. Change position when clarification is made
    17. Under tension make conflict reducing remarks
    18. State your thoughts or opinion for clarification
    19. Give needed information
    20. Seek clues to acceptable solutions

To Improve Group Solidarity:
    21. Show approval by gestures, posture, or facial expression
    22. Show politeness or friendliness
    23. State your feeling about others usefully

To Satisfy Your Personal Needs:
    24. State your feelings destructively
    25. Ask non-pertinent questions
    26. Attempt to sell your viewpoints, regardless
    27. Interrupt unnecessarily
    28. Talk excessively, reminisce, tell stories, talk with neighbors
    29. Try to impress others
    30. Repeat yourself or others
    31. Backtrack when opposed
    32. Become antagonistic
    33. Read
    34. Be apathetic, preoccupied, withdrawn, hurt
    35. Show boredom or tension by doodling, nail-biting, shifting in chair, etc.

We next point out that items 1 through 6 and item 11 are the facilitator's tools and that he tries to restrict himself to those activities. Then we mention that these activities should also be performed by discussants, along with all the others through item 23, and that all of them are necessary for a good discussion to reach its goal. We emphasize the special importance of item 11, listening, explaining that intent listening is the key to everything the facilitator and the useful discussants say and do, and that real listening stops the instant a person lets his own concerns interfere. We talk very briefly at this point because we have found that explanations have much more meaning for the trainees after we have demonstrated facilitating than before.

We then divide the trainees into groups, and explain first that we will facilitate a demonstration discussion by members of one group while all the others observe. Then each group will begin a discussion, each member taking a turn at practicing facilitating for his group for fifteen or twenty minutes. Next, we give the members of each group a few minutes to get acquainted with each other.

After this getting acquainted, we ask for the attention of all the groups and, before indicating which group will be used for the demonstration, explain that all non-discussants will be observers, who should concentrate primarily on our performance as facilitator and score our activities on the form. They do this, we explain, by listening to us, watching us and making a mark (') on the appropriate line of the form for each question we ask, statement we make or action they see us take. We ask them also to listen for, and note, the moments when a group member performs either item 12, "Draws others into the discussion," or 13, "Builds on another's contributions."
These activities have several purposes:

1. To stimulate the trainees' awareness of the intricacy of a good discussion and the large number of activities needed to make it good.
2. To give identity to each of the items on the form so the trainees can begin to use them as tools in analyzing a discussion.
3. To focus attention on two activities, items 12 and 13, which are keys both to progress in a discussion and to building solidarity in a group—and which in most groups occur all too infrequently.
4. To involve the trainees in concentrating on the conduct of a discussion instead of on its content.

5. To show them how to analyze a facilitator's activities.
6. To demonstrate that the facilitator not only expects and accepts criticism, but invites it.

Demonstration

We now select one of the groups for the initial discussion, explain that the training is to be conducted by problem solving and ask everyone in that group to suggest problems, or situations they would like to change, in which they think all the trainees have an interest. Across the top of the flip chart we write, "Suggested Problems." Then we usually ask, "Who wants to give us the first one?" or some similar open invitation. If none comes immediately we simply wait, perhaps smiling, demonstrating that silence doesn't bother us.

When the first suggestion comes, we write or print it with a magic marker on the flip sheet as number one, entering it verbatim if it has been stated in a few words. If the statement was not succinct, we ask the submitting member to rephrase it concisely. If that proves impossible, we ask the other members to try. If one does, we write it and ask the originator, "Does this say what you mean?" If no trainee can put it briefly, we try it ourselves and then change it until the members are satisfied. Usually phrases of three to six words can state the idea clearly enough to be understood later. In each case we change the wording on the flip sheet until the group is satisfied. Our record should be legible, of course, and the letters large enough for all to see.

If the discussion on the suggested problem has not brought out its significance, we ask the group, "What is this about?" or "Can you explain this a bit more?" When we feel that the group understands that suggestion, we invite a second one, which we handle the same way, then a third, a fourth and others until the list includes some that seem to be of general interest and the pace of incoming suggestions slackens, usually after about five or six.

At this point, we ask the members who have observed the listing of suggestions for their comments on our activities. Usually this starts with two or three of them mentioning our having taken all or almost all of the actions given as items 1 through 6, sometimes giving a count of instances of each. Occasionally, instead, the first comment comes from a member who delightedly reports a negative act, perhaps interrupting unnecessarily. We grin and show the acceptability of criticism by saying something like, "I'm glad you noticed that. I make plenty of mistakes. Who was it that I cut off and what did we miss?" If there are no such negative comments, we invite them.

The next step is selecting the first discussion subject from the suggested list. We explain that to find out which subject has the most general interest, we will point to each of the suggestions, in turn, and ask all the trainees to raise their hands at each proposal which interests them. As we do this, we record the total number of hands for each. This process eliminates subjects of narrow interest and usually identifies the one most members prefer. If two or three are in the running, a brief discussion can normally put them in priority order. In the unusual event that the selection is difficult, we have the group specify criteria to use in testing them. The few times we have had to do this the criteria have been: (1) importance to the community, (2) urgency and (3) the amount of solid information the members of the group have. However, the selection of both criteria and subject is the group's responsibility, not the facilitator's.

If there will be more than one group, an alternative is available. The participants can pick more than one subject and rearrange the groups so each one has his choice. However, we remind them that skill practice, not problem solving, is the purpose of the course and that, for lack of time, some of the problems tackled will not be carried through completely.

With the subject chosen, we ask for questions which the trainees have so far about the facilitator role. When those questions have been discussed, the trainees reassemble in groups, either those previously established or new ones arranged so they can focus on different subjects.

Beginning Practice

Each group's trainer tells the members that, in analyzing the selected problem, each member will take a fifteen- to twenty-minute turn as facilitator, and asks for a volunteer to start. If, after several seconds (which may seem very long to a person unused to silence in a group), no one volunteers, the group trainer reminds the members that that is why they are here and, as encouragement, that the first round practices will be short. Then, if necessary, he waits again. If the group tries to pressure one member, he does not intervene, but waits for that person to accept the challenge or someone else to volunteer.

When a member has accepted or volunteered, the trainer explains that the first focus of the group will be to bring out and list the symptoms of the situation the members would like to change, and that as trainer he has a dual role: to serve as the group's first observer and to intervene in the discussion if he thinks it useful. As he turns the session over to the facilitator, he gives one important guideline: during the early discussion stages, of which this is the first, no proposed solutions of the problem are admissible. Solutions may not be considered until the situation has been thoroughly explored, so the facilitator should ask the suggester to bring up his idea again when that point is reached.

The facilitator begins by inviting the other members to suggest symptoms. As each one is mentioned he follows the pattern set by the trainer in the demonstration session (when the subject was selected). If the symptom is worded briefly he puts it on the flip chart verbatim. If it is longer he obtains or makes a concise version and, as he finishes writing it, asks, "Does anyone disagree?" If anyone does, discussion ensues and he changes the wording until it satisfies the group or, much less frequently, the group rules it out.

This use of the flip chart is basic to the whole facilitation process. It keeps the discussion in a kind of show window, assuring each member full opportunity to work out, with the group, changes he believes desirable. Thus it is a continuing demonstration of fairness. It also becomes a visible record of points on which the group has agreed. That visible record helps keep the later discussion on track, since at any point any member can say, "But we covered that back under point three [or whatever it is]," "How does that relate to what we decided on point six?" or, "Looking at what we have on the chart, I wonder if this is the direction we want to go." If the facilitator thinks such a question is pertinent and no one else raises it, he does.

When a group completes the listing of symptoms or at the end of fifteen minutes, whichever comes first, the trainer takes over the discussion to lead an evaluation of the facilitator's activity. As observer he has made notes of opportunities he thinks the facilitator missed, what he sees as errors the facilitator made, activities in the group which need correcting or, alternatively, were worth underlining as examples of good performance. However, he does not mention any of these, because his purpose is to have the group evaluate first. He can help them fill in any gaps later.

He begins the evaluation by asking the facilitator, "How did you feel?" The facilitator usually admits some discomfort and expresses doubts about one or two of his decisions. Other members comment and the evaluation is under way. If, instead, his remarks do not generate a response, the trainer asks the others, "Well, how *did* he do?" If this brings only favorable, supportive comments, he then asks one of several questions, whichever seems pertinent. "Were there any moments when any of you wanted to say something but couldn't break in?" "Did the facilitator intervene too much?" "Did the facilitator miss any chances to . . . ?" A five- to ten-minute discussion ensues, bringing out matters the trainees need to know as well as alerting them to ways in which the facilitator could have helped the group more. The trainer then asks for instances when a member drew another member into the discussion or built on another's contribution. If any such actions are reported, the group briefly considers what impact they had, either on progress in problem solving or on the feeling of members.

After that evaluation, the second facilitator takes charge and the first one serves as observer, filling the same role that the trainer did during the previous period.

When the group finishes the list of symptoms (point la on Form 1, "A Pattern for Problem Solving," Appendix, Chapter 13), the discussion moves on to reaching agreement on the essential problem indicated by the symptoms (point 1b on Form 1). The prohibition against discussing solutions continues until the group reaches Recommendations, point 4. Normally trainees become used to it quickly and it presents no difficulty.

These two intermingled processes, changing facilitators and observers frequently while working through the steps of the problem-solving pattern, continue until each trainee has had a chance to facilitate and have his facilitating evaluated. Usually the trainee's period as observer is almost as important as his facilitator practice. During it he gets his first conscious look at a discussion in process, becomes aware of a number of factors for the first time and thereafter begins to think of the process in a much more knowledgeable fashion.

Usually, three or four trainees complete their first practice in the first two-and-a-half-hour session. The trainer's chief concern in that session is neither how many do so nor how far along the group moves in the problem-solving process. His real interest is in having penetrating discussion develop among the trainees about matters that concern them regarding facilitating.

At the end of the first session, the trainer gives each trainee copies of Form 1, "A Pattern for Problem Solving," Form 7, "Some Clues

to Facilitating," Form 8, "Cutting in on a Long-Winded Speaker,"
and Form 9, "Suggested Questions for Observers."*

The problem-solving pattern of Form 1 helps focus discussion in
an orderly fashion and is an important tool for facilitators to have.
We use it in all our facilitator training sessions unless the planning
group has worked out its own pattern for the conference discussion
groups. For example, see the guidelines which the planners of the
Fairfax County program to develop goals for the county gave their
work groups for their first and second meetings (Chapter 6).

Later Practice

The second session opens with all members discussing with the
trainer their questions about the first session's practice and the forms
he has given them. Then they resume the combination skill practice-
problem-solving activity started in the first meeting. When each member of a group has finished his fifteen- to twenty-minute first practice
and had the group evaluate it, a second round starts.

This time the practice periods are longer, usually twenty-five to
thirty minutes, and the first observers use question 5 of Form 9, with
its subheadings, as their guide. This means that, instead of count-
ing instances when the facilitator takes those actions, the observer
focuses on what happens when the facilitator intervenes—or when he
thinks the facilitator should have taken action but didn't. He makes
fragmentary notes for the evaluation. Later observers use other
questions from Form 9, whichever each finds appropriate. The
evaluation follows the same pattern as before but may be a bit longer,
ten to fifteen minutes, and normally is more penetrating.

The impact of the individual practice periods is cumulative.
Every member learns from the experience of each facilitator. On
the first round, most trainees are insecure and uncomfortable, those
with much experience as discussion leaders often more so than others
because they are abandoning old habits for imperfectly known
and, to them, untried techniques. Other experienced leaders sometimes start by using their old habits, directing the group closely or
intervening after each remark. This causes the trainer to intervene
by asking the group, "What's happening here?" and so leads to an
interim evaluation, after which practice is resumed. By the time a
trainee takes his second turn, he has usually planned ahead to offset
his first round weaknesses and the process is no longer strange, so

* For these forms, see Appendix, Chapters 13, 14.

he is comfortable with it (or even beginning to enjoy it), though not as secure as he will become as he facilitates actual discussions.

A third round of practice can do much toward helping a trainee achieve security but we are not able to arrange it as often as we would like. Our trainees are almost always people active in communities or organizations and have to be persuaded to commit time for three training sessions in something they think they already know ("I know how to run a meeting; I've run dozens [or hundreds] of them"), let alone four. By the time they become involved and would like a third round, we usually find it impossible to schedule extra sessions which enough of them can attend before the date of the conference in which they are to serve.

When enough trainees want a third round, a consolidation of groups is usually necessary, forcing some members to shift to a problem new to them, or making all continuing members choose a new problem. At this stage some trainees find it frustrating to give up the old one. We remind them again that the problems are only vehicles for practice and encourage those who wish to finish a particular problem to get together at a different time to do so. The last training session, whether it is the second, third or fourth, ends with a question period to learn and throw new light on trainee concerns about facilitating which have not come out earlier.

Writing on the Flip Chart

Knowing what to write on the flip chart and when to write it are important enough, we feel, for us to treat them separately from the rest of our facilitator training. They are relatively easy when the group is making a list (whether of possible problems or symptoms to be explored, barriers in the way of working toward a goal, criteria to help in making a decision or some similar situation). At this stage the discussion is usually pertinent and the suggestions specific. When the interaction is of this type, an alert facilitator has little difficulty in catching the essence of suggestions in three- to six-word phrases and then making the changes the discussants wish. If he does have trouble, the others are focusing closely enough on the topic to help him.

Unfortunately, in other stages, the going is not that simple. Groups may take a little time to settle down, the discussion may drift, members may indulge in some of those anti-productive activities mentioned earlier. Even when the members are working together well, some of them will produce non-pertinent thoughts and ideas that seem to be completely at cross-purposes with what the facilitator thinks the group is trying to accomplish at the time.

Our first suggestion here is one we make repeatedly: listen intently for the essential point of what the speaker is saying (or trying to say). If he's brief but you feel sure that his point does not contribute, thank him and let it drop unless another member picks it up. If it seems worth capturing, when you think you have caught it, ask him, "Joe, do you mean . . . ?", "Let me see if I understand. Is your point . . . ?" or "I think I'm with you but I'm not sure. Are you telling us . . . ?" If you aren't sure, or you begin to wonder if he really has a point to make, toss it to the group: "What does someone else think of what Joe's telling us?" Whichever way, he gets some degree of recognition and you have given the group a chance to decide if the point is worth having. This sort of direction could have been very useful in making the sophomore youth conference at Fairfax City High School more productive (see Chapter 2, "Approaches to Problems of Youth").

If the discussion begins to be prolonged, put something, almost anything pertinent, on the flip sheet and invite the others to change it. This gives the discussion a focal point and the discussants a feeling of both movement and participation. If, on the other hand, you write nothing, they are apt to feel that they are making no progress and that you are blocking them—which, in fact, you may be doing.

Listening intently, of course, is not an easy trick. As we said earlier, listening stops the instant the listener begins to relate something he hears to his own experience or thought, or starts to prepare a comment in his mind. Everyone has both these habits and we know only one answer: self-training. Facilitating can be a great help with that since intent listening is essential to a good job and being caught woolgathering in public is embarrassing.

But listening well (and it's very tough to do it continuously) is only the beginning. The facilitator must simultaneously judge the worth of what he hears. That skill, too, requires practice unless he has already learned it and uses it frequently. Again, facilitating helps, particularly when the group gives an honest evaluation at the end of the meeting.

A key aspect of judging is how well what the member says fits into what the group is trying to do. Is it a contribution useful as it stands or does it need reshaping to help the discussion along? Happily, the facilitator can get help. He can put the thought on the chart and ask the group, "Would this help us more if we put it differently?"

So far, we have assumed that the discussion is proceeding at an easy pace. But there are times when it gets too rapid for the facilitator to keep up. Should he intervene, thus slowing it down and perhaps wrecking it? What are his options? (1) He can take that chance. (2) He can gamble that he can pick out the highlights (but when he starts writing he stops listening). (3) He can put down fragments as reminders and when the tempo slackens say, "That was a live bit, I could only get pieces of it. Let's go back and see if we can put together what we want in the record."

Then there are times when the tempo is easy enough to follow but the discussion is so intense that the members have forgotten there is a flip chart (or a facilitator). He writes and no one reads, but what is going on seems worthwhile and he doesn't want to take a chance of spoiling it. The answer here is easier. He can keep on recording until the intense period is over or until he thinks an interruption will do no harm (or might even be useful). Then he can ask the group to review what he has written and correct what he got wrong.

Breaking the Rules

On rare occasions, we break our own rules. For example, let's take our basic rule that we accept no suggested solutions until the problem and goal have been agreed upon and the barriers explored. Sometimes, out of the blue, comes a thought too good to be lost or a possibly useful contribution from a member we want to encourage. If we have established that rule with the group, instead of asking him to hold it until we reach the right point, we may flip the top sheet over and put his idea on a blank one for future reference. Sometimes that opens a Pandora's box and we find ourselves putting down a flow of suggestions for future reference to prevent other members feeling slighted. Or we may have a seesaw situation, swinging back and forth between present and future pages, for a time. To keep those situations to a minimum we follow our rule—except when we decide that breaking it is worth the gamble. But even then we never let the group get into a continuing discussion of a suggested solution before the problem, goal and barriers have been thoroughly explored.

A second example of rule breaking relates to our guideline that in problem solving we list symptoms and agree on the essential problem before we go on to the goal. When the group finds agreement on the essential problem difficult to reach, it is sometimes useful to put it aside and work on the goal instead.

If the members can agree on the goal they can either bypass getting agreement on the problem or go back to it if it later becomes necessary as a takeoff point in their thinking.

Of a different nature is our implication that what the facilitator writes on the flip chart is always in response to a statement from another member. While this is generally true, a facilitator can sometimes reinforce one of his questions by writing it. If a group is stuck on dead center or we are trying to bring in a thought to give shape to a random discussion, this emphasis, because it is rare, can sometimes get more attention than an unreinforced question. Other times when it can be useful are when the facilitator is trying to bring in a viewpoint that the group has ignored persistently, or to introduce a possible way out when deadlocked factions are determined to ignore what anyone else says.

Training Resource People and Reporters

With resource people, alas, the need for training is great. People who know much about a subject often can't stop talking when they have answered a question or made a pertinent suggestion. One thing suggests another that their listeners "ought to know." If training to help resource people avoid this well-intentioned excess is not feasible (or successful) the best alternative is an agreement between the facilitator and resource person on the role each is to take, including the facilitator's responsibility to interrupt when he believes it useful ("Does that cover the essentials?") and the resource person's willingness to give way.

The best technique for training resource people and reporters, when it is feasible, is to involve them in the second or third facilitator training session. This lengthens and complicates the session a bit but it gives all of the facilitating team members an opportunity to practice their roles together. However, this happy combination is seldom possible. Resource people are rarely available or able to give the additional time, and, since it is generally assumed that anyone can be a competent reporter without training, sponsors who want reporters usually do not select them enough in advance.

When we *are* able to get them for a facilitator training session, we give them our "Guidelines for Resource People," Form 2, and "Hints for Reporters," Form 10 (see Appendices, Chapters 13 and 14) to follow during the session. When the group evaluates facilitator trainees it also evaluates the resource persons' activities and twice —about halfway through and at the end—we have the reporters give us the highlights they have recorded so the group can evaluate their performance, too.

An alternative is to hold a session shortly before the conference for just the resource people and reporters. In this we give them the "Guidelines," Form 2, and "Hints," Form 10, then ask the resource people what difficulties they anticipate in following the guidelines. If they claim to expect none we follow up with questions along the line of, "How can you be sure to keep your comments brief enough so they use only a minute portion of the group's time?" We can't guarantee that the answers will control egocentric authorities but the discussion does get into their consciousness to some degree that brevity is the virtue of intervention.

If the reporters also anticipate no problems we wait until they have compared their highlights after the end of the discussion—then we ask them what difficulties they had and how they solved them. Finally, when we are unable to get these people for a training session, we simply give them the appropriate guidelines with a few words of encouragement and hope for the best.

What Usually Happens with Reporters

Actually, we normally obtain and train reporters in advance only when the sponsors plan to put out a report on the conference and can provide sufficient staff to do so, or for some other reason need firm data.

Most groups include at least one person who likes to take notes, usually does it fairly well and rarely looks at them afterwards. So, unless the sponsors have a special reason for using trained reporters, we simply tell the facilitators to ask for volunteer recorders and normally have little difficulty in obtaining reasonably adequate notes from them. We call them recorders instead of reporters because the sponsors use their raw notes rather than asking them to reorganize them into prepared reports. In case, however, you need reporters, Form 10 includes a suggested worksheet.

Training Discussants

Usually, we have no opportunity to train discussants in a one-day or even two-day conference. If the sponsors are naïve, normally they have a list of subjects on which they want name speakers. If they are more knowing they want firm information from knowledgeable people. In either case, as we have said before, we almost always find ourselves fighting to keep the speaking and question-answering periods short enough to give discussion groups a reason-able opportunity to explore their problems. That means we find it very difficult to get fifteen minutes for two demonstrations in which to show the difference between a discussion which is a typical every-man-for-himself free-for-all and an astute facilitator-led one.

When we can get time, we ask the group which is planning the conference to pick a minute portion of the problem and have five or six members ready to give two short skits which will demonstrate the different methods. They don't write anything, so their planning is brief. They decide what issue they will discuss, then pick a chairman for the skits, determine what type of participant each member will be and what viewpoint he will present. In the first, five-minute skit, they do a typically combative meeting, with perhaps a little extra voice-raising. In the second, ten-minute one, they propose and the facilitator rapidly lists the symptoms of the situation they are propos-ing to change, then determine the heart of the problem. They present the two spontaneous skits just before the participants go to their discussion groups. The conference chairman then sends people off to their groups, expressing the hope that they'll succeed in using the second pattern—which they almost always do.

Whether or not we are able to use the skits, when the participants reach their groups, each facilitator gives them a brief statement about his job, such as the one we used in the conference which explored the proposed changes in the Virginia Constitution, and asks for ques-tions about it. (See Form 3, Appendix, Chapter 13.) We make this handout short and quickly readable so it will not tempt the members to shift their attention away from the discussion. When a conference starts in the evening and goes into the next day, at the close of the evening session each member receives a copy of Form 11, "Sug-gestions for Discussants." This timing follows a precept of the Agri-cultural Extension Service, based on its long experience, that handouts at the beginning or during a session tend to be distracting.

Role Playing

Role playing is an excellent technique to use in analyzing situa-tions, particularly when they have a high emotional content, because it can produce insights which make the analysis far more penetrating than the usual direct discussion. We reported using it for problem analysis in planning a conference, Chapter 13, and in supervisory training, Chapter 9, "For Better Local Government." It is also superb in helping a person begin to understand the feelings of another and we told how we used it that way in our pages on the Vienna Teen Center and on job coaching.

We include material on it in Chapter 16, "Help for Continuing Groups," rather than this chapter, for these reasons:

1. It is rarely usable in the types of conferences we have discussed (as distinct from training), but can be highly valuable in any group which meets a number of times.

2. It must be directed with great skill, which we do not have time to develop in our trainees during the facilitator training for those conferences.

Principal Tools of Facilitating—A Summary

Tools	and their	*Uses*
1. Five- or six-person groups		—give everyone a chance. —facilitate interaction. —emphasize thinking.
2. Listening intently		—gives the facilitator clues to what actions to take.
3. The penetrating question addressed to all		—stimulates thinking. —invites participation.
4. The personally addressed question (used infrequently)		—breaks the discussion pattern. —puts the facilitator in control.
5. The visible record		—focuses attention. —increases concentration. —facilitates orderly analysis. —discourages backtracking and wandering.

6. Role playing		—helps
		  understanding.
		  planning.
		  testing.
		—is a safety valve.
		—throws light on
		  emotional problems.
		  proposed courses of action.

7. Summarizing   —helps the group understand where it is.
                                    —helps get the discussion off dead center.
                                    —puts the facilitator in control.

8. Testing for consensus   —helps the facilitator know
                                     what views still need to be heard.
                                     when the group is ready to move on.

9. Evaluation   —provides opportunities for members to
                                     point out possible improvements.
                                     plan how to accomplish them.

Extra Dividends—from Two Concurrent Training Groups

Although the focus of training sessions is training, they sometimes produce unexpected and valuable thoughts. During the period when we were training job coaches (Chapter 3), we also gave facilitator training to three women from Leagues of Women Voters and two nuns who were active in social group work. The latter five picked parent–teen-ager relations as their problem to work on during training and we were delighted with the degree to which the exploratory sessions of the two groups produced insight-giving ideas that sometimes complemented and sometimes almost duplicated each other. These came out in such simple, and we think easily understandable, form that we feel compelled to pass them on even though many of them will not be new to thoughtful people.

1. Some of the thoughts have general application, as these on obstacles to listening which prevent the listener getting the real message:
   a. Substituting one's own experience for what the other person says.
   b. Pretending to listen.
   c. Letting the other's words get in the way of the significance of what he is saying.
   d. Being unable to suppress a tendency to react verbally.

      e. Being unable to suppress a tendency to give advice.

      f. Mentally preparing a counter charge.

2. Hopefully, when people listen well, they will be able to understand and feel with the person speaking.

      a. Previous similar experience is valuable, but not the only way.

      b. Also helpful are:

          —Avoiding preconceptions so you can listen and watch:

             —For significant nuances which may be clues.

             —For common ground.

          —Being eager.

          —Giving empathy.

          —Using your intuition.

3. Those discussions on listening led into how to build rapport when one person seems not to want to communicate. From one group came these ideas:

      a. Recognize that the person is not ready to communicate.

      b. Watch for clues which can indicate ways to help him:

          —Reduce his insecurity.

          —Increase his readiness to communicate.

          —Build his ability to take responsibility.

      c. Capture opportunities to help by:

          —Expressing *real* interest.

          —Being at ease.

          —Listening.

4. The other group's thoughts were in the same spirit, and were somewhat more tangible:

      a. Work on a project together.

      b. Give minimum supervision.

      c. When listening, be open to the present moment.

      d. Be sensitive to timing.

      e. If these don't work, remove yourself from the situation, at least temporarily.

5. Finally, came this thinking, under the heading of boundaries of communication between parents and teen-agers, most of which we found equally applicable when we substituted coach for parent and worker for teen-ager:

      a. Parental (coach's) interest, if too solicitous, turns off the teen-ager (worker).

      b. Resources available to help parents (coaches):

          —Parent (coach) education.

—Learning that there is an informal social structure in every group which can have positive value, instead of negative, if the parent (coach) is able to keep in touch with it and work with its leaders.

—Communication among parents whose children are friends.

15

MAKING THE PLAN WORK

Before the Conference

How Many People Will Come?

The invitations to a conference may bring a flood of registrations. Even so, some of the discussants the planners most want may not reply. At the other extreme, a few replies may come in promptly, followed by a period when there are virtually none—and those that have come are from people who have previously said they will attend.

In any case, a follow-up can ease the planners' tensions and get more of the discussants they want—or adequate replacements for some who really can't come. We find that the best follow-up occurs when each planner phones the people he or she put on the invitation list. If some of the planners haven't the time to call all of their nominees, we ask each one to call the most important and someone else to call the others. Phoning is much more useful than a follow-up letter. At times we have used letters, but phone calls, being more flexible and permitting discussion, produce better and faster replies.

The frequency with which invitations actually or presumably have not been received is often surprising. Surprising, too, are the number which remain unopened or have been put aside for a last-minute decision. Then there are those that require approval by an organization's membership or executive board, which may not meet again

until after the conference. The personal call permits further
follow-up to cope with these situations.

What Details Must We Take Care Of?

While some planners are working on the number and composition
of the discussion groups, others must be making the down-to-earth
arrangements for the conference sessions, including such essential
matters as these:

1. *Audio-visual aids*
    —Which ones do we need for which sessions?
    —Where will they come from?
    —Who brings them to the conference rooms?
    —Who sets them up and assures that they are working
      properly?
    —Who needs to be on hand during the sessions to assure
      their continued working?
    —Who will be responsible for disconnecting them and re-
      turning them to their sources?

2. *Handouts*
    —What ones do we want:
      —For their content?
      —For information about the conference, its activities
        and participants?
      —For guidance in discussions?
    —Who will draft which ones?
    —Who will review which ones?
    —How do we reproduce them?
    —What's our deadline for obtaining them?
    —When and how shall we distribute them?

In answer to this, as mentioned earlier, our experience supports
the long-standing U. S. Department of Agriculture Extension Service finding that those given out at the beginning of a session often
distract the attention of some of the participants. But there are some
things which people should have at the beginning and advance mailing is expensive—and what percentage of the registrants will read
material sent them in advance? We usually compromise. We mail in
advance—as soon as we receive a registration—the papers necessary
to knowledgeable participation in the conference. Hopefully we mention in the transmittal the parts that are most important. We often
add a map showing the conference location and layout.

When the discussants check in for the opening session and receive or make their name tags, we give them the revised agenda and a paper showing the planned numbers and locations of the discussion groups with their assigned functionaries and discussants. Both these papers are usually hot off the reproducing machine, with next-to-last-minute changes. The last-minute ones have to be announced at the end of the opening session.

Often we have handouts for small discussion groups, containing facts or reports of studies. Some are to stimulate discussion, others to provide specific information. They carry titles such as these:

—"Excerpts from the Governor's Council of the Environment report: *The State of Virginia's Environment*"
—"Comparative Fiscal Facts—Virginia and Adjoining States"
—"Summary of Population Projects"

If we have not mailed these papers in advance, we hand out those for morning discussions at the end of the opening general session and those for afternoon sessions just before lunch, thus giving the discussants a little time for that first quick glance which satisfies curiosity and, for those who prefer it, enough to dig deeper over coffee or lunch instead of friendly conversation.

The simpler, easier technique, of course, is to put all reading material and handouts in a folder or envelope and distribute them as the discussants check in. If the sponsors want it that way we do it, but our experience is that the gradual distribution gets better results. Though the one-time handout is neater and looks more professional, we watch people noisily thumb through their piles of paper to find the right one at a particular moment, not find it, quietly (but not quietly enough) get help from a neighbor, finally locate it and rustle it to the top of the pile—then determine its content while ignoring what the speaker or other participants say, or perhaps find that the others have gone on to the next sheet.

3. *Signs*

Should we put up signs showing participants where to go for the sessions (instead of or in addition to a map or layout sent in advance)? If so, what sizes should they be, where do they go, who makes them, who puts them up?

4. *Transportation*

Are there people for whom we must provide transportation? Speakers to and from an airport? Participants without cars? If so, who will be responsible for which?

5. *What About Meals and Coffee Breaks?*

As the follow-up calls to invitees near completion, the plan-

ners reach the deadline for deciding the number of people
to be fed and for whom to make mid-session Cokes and coffee
available. These are always difficult guesses. Usually we can
arrange to pay for a minimum number of whom we feel reasonably sure, with contingent responsibility for up to 10 per
cent more. In this connection, we have learned that if the
number of participants runs near or over 100, a meal served
by enough waiters or waitresses is faster and more relaxing
than buffet style—assuming that doesn't put the price higher
than we think the participants will be willing to pay.

The arrangements for coffee and Coke work best for us
when they are available throughout a morning session and
during the middle of an afternoon one. This requires that
someone, usually the head registrar, keep an eye on the supply during the morning to see that neither coffee nor cups
run out. And since charging for individual cups is both difficult and resented, we include the estimated cost in the lunch
or dinner price.

How Many Discussion Groups?—And Who Comprise Them?

Early in the planning stage we had to estimate the number of discussion groups that seemed likely, so we could know the approxi-
mate number of facilitators and resource people to provide. Now
we have to settle on an actual number and assign the subjects, facilitators and resource people to the rooms to be used. This is another
gamble. We must estimate, from the replies we have received, how
many participants will want to discuss each subject and arrange the
groups accordingly.

We try to put in each group a range of participants who represent
all important viewpoints on the subject. This can be difficult when
most of those who express interest in a subject tend to have similar
views. Unless the two or three planners who help us set up the groups
recognize the names of persons with different thinking, we ask the
planners to go back to the telephone and draw in the additional people needed for multi-sided explorations.

In planning the discussion groups we use a system devised by
the administrative assistant of the George Mason University Community Education Program. It requires a bit of clerical time but saves
much confusion and backtracking. We type address labels in dupli-
cate, or in triplicate if we expect to mail reading materials to those
accepting. When invitations go out we use the duplicates to make

a five-by-eight registration card for each invitee, and file the triplicates until we need them.

When we receive a registration, on that person's five-by-eight card we note payment of fee, any change in address or title, plus discussion group choices. *In addition,* we make a yellow construction paper chit or card showing the person's name, organization (or other pertinent identification) and first choice of discussion subject, a green one for his second choice and a red one for his third. When the time comes to arrange the groups, we start by sorting the yellow pile to find the way people's first choices are distributed. We then re-sort the yellow cards into tentative groups, using our basic criteria of group size and distribution of viewpoints, to give as many people as possible their first choice.

When we need to use other choices to help balance groups, to fill in we run quickly through the green pile to find second choices we can use and, if necessary, through the red third choices (both sorted alphabetically). It is when even these don't appear to provide balance that we ask the sponsors to find additional people. If we use a person's second or third choice, we pull his yellow (first choice) card from the group in which the original sorting had put him and place his green or red one in the appropriate group, so only one colored card represents each person when we prepare the typed lists of discussion group members.

When we use the red third choices we call the people involved to explain what has happened and ask their permission. We find that people usually respond quite honestly—asking us not to put them there if they have an intense interest in their first or second choices, assenting if the third choice was not just to fill a blank but has real meaning for them. When we need to use a person's second choice we try to call him but usually we don't have time to follow up the call as persistently as with third choices because there may be quite a few of the second ones and the assignment process tends to be a last-minute thing. There have been occasions when we've wished we had persisted in reaching such people—though, fortunately, not many.

In spite of these efforts we don't always succeed in keeping groups either as well balanced as we'd like or at our ideal size of five to seven discussants, plus the facilitator and resource person. Last-minute changes by discussants can distort the most carefully made plans. To restore balance we can only make quick fill-ins or rely on our facilitators and resource people to initiate questions which can keep the discussion penetrating and unbiased.

To help the facilitators prepare for this possibility and to give them background to help their thinking in raising questions, we normally have a warm-up session with them on the purposes of the conference. We also give them a memo on the focus of the discussion and guidance in the mechanics of their roles (see Appendix, Chapter 15).

Attendance much larger or smaller than our estimates can lead us to combine groups of fewer than four discussants or split those which have more than eight, if most discussants know their subject well, or ten if they do not. To provide for the latter situation we try always to have 10 to 15 per cent more facilitators available than needed for the number of discussion groups planned, and almost always use some of them either for this reason or to replace someone not able to appear. We ask our best facilitators to serve in this capacity—people who can grasp quickly what is going on in a discussion if they are at all familiar with the content, and who do not hesitate to ask questions which will put them on the beam if they are not.

Assuring the availability of resource people is a tougher problem. Unlike the facilitators, they need to know their subjects thoroughly, so usually we cannot shift them from one subject to another to meet last-minute needs. As we mentioned earlier, to assure that we have enough resource people we try to find standbys among the discussants or to recruit knowledgeable local people who will be willing to be either discussants or resources.

Checking in the Registrants

Checking in registrants may seem a bit of minutia but it can become a headache. Most participants tend to arrive within the ten minutes before and the ten minutes after the announced starting time—and to be impatient if they can't be checked in promptly. Those who have not registered in advance or who are not assigned to discussion groups need special handling to prevent their delaying others. Then there are those not satisfied with their discussion groups. We may not have been able to talk with them in advance about not giving them their first choices, or they may simply have changed their minds. There are also the latecomers—we have had people appear as late as a half-hour before the close of an all-day meeting.

Our techniques for smoothing such problems are these:

1. We provide an unflappable chief registrar to whom all non-registered or difficult discussants can be referred, and a number of assistants if the conference is large. We find that when

we divide the list of participants alphabetically or in some other appropriate fashion, in the peak twenty-minute period an assistant who refers all non-routine people to the chief registrar can check off about thirty, fill out their name tags and see that they get copies of the agenda and other handouts. Incidentally, we never type name tags. Instead, as mentioned before, we print, or have each person print, the name he likes to be called, using a flip chart marker to make letters large enough to be read across a discussion room.

2. Signs, prominently displayed, show where people are to go. Each registrar has the five-by-eight registration cards, alphabetically arranged, for the advance registrants he or she is to check in. As each participant arrives the registrar pulls his card, with its note showing whether or not he has paid, and refers the unpaid arrivals to the chief registrar. We give each arriving discussant a revised agenda, a copy of the list showing discussion group assignments and, if the sponsor wishes, an alphabetic list of all pre-registered participants, with addresses and telephone numbers.

3. The chief registrar, to whom those not previously registered are referred, keeps a master list of discussion group assignments. She can thus tell which discussion groups are being over-subscribed as she assigns last-minute arrivals to their first or second choice of group. When a quiet moment comes, she refiles, alphabetically in separate pack, the five-by-eight cards for those who have arrived, including substitutes for the original registrants. This pack of cards for check-in registrants provides a quick reference of actual attendance and is the basis for a list of them when the sponsors wish it.

4. Before and after the peak check-in period, one of the assistants (or the one assistant, if the conference is small) can be available to help smooth the myriad minor crises created by poor planning or follow-through, people's forgetfulness or instability, transportation problems, latecomers and the like.

5. We notify the facilitators and resource people (including standbys) to bypass the main check-in point and come instead to another room. There we greet them and see that they get all the necessary materials and supplies which are not waiting for them in the discussion rooms. Also, we check them on our master lists. As the arrivals build up and they are getting acquainted with each other or renewing old ties, we find out

which ones have not checked in with us, have them sought
and arrange to replace those who actually have not appeared.

Setting Up the Discussion Rooms

Setting up the discussion rooms is another bit of minutia which
takes attention. We get our registrars, or similarly interested people, to do this job the evening before the conference (or, less comfortably, very early in the morning before it starts), and have the
registrars do a follow-up round between morning and afternoon discussions to replace used flip chart sheets and markers which have
disappeared.

The process itself is simple but we've learned that it takes more
time than we originally expected. We send people in pairs, each pair
to do several rooms. In each room they first select a place to hang
flip sheets—preferably a long, clear wall away from windows so as
few people as possible will have to face the light. They then arrange
chairs for the expected number of participants in a semicircle
facing the center of the wall, and there hang five or six flip sheets.
They put these one on top of another, using tabs of half-inch-wide
masking tape with the tabs of each sheet separated from those of
the others. This makes a pad, from which the facilitator can lift each
completed sheet, and rehang it where the discussants can still see it,
without disturbing the sheets below. We do this rather than hang
them separately because markers sometimes penetrate more than one
sheet and we prefer slightly tainted sheets to the cost of repainting
damaged walls. So, obviously, we don't write on last sheets.

Another precaution is to let the upper ends of the tabs curl away
from the wall instead of being pressed against it, to make their re-
moval easier and prevent the chance of their being pulled off in a
way which takes strips of paint with them. The last step is to leave
two markers, a few extra flip sheets and a half-dozen two- or two-
and-a-half-inch-long strips of masking tape in case the facilitator
needs them.

During the Conference

Our work during a conference is primarily behind the scenes. Out
front are the sponsors (whose conference it is), the speakers, the
registrars, the resource people and the facilitators. Our job is to back
them up, smooth the way for them, quickly find (or become) re-

placements for them when necessary and, in general, see that crises are met.

Opening Moments

We and the chief registrar arrive forty-five minutes to an hour before the announced starting time. Our first job is to see that the physical arrangements we requested have been or are being made— and to get them made if they are not. Are necessary signs posted both outside and inside? Is the coffee setup ready to go? Are the registration tables and the speakers' platform as we want them? Are microphones, and recording or projection equipment when it is being used, where we want them and ready to operate? Are the discussion rooms unlocked and ready? Are all the room temperatures o.k.? If any of these are amiss, with whom do we get in touch, and how?

Registration Time for Facilitators and Resource People

As the chief registrar and some sponsors greet the arriving participants, they send on to us any facilitators or resource people who mistakenly wait to check in with the discussants. In a room close to the reception tables we have hung a master list—flip sheets carrying columns of pertinent information about the discussion groups: their numbers, discussion subjects and rooms, and the names of the facilitators and resource people assigned to each. In front of the list we greet them and give them name tags, plus whatever handouts are necessary. After they have noted their assignments and teammates, when possible we introduce teammates who haven't met before and ask them to do a bit of joint planning. We try to have them do this in advance but there are always some who didn't get to the orientation session. Since our whole operation functions on a shoestring we cannot pay these people, and give them only their lunch, so we do not feel free to ask them for as much time as we would like.

Opening Session

Our opening session usually differs little from that of many conferences. All discussants, resource people and facilitators meet to hear a brief statement of welcome and a keynote talk (also, we always hope, brief), followed by whatever background talks the sponsors and we have agreed upon. We hear little of this. When the arrivals slacken, our first priority is to compare the actual arrivals with the discussion group plans and make necessary changes.

Some groups may be smaller than planned, others too large. If a

group has more than ten discussants we break it into two—
provided we can get a reasonable spread of viewpoints in each and
supply them with facilitators and resource persons. If we had planned
more than one group on a subject and one of them has fewer than
four discussants we do one of three things: add an appropriate discussant or two from other groups, combine it with another small
group or distribute its members among the other groups. In the latter
two situations we can use the resource person, and perhaps the
facilitator, of the vacated group as discussants in others. In making
changes, in afternoon groups we have learned to adjust for the 15
to 20 per cent of the discussants who usually disappear after lunch.
After planning these changes and the accompanying shifts in room
assignments we re-do the master list of discussion groups, which
we used earlier to orient the facilitators and resource people, and
hang the revised lists where everyone can study them during the
coffee break which follows the opening session. When necessary, we
also post a list of changed assignments of participants. Then, during
the coffee break, we stay near the lists to explain the reasons for
changes.

Morning Discussions

After the opening session, when the morning discussions start,
we normally wait at the reception tables for fifteen to twenty minutes. This gives the discussions time to get under way, for any new
crises to arise and for additional people to come in and be assigned
to groups. Then each of us takes a different list of discussion groups
and goes on a round of visits. We stay in each one long enough to
get some feel of how it is going, usually ten to fifteen minutes. But
if two people in a group are having a controversy or one person is
stating his thinking at length we stay until more general discussion is
resumed. We do not intervene unless asked or the facilitator sends us
a usually non-verbal appeal for help. We want to see how the group
and the facilitator handle any difficult situations so we can give the
latter suggestions, if advisable, before the afternoon sessions. Such
episodes are a normal part of most discussions and even skilled
facilitators cannot always prevent them or break them up easily. If
we have suggestions, we usually drop them lightly into a noon
conversation which begins with the facilitator telling us how he felt
about the morning session.

If, while we are observing, a discussant asks us a question of fact,
we answer it briefly and leave with a smile before a whole series

erupts. Any questions of opinion we turn back to the group—and leave. The content of the discussions is not our job. We have learned not to let ourselves get involved in a discussion and even not to stay long in one room. The usual result, if we do, is either to take over the facilitator role or be seen as a partisan, neither of which is good.

If the afternoon groups and subjects are to differ from those in the morning, at the end of the morning discussions the facilitators bring their flip sheets to us in our headquarters room, where we met them and the resource people earlier. We see that the materials are clearly designated by discussion group number, subject and page number—then turn them over to the persons who have agreed to take whatever further action the sponsors want during the conference or after it.

Reporting Discussions

The decision regarding the reporting of discussion content or recommendations is the sponsor's and it is guided by their purpose. If they simply want to stimulate interest in the subject by those present, there may be no need for any report or, at most, a verbal one to the participants. However, if the sponsors want to reach people not there, or use the conference as a basis for action, they may want a reproduced report for mailing, sometimes plus recognition in the public news media. Arrangements for either of these should have been made during the planning stage (Chapter 13). At the conference the only activities necessary should be taking proper care of news media representatives and seeing that the flip sheets, recorders' notes and other materials on which a reproduced report is to be based get into the hands of the person responsible for producing it. This usually means obtaining the recorders' notes when they finish with them and putting them with the related flip sheets, then turning these materials over to the designated person.

If the afternoon discussions are to be a continuation of the morning ones, no midday report is made. The facilitators leave the morning materials just as they are in the discussion rooms for reference during the afternoon. However, if in the afternoon different groups will discuss the same subjects as in the morning, the facilitators normally bring the materials to us so we can check the identification and give them to the reporters. We could, of course, have them left in the discussion rooms but we find that the afternoon groups have their own takeoff points and directions, so reference to what the morning groups did is more often distracting than useful.

Lunch

The luncheon break is our personal opportunity to get participants' comments on the morning session. We listen to little knots of people, sometimes ask questions of individuals whose opinions are deemed important and try to sit at lunch tables with people whose reactions to their discussions we think will be useful. Because their interest is in the content of their sessions while ours is primarily in the sessions' quality as discussions and in how well they were conducted, we have to listen carefully for clues. Infrequently, we ask questions to clarify what we think we have heard. However, since such questions tend to change the course of discussion, we only do this if the clarification is really important to us. On the other hand, if we find that we have picked a luncheon group whose conversation moves to something outside the conference, we take that as an indication that their morning sessions were not stimulating enough and feel free to try to find out why.

Afternoon Sessions

Since the end of lunch is the time when people disappear, we try to get reaction sheets from those we know are planning to leave. Also, at the beginning of the afternoon sessions we circulate very quickly to appraise the size of the groups and, wherever we know the people well enough to judge, their composition. If departed discussants have left a group too small for good discussion or left gaps in the spread of viewpoints, we ask those remaining whether they wish to continue as is, combine with another group on the same subject (if one or more exists and the combination will not be too large) or disperse to other subjects.

Usually they do not want to change but if their choices are to join other groups, we check with the members of those groups to be sure the change is agreeable. They rarely say no but are apt to resent the newcomers if not asked. If a group decides to disperse, we ask that each person explain the situation to the group he picks and request permission to join.

Either the second or third situation, of course, leaves the facilitators and resource people free to pick other subjects or leave the conference. If any do leave we make sure that before each goes he has talked with his group's recorder and turned over to him or us the flip sheets and recorder's notes from their morning session.

After the Afternoon Discussions

After the close of the afternoon discussions, the facilitators bring us their flip sheets and we organize them to turn over to the sponsors.

Usually the intensely interested discussants reassemble for a closing general session. Most often the purpose is to hear brief reports of the discussions, and perhaps to determine next steps. Alternatives are a stem-winding talk or submission of questions not yet answered to a panel of resource people. If there is such a session we join it as soon as the group reports and materials are all in and we have heard what the facilitators, and perhaps the resource people, want to tell us about their discussions.

If, as sometimes happens, there is no closing general session, the discussions end at various times. We, and some sponsors, wait for the facilitators to turn in their materials. When the number of groups still discussing is the same as those of us waiting, we disperse. Each of us sits in on the close of one discussion and collects the materials and comments when it ends.

When the last hot argument has been concluded and the materials turned in, we roll up the flip sheets, assemble reports and hand them over to the person chosen by the sponsors to be responsible for whatever is to be done with them. We keep the evaluation sheets temporarily to look over, and summarize, if we wish, then give them also to the responsible person. At one time we didn't always do this, but we found, as mentioned before, that if we didn't, either we never saw them or got them so much later that their value to us was largely dissipated.

Finally, we make a round of the discussion rooms to pick up markers, unused flip sheets and such rolls of tape as may have been left.

Keeping Going

Our role after a conference varies with what the sponsors want. Often they wish to put out a report after getting the participants' concurrence in its contents. This means the preparation and mailing of a preliminary draft (in which we may or may not be involved), with a follow-up conference to discuss and revise its contents. The participants who attend are usually only a fraction of those at the basic conference—people who want to be sure that a pet viewpoint is put in language they think sufficiently strong. If the draft goes out in advance, a half day usually gives enough time for this stage. If indications are that no more than fifteen or twenty will attend, we nor-

mally suggest just one general session, with the portions of the draft
reviewed in whatever order the sponsors think will be most effective.
A more sizable group calls for concurrent seventy-five- to ninety-
minute discussions, one for each portion of the draft, followed by
a general session in which the decisions of each group are reviewed in
turn.

Whichever way the follow-up is handled, the major danger is that
one or more persistent advocates of a special position may prevail
over the wishes of most of the original participants. To help prevent
this in small groups, we provide facilitators if requested. In the general discussion there are usually enough balancing voices to have a
generally accepted position adopted, but we furnish a facilitator for
that too if the sponsors wish.

If the Conference Is Just the Beginning

A completely different situation occurs when the purpose of the
conference is to initiate continuing exploratory or action groups. In
the Fairfax Goals Program, for example, the facilitators were committed to conducting the first post-conference meeting of their
groups. This was to assist the groups in organizing themselves for
the two-month study which the members had agreed to under-
take. Some groups asked the facilitator to continue in that role and
he or she agreed; in others the facilitators dropped out, became reporters or continued as group members, as did some of the resource
people. On three subjects which started with two groups each, the
groups elected to join their counterparts. Almost all groups drew in
people who had not been in the takeoff conference and represented
needed viewpoints. Each group proceeded in its own fashion, organizing and conducting its study in whatever way seemed best to its
members.

Almost always, continuity depends on the dedication of one or
a few members. Usually, one person who believes thoroughly in the
purpose of an activity, plus two or three who are interested and willing to do supporting jobs, can involve enough others to carry it along
through a succession of phases. Planning, contacting other people
and bringing them into the effort, getting announcements into local
papers and on radio stations, even getting support from businesses
for some purposes, can be done with very little money or none at
all. Usually a volunteer is even willing to do the time-consuming
job of drafting a conference report and some participating organization will reproduce it.

However, if the report is to become a springboard for action, a cheaply produced job will not do. Only the most zealous adherents will even bother to read it. A report that will catch the eye and interest of the people who have the power to carry out the desired action, or others who can persuade them to do it, cannot be routine. A capable writer must write it with those people in mind. A knowledgeable layout person must design a format which will attract them, get fitting cuts or photographs and see that the resulting product has the pulling power desired. Usually, these activities take money which the devoted cadre must obtain. Depending on the situation, it may come from interested friends or businesses, group enterprises as traditional as bake sales or, less often, grants of foundation or governmental funds.

The Fairfax County Goals Program is an example of involving key people very early in the process and getting organization help. The chairman of the county Board of Supervisors started by getting agreement from the Board that such a program was desirable. He appointed a committee of six leading citizens to begin it. After lengthy study they decided that substantial citizen involvement was necessary and asked us to help. Together, we decided to work through the county's active citizen organizations and businesses to develop a set of goals, supporting objectives and specific targets which the voters could be expected to support.

All this took individuals' time and effort but no cash. The use of county funds began with the mailing of an invitation to organization leaders to review and critique the proposed study plan, an evening meeting for which George Mason University furnished the facilities. The county mailed the opening conference invitations, and the registration fee paid for the lunches of the discussants and functionaries. George Mason University again furnished the facilities. County employees received overtime pay for organizing the replies to the invitations and making follow-up calls. We helped plan the various exploratory discussion groups. At the end of their two-month study period each group submitted its report in reproducible form at the expense of an organization for which one of the participants worked. The county reproduced the reports and mailed them to all participants. George Mason University furnished the facilities for a series of follow-up meetings at which participants gave their suggestions for improving the reports. (See Chapter 6.)

The Prince William County Job Fair is a simpler example of the involvement of key people. The initial request came from IBM,

248 HOW WE DO IT

the county's largest industrial employer. Planning group members were representatives of several employers, the state employment service, the executive directors of the two Chambers of Commerce, the school system's vocational education co-ordinator and three people in close touch with potential employees. The people needed for a successful job were all there.

When the economic recession made another successful job fair seem impossible, the planning group members felt a responsibility to find other ways to improve the employment situation and created a continuing organization, with the first result being steps taken toward establishing a long-needed office of the state employment service at the county seat.

The two successful job fairs in Loudoun County, on the other hand, lacking adequate support from the local business community, led to no lasting organization and no further developments.

Again on the positive side, our sessions with a Loudoun Association for Retarded Children came about because the association had been making no progress. Each member was highly involved, but his interest was too personal, too tied to his own situation. Our problem-solving approach enabled the group to focus on essential matters of common interest and through them to create a constructive program. The association carried out the program effectively and has continued to operate successfully ever since. The dedication had been there but not the knowledge of how to use it. Since we helped the members learn that, they have been able to proceed well.

Evaluation

Because we work with a tiny budget, expensive evaluations of our activities are beyond our means. Yet we are very aware of the importance of continuously assessing how well (or how poorly) we are doing. We use three rough gauges which give us valuable and inexpensive help in judging our effectiveness, and we recommend these gauges to others:

1. An evaluation sheet, such as Forms 4, 5 and 6 (see Appendix, Chapter 13), filled out by each participant at the end of a program.
2. Obvious results—in our case, for example, we look at such as these:
   a. The degree to which the Fairfax County Board of Supervisors included in its new ordinances and regulations on erosion and siltation the recommendations of our con-

ference, or the number of positions filled as a direct result of our job fairs.

b. The growth of one project out of another, such as the succession of job fairs followed by the creation of the Prince William Area Employment Advisory Committee, the annual conferences for legislators which grew out of our 1967 conference on the report of the Fairfax County Zoning Procedures Study Committee, the continuing relationship with the Northern Virginia Planning District Commission that developed from our first conference on Growth in the Northern Virginia area.

3. The quality of participation in the group's activities. In our Community Education Program, for example, we watch the intensity of discussion, the depth of its penetration and the degree of understanding which its results indicate the members have achieved.

16

HELP FOR CONTINUING GROUPS

Most of the experiences we report in this book have been with groups which have met only a few times, usually in one-, two- or three-day conferences. However, in addition to our earlier experience with continuing groups, we have also worked with them in the Loudoun and Fairfax goals studies, the planning groups for the conferences and job fairs, and the training groups in facilitating, reporting, supervising and job coaching.

In this experience we have found that a group which continues successfully has at least one highly dedicated member with enough energy to persuade others to maintain their efforts through periods of slack interest. In an established organization, as the interest of this person or small group begins to wane, many group members become frustrated unless new leaders take over. In a less formal group, if the same spark plug does a good job no other member may want the responsibility and he/she may continue for years.

In addition to this key figure we have found five techniques very useful in helping groups develop and continue strongly. These techniques, which we discuss below, are decision making, working with difficult discussants, role playing, appraising progress and evaluating group performance.

Making Group Decisions

In the type of discussion we use, decisions in continuing small groups are made by consensus instead of majority vote. A meeting does not end with a disgruntled minority resolved to oppose a decision it disliked or, at best, determined not to help in implementing it. One result is that all members are more apt to carry out effectively a decision in which they have concurred.

Reaching a consensus is feasible because the members of a small group can explore their differences, determine the common ground within the areas of disagreement and build on that ground. This process is more difficult in a sizable group and impossible in a very large one. It is not a compromise but an integration of constructive ideas which occurs as discussion reveals the limitations within which each participant is thinking. Other discussants can remove some of those barriers or open ways around them by concessions or perceptive thinking. Restrictions they cannot budge come to apply to the entire group. The members, as they discuss, develop plans based on the areas of agreement while respecting the points on which agreement is, at least for the time, impossible.

This process happens every time we help plan an activity. Each planner always starts with a wide range of ideas as to what kind of activity it should be; who should participate; how, where and when it should be conducted; and what preparatory steps are needed. Our insistence that they first agree on what specific results they, as a group, want to achieve upsets those apple carts. It works like a kaleidoscope, shaking their preconceived ideas into a variety of different patterns.

Most of the planners have come with general, rather unclear, thoughts of what they want to accomplish. When forced to think through those ideas from unanticipated viewpoints and match them with the goals of the other members, they leave their defenses behind and are on new, exciting ground. This opens the way to put fresh ideas together into creative, joint thinking. When, occasionally, one member does know clearly and specifically what he or she wants the activity to accomplish, that concept quickly goes on the flip chart. Then it is up to us, as facilitators, to see that the others do not swallow the concept whole but have enough time and opportunity to pull their thoughts together and use it as a jumping-off point or a springboard.

Once the group has agreed on specific goals, or a goal with specific components, those become major determining factors in all subsequent decisions. The goals, and the fact that we have agreed on them, tend to pull us together and establish a control over our thinking. The preconceived ideas come up in unexpected contexts. Seen in that new way, some are so inappropriate they are barely mentioned. Others are suggested, quickly tested and passed over. Still others are obviously appropriate and are just as quickly adopted. The remaining ones need and get thorough exploration.

That kind of discussion has become possible because the members have learned, in reaching agreement on the goals, that their thinking is not ignored, brushed off or knocked down, but heard and weighed fairly in a meaningful context. They have found that their confreres also have ideas worth listening to and thinking about; that instead of banging heads in an ego-displaying contest, they are all working together. And they have discovered that the group is producing something much sounder than even the brightest of them would have done alone.

Not that the path is smooth or the discussions all sweetness and light. This process is not easy. Valid but conflicting aspirations, feelings and opinions continue to exist. So do opposing facts and situations. Listening intently to find common ground to which everyone can adjust takes much patience, particularly at the beginning.

In a continuing group, substitute discussants can be especially difficult. They are a much worse strain on the regular members' patience than a new participant. The latter has been invited, and his or her arrival planned, because the group decided that it needed a new viewpoint. The previous members are set to go over old ground and look at it in a new fashion. But the substitute, alas, arrives as a surprise and must be read in, grudgingly, without the others knowing how much background he or she has. He has not been immersed in their techniques and spirit—and their prior agreements do not exist for him. Some of his views and positions may conflict with those of the regular member. Must the group re-examine and perhaps change decisions already made? That, of course, depends on whether he is temporary or permanent. But even if temporary he can't be ignored, so that session can easily turn out to be virtually useless. Try early in the game for an agreement not to permit temporary substitutes, but instead to go over next time with the permanent member any ground he may have missed.

In spite of difficulties such as these, continuing members often experience an unexpected and gratifying reward—one by one they become aware of a warm, satisfying realization that all the group members are creating something unusual and useful. But next meeting, that feeling has worn off and relapses occur. The day when everything clicks is rare.

Working with Difficult Discussants

The Strausses, in their *New Ways to Better Meetings,** give considerable space to dealing with discussants, describing a variety of "Nuisance Types" and "Destructive Types" in a chapter called "What's Wrong With Our Meetings?"

We have found relatively little difficulty in working with responsible citizen leaders. We think this is due partly to the fact that the people who have participated in our planning groups and meetings are, generally speaking, both busy enough to be conscious of wasted time and much interested in the problems they are discussing. This, combined with the spirit and conduct of our sessions, tends to restrict activities that are primarily negative. Even people who are dominators in other groups usually respond constructively to the challenge one of our conferences presents and the effort of the group to meet it. For those who do not, we list in Form 8 (see Appendix, Chapter 14) several suggested actions.

Accordingly, we do not think it necessary to say any more here than to suggest that in this kind of setting, if the other members listen to a difficult but interested citizen with respect and make real attempts to understand his position, the chances of his remaining a nuisance or becoming a destroyer are small.

Role Playing

What Role Playing Is and How It Is Used

Role playing is a specialized tool used primarily to help members of a group find clues to help solve the knotty difficulty at the heart of a problem which has them baffled. It usually stirs intense interest, is often highly amusing and can lead to dramatic breakthroughs. A normal secondary result is improvement in the members' understand-

* Strauss, Bert and Frances, *New Ways to Better Meetings* (New York: Viking Press, 1951 and 1964; London: Tavistock Publications, 1966), $3.95.

ing of good participation, making them better discussants, but that is
a by-product.

Role playing also differs from psycho-drama, encounter groups and
the like since its focus is not on a person but on a situation. Where
the purpose of those activities is to help an individual understand
himself or herself better and function more satisfactorily as a total
man or woman, role playing is aimed simply at the situation the group
is exploring. However, sometimes participants gain valuable information about how they function in certain circumstances and how they
might improve.

One of Bert Strauss's favorite episodes occurred several years
ago, when he was working as an advisor on public administration in
what was then a British African colony. He spent a week with a group
of seventeen black men and another with a dozen black women who
had been in training for some weeks to do community development
work in villages. The situation he remembers with special pleasure
occurred with the men. He started by explaining that he had been
asked to help them prepare for their new jobs but couldn't do so
until he knew what difficulties they expected to encounter and were
disturbed about. They told him they had learned that their first problem on going into a village would be to get the support of the dom-
inant citizens. But how would they do it?

"Who will they be?" he asked.

"The headman, the politician, the schoolmaster, a retired government messenger or an African shop owner if there is one of either,"
came the answers (most shop owners were Indian).

They agreed that the politician would be the hardest to reach and
were completely stumped as to how to go about it. Strauss, knowing
that they had a kind of role playing in their tradition and having
used it successfully with another group, suggested that they try it.
They concurred and one quickly volunteered to be the politician. A
second, obviously torn between desire for the limelight and fear of the
role, agreed after some urging by the group to play the community
developer who would try to get the politician's support. The group
set the scene in the politician's hut, where he would be drinking
beer in the late afternoon.

Both men warmed up to their roles rapidly. The politician wal-
lowed in the opportunity to trot out every put-down that had ever
been used on him and each of his sallies brought uproarious laughter.
The community developer got in some good cracks, too, and the
room resounded with shrieks and chortles but it soon became evident

that the politician was not about to give an inch. Two more pairs drew more laughs but no progress. The facilitator then split them into three subgroups and asked each to list the types of resistance the three politicians had shown. Fifteen minutes later the following list was on the flip chart:

1. He was against anything the existing British Government supported.
2. He thought the community developer a government spy.
3. He wanted to postpone action until his party came to power.
4. He feared the loss of his own prestige.
5. He did not want the other villagers to advance.
6. He thought the community developer was afraid to show which of the two African political parties he favored.
7. He claimed the people were too poor to help with a community development project.
8. He claimed to misunderstand, either saying community development was confined to certain areas, or that a project would take people to work in town, which he opposed.

The group members, having brought these specific types of resistance to light, could then tackle each of them individually, starting with "How can I show him I'm not a spy?" And they gained good insight as to how to handle them, using discussion and more role playing.

Another very effective use of role playing is to help people gain insight into the effects and causes of their own actions and those of others in specific situations. In the training course Strauss runs twice a year for first-line governmental supervisors, a frequent problem is the inability of some of them to direct their subordinates successfully. Others are unable to get along with their bosses, or with supervisors of other sections with whom they must work. Those who ask for help with these problems usually present them as arising from situations they cannot change or personality quirks of the other person involved. When a group has explored these aspects of the situation and not found helpful clues, role playing has been useful.

By that time, the members know quite well both the circumstances and the opposing person as the presenter sees them. Jointly, they plan a confrontation. Depending on the presenter's willingness, the role play may start with him playing either himself or his opponent, or with two other members playing those active roles while he observes. The facilitator stops it as soon as the proponent has obtained a concession, clearly is not likely to, or after about ten minutes if progress is inconclusive. After the play, the group evaluates what impact the proponent (or the person playing his role) had, how he succeeded if he did, or, if he did not, what opportunities he missed or bungled. That situation or another growing out of it may be played several times, with the presenter in each of the three roles at least once, each play producing a different course of interrelationships or possible actions.

The members not taking one of the active roles watch and listen for indications of answers to questions such as these:

1. What progress did the supervisor make? How?
2. What were the players' significant reactions to each other's remarks?
3. What were the supervisor's remarks that helped? That hindered?
4. What kinds of resistance did the other player show?
5. What important points did the supervisor pick up? Fail to pick up?
6. What other opportunities did he utilize? Or miss?
7. Were there any obvious angles overlooked?
8. Did any new problems arise out of that scene?

Each time the play is cut off, discussion begins with the facilitator asking the players to give their reactions to some of those questions; then the observers join them in a discussion which often leads to such other questions as "How did you feel when she said . . . ?" or "Did you notice the look he gave you when you . . . ?" This review normally helps the presenter's insight and lays the groundwork for the next replay, another scene or the conclusions and actions, if any, which the group recommends to him.

Sooner or later, and usually sooner, the presenter begins to see himself a little from the outside—what some of his weaknesses are, how he contributes to the problem, what changes in his attitude and approach might alleviate the situation. The other members draw their own lessons. They see that some of what has gone on applies to them or to their relationships with people they work with. That fresh view of their own situations can start a whole process of creative thinking to help them break the boundary which has been confining them and forcing them to repeat and repeat their mistakes and bad habits.

On a later problem, the facilitator gives every group member an active part in the experience by shifting to multiple role playing. As usual, this starts when a situation needs more insight than discussion reveals. After the exploratory stages, when the group has learned about the problem and needs to find a way through a situation to which it has no clues, he divides it into subgroups of three or four members. He has each subgroup play and evaluate the confrontation enough times so each member can take each of the three roles: proponent, opponent and observer. When they have finished, each subgroup thinks through what the members have learned, then reports whatever insights they gained and suggestions they have.

Other Examples of Situations in Which Role Playing Can Be Useful

In a planning group, role playing can help the members appraise how the proposals they have developed may be received. They determine what individuals have the power to make or break the carrying out of the proposals. Then they dramatize a situation in which these people first hear of them. For example, the role players could be citizens trying to assess the reactions of city council members to a plan the citizens want enacted. Or they could be council members in their august chamber trying to gauge the impact on citizen groups of an action the council is proposing to take. Role playing can be useful to ranking members of an organization staff who want action from their governing board, salesmen testing customer reaction or union leaders focusing on management thinking.

Whatever the situation, in a planning group enough members to represent the target people agree to take those roles, warm up by deciding under what circumstances they, as the target people, would learn of the proposed action. Then they move into discussion, giving the reactions they would expect those persons to have and discussing them from those viewpoints. They may even develop plans for counter-actions. Usually, the players, without knowing just when, identify themselves with their roles and begin to respond as they would if they were actually on the receiving end. The result is that they expand their own understanding as well as help the group clarify the problem. The members not playing roles are alert, as observers, to the resistances which come to light. The subsequent discussion revolves around those resistances, leading to re-planning to reduce them, and to defeat the counter-plan if one was developed.

Then the group, by testing revised or different plans in the same way, can gauge their relative effectiveness and take that into account in making its decision.

Used in this way, in many circumstances role playing can help participants get a better understanding of the possible thinking or reactions of people with whom the group members work and live or whom they plan to approach. It can also help greatly in preparing members to meet special situations, as we reported earlier on training mostly middle-aged, middle-class white people to be job coaches for newly hired black teen-agers (Chapter 3). A variation of that purpose is to help someone (or ones) improve a personal skill, such as conversing or negotiating.

In a completely different vein, groups sometimes use role playing simply to help an irritated member calm down or an adamant one begin to understand the others' viewpoint. Not surprisingly, members of the majority usually gain some useful insights in the process.

Why Role Playing Works

Role playing gets results for much the same reasons as our group-centered meetings: the members are free to respond to each other spontaneously and join in working toward goals they want to reach. They all participate, some in active roles with the others observing them closely for useful leads so, together, they can make an intensive analysis of whatever happened.

A cliché we all know holds that most of us have a bit of ham actor inside. Like many clichés it contains much truth. Putting on a show is fun, as every good storyteller is aware. Our adrenaline rises, our mind and eyes light up, the attention focused on us spurs us on and remarks begin to come of their own accord. It's fun, too, to think ourselves outside of our own skins and into someone else's. We may think, for example, "If I were the old battle-ax who always takes over the civic association meetings, what would I be shooting for in this dilemma?" "If I were a suspicious tight-mouth like that woman up the street, what would I think about these proposals?" "If I were like Bill E., who weighs everything with great care before he talks, what points would I pick out and try to fit together?"

Role playing creates opportunities for the players to do these things, to have these infrequent feelings. Once the ice of initial self-consciousness is broken most everyone wants to get into the act. As observers, our appraisal of the impact the players are having on each other leads us to thinking of ways to do it better, so, in the next play, some of us try our approaches. Most everyone makes a contribution. A failure is as good as a success because each can be analyzed fruitfully in the search for a better approach. Suddenly we realize that we are learning about ourselves as well as about others. Sometimes we find ourselves reacting in surprising ways. Another person's attitude or expression may put our backs up—or open a path in our thinking. Or we may recall a time when we reacted just as someone else is doing right now and realize its significance for the first time. In short, role playing can be an enjoyable, valuable personal experience as well as an aid to problem solving. In fact, it can be so enjoyable that a frequent, though minor difficulty is that often people don't want to stop. With the purpose of the role play accomplished, the facilitator may have to nudge, push or pull the group back to the problem itself. Even when the members have presumably refocused on the problem, a few casual remarks may show that some minds are still working on one aspect or another of the role play.

Conditions for Effective Role Playing

Role playing is most useful when a scene involves only two, three or perhaps four players. With a larger number, pot shots from several people tend to prevent the consistent line of discussion needed for a penetrating result. The small number is appropriate, anyway, since most human relations problems involve only a few individuals directly, and the fewer there are in the play the more easily the observers can recognize significant feelings and other pertinent factors.

The problem should be valid and actual. If synthetic or outdated it lacks the reality needed to give the play (and the players) a cutting edge. It also needs to be clear and specific. When related problems are tackled together the action is apt to shift from one to another without revealing much of significance about any of them.

Obviously, the better at least one of the participants knows the situation, the more valuable the result is likely to be. Our training of job coaches, for example (Chapter 3) would have been worth little without the know-how of our black ghetto graduates. In exploring a supervisor's problem, his view of the others involved is essential to the play—and often to the solution, since the cause of the problem may be his conception of them, of himself or of their relationship. Just as obviously, the higher the degree to which both players and observers can realize how the characters being played might feel, the better the level of their understanding.

Directing Role Playing

The first step in starting to role play is to define precisely both the situation and the goal(s) of the protagonist(s). The next is an adequate warm-up. When used as we have described it here, to penetrate a dilemma a group is already exploring, that exploration itself provides the groundwork for clarifying the situation and does the major part of getting the participants well involved. The next hurdle is casting. Some members will be reluctant to take roles at the beginning. We don't force them. We keep as observers anyone who feels inarticulate, is timid, afraid of being hurt or for any other reason seems to fear that something he wants concealed may be revealed. Some of them will unfreeze later and none will object to the anonymity of multiple role playing. If any member feels unpopular with the group, whether he actually is or not, we don't let him take an unpopular role. Other than that, we let people volunteer—even though it may take a few minutes for the first ones to do so.

Before the players begin they or the group decide where, when and under what circumstances the play is to occur. They also determine two or three key characteristics of the people they are to play. Perhaps one person is warm and well informed, but too casual. Another may be a tough driver or bargainer; a third, one who gets lost in details: whatever the group sees in the characters involved. Such bits are adequate because each play brings out more characteristics and each time the group evaluates, it checks them by asking a question such as, "Is that what he is like?"

Once the play has begun, the facilitator must make quick decisions. When should he intervene as an alter ego (speaking for one of the players to bring out a needed thought that is not being expressed)? When to end that scene? How to get the group to produce an insightful evaluation? What to do next? What seems the best way to penetrate what is still obscure or confused? The same scene, with the players exchanging roles? With different players? A different scene, perhaps with some change of characters suggested by the previous play? The final decision, of course, is to determine when this vein has been mined sufficiently. When have we learned enough to go back to our problem? (With multiple role playing, of course, this kind of close direction is impossible. Instead, the facilitator sets up a time schedule and depends on the various groups to produce useful leads.)

Although most of us have done some role playing in our past, from childhood play of house or cops and robbers through charades to adult parlor games, directing it successfully requires a sensitivity that most of us must learn. Even for those who have that sensitivity, acquiring the skill to make these decisions well and promptly requires practice.† One way to start is to take a very simple situation, such as asking the boss for a raise. In a completely private session, three or four people who know the boss can try to evaluate various ways of approaching him. Parents and a child can test approaches to a teacher with whom the latter is having difficulty. A family can try means they might use to reach a problem neighbor, relative or friend. As the participants work through their situation, play and evaluate it, change roles and re-evaluate, they begin to get the feel of what some of them can do with role playing and, after a few such experiences, be ready to try their skill in a less personal, more public situation with a larger group.

A Different Kind of Role Playing

People sometimes apply the term role playing to a partially prepared skit, usually used to demonstrate how a group-centered discussion works. Perhaps a continuing group such as we are writing about here reaches the point of setting up a large meeting with small subgroups and would like to have them discuss in a group-centered fashion.

The overall plan of the large meeting could include a demonstration with these three continuous steps:

1. When the total group is about to break for discussions, a brief preparatory talk by a member of the continuing group in which he or she distributes copies of our form "How Good a Discussant Are You?" (Chapter 14) and briefly invites the listeners' attention to the difference in attitude between the constructive actions (items 1–23) which make for successful discussion and the destructive ones (items 24–34) which prevent it. He then mentions the coming skit and tells the listeners what they are to do while watching it.

† Another way to start is by participating in several good training sessions. In the United States these, or information about where to find them, should be available from a nearby human relations, mental health or psycho-drama center; the psychology, education or business department of a university, the personnel department of a large corporation; or a Girl Scout Council or regional office. If not, an inquiry to University Associates, Post Office Box 615, Iowa City, Iowa 52240; the Institute for Social Research, University of Michigan, Ann Arbor, Michigan; or the NTL Institute for Applied Behavioral Science, 1815 N. Ft. Myer Drive, Arlington, Virginia 22209, should produce a good address not too far away.

2. Five or six members of the continuing group give a ten- to twelve-minute demonstration, with the audience members watching their performance for any of the negative items and some of the outstandingly constructive ones, say items 1 through 6 for the facilitator and those plus items 6, 7 and 8, 11 through 13 and 21 through 23 for the other discussants.

3. After the skit the subgroups assemble as directed, each with a member of the continuing group as its facilitator, and another as observer if possible.

4. Each subgroup begins with a discussion of what its members saw and heard in the demonstration, leading (hopefully) to agreement that they will do their best to discuss accordingly. Another useful agreement would be to evaluate their upcoming discussion at about the halfway point. In the absence of an observer, the facilitator would lead that evaluation.

In preparing the skit, the members of the continuing group first select a hot problem directly related to the purpose of the meeting. Next they decide what stage of our discussion pattern (see Form 1) they will use, i.e., will they be seeking agreement on the problem, on the goal or, having pre-listed the barriers they must break to reach the goal, will they propose recommendations and test them against the barriers? The decision as to which stage to use should depend on their appraisal of the one most useful to them with their audience.

The continuing group then decides the natures of the skit's characters and their attitudes. Finally, in preparation, the members determine who will play each character. Since the essence of a successful skit is spontaneity, the group does NOT write it and the participants do NOT rehearse it. Instead, they trust their discussion skills to create a live, impressive demonstration.

Just before beginning the skit, its facilitator lists the major steps in the Form 1 discussion pattern for the audience and tells them which step his group will discuss. Then, in opening the discussion, he summarizes the group's previous decisions. For example, he (she) might say, "Last time we met, we decided to use the discussion pattern I've just outlined so our job today is to agree on what our problem is" or "In our earlier meetings we agreed that the problem we wanted to tackle is ——, that our goal is ——, and we then listed the barriers [shown on a screen through a projector so the type is large enough for the audience to read] between us and our goal. Today our job is to agree on what we want to recommend."

The group then plays its skit and the other steps in the overall plan follow.

What Are We Accomplishing?

Every continuing group needs to look at itself from time to time to be sure that it is accomplishing what it wishes—and as well as it wishes. Businesses, executive branches of governments and other formal organizations go through the motions of doing this as a matter of routine in their annual budgetary planning. Small, informal groups are less apt to have an established procedure for it and, in its absence, tend to forget the need until a crisis forces it to their urgent attention.

Though our Community Education Program has been very small, the annual budget request has required us to evaluate annually. We have also looked at ourselves at intermediate times—usually when an activity has disappointed us or, conversely, when we have felt we had accomplished something valuable and needed to think through what it might lead to. On all those occasions we have asked ourselves fundamental questions which any group can profitably ask of itself:

1. Are we still aiming for the same goals, both long-range and interim?
2. Are we where we planned to be?
3. Where we are behind or on an undesirable course, why?
4. What mistakes can we learn to avoid? And how?
5. Where we are ahead, what can we learn and apply in other activities?
6. Do we need to improve the quality of anything we're doing? How can we?
7. Are there any activities we should stop? Any we should start?

One question we happily have not had to ask ourselves is "What can we do about difficult members?" Though we all have our peculiarities, we also have enough goodwill to live with them for the sake of our common goals. All groups are not that lucky.

How Well Are We Working Together?

Post-meeting evaluation is the key to improving the session-to-session performance of a small continuing group—but this type of appraisal is more intensive than that mentioned in our previous chapter and, at least at the beginning we do it without an observer.

For effective evaluation, a group should not be larger than twelve or thirteen persons, including the facilitator, and an observer when one is used. Planning groups such as those we use in developing our activities are a good example. So are study groups such as those in the Fairfax Goals Program, and governing and advisory groups of organizations. The evaluation techniques we discuss here can also apply to organization staffs when the boss is willing and able to waive his authority as a traditional chairman. They can be valuable, too, when large groups have been broken into subgroups. We have not used evaluations with groups which met only once or twice, or are primarily seeking information.

The first requisite for using this kind of evaluation successfully is the willingness of the members to participate freely and fully. This includes their taking whatever time the evaluation requires and learning to accept constructive comments without being defensive. Usually, a group doesn't reach this point until some of its influential members become unhappy enough with its progress to persuade the others that some kind of review is needed. They may get agreement for it in a meeting or in private conversations—or, if they sense enough general dissatisfaction to indicate little opposition they may simply start, assuming that all the members will welcome the idea.

With or without prior agreement, an easy way to begin is to ask each member to fill out an evaluation sheet at the end of a meeting. A simple, wide-open one like our Forms 4 or 5 (see Appendix, Chapter 13) does not indicate any biases the originators may have—and so is unlikely to antagonize other members. Anonymity is also desirable at this point to encourage the members to give their thoughts frankly. If the start is made without group agreement, the facilitator or chairman can explain that some members have expressed dissatisfaction and that he wants to find out how everyone feels. In any event, after the meeting he has all the sheets reproduced and distributed to all group members (with an explanatory statement to those who were absent). Before the next meeting he or another member makes a tabulation of the comments and puts it on a flip sheet.

At the next meeting, discussion of those comments is the first order of business—and may become the only one if the group gets into planning corrective measures. Usually the comments will not have named specific individuals, acts or remarks. If two or three of the leading members can see themselves as guilty of one or more destructive points mentioned, their quick admission of those deficiencies can set a constructive tone. "The point about some members taking too much time probably means my getting so interested in the idea of —— that I couldn't stop trying to get it across," or, "When I read the comments I was shocked to realize that the one about 'one member making a nuisance of himself by interrupting' meant me."

Such admissions make it difficult for other members to be defensive about comments they believe were aimed at them, and instead open the way for them to begin to see those remarks as opportunities for improvement. This may not be easy. When someone points out one of our negative habits to us, our first reaction is apt to be disbelief ("I'm not really like that" or "How could anyone think that of *me?*"). When others indicate the same thing we may give a grudging admission of its truth ("If they all feel that way there may be something to it").

If I'm apt to be impatient in discussions and interrupt frequently, having it called to my attention can sooner or later make me resolve to do better—but I'll probably have to be caught in the act and pinned down a few more times before I can train myself to ignore minor points I'd like to change, to hold myself to those I believe really important and give other members adequate chances to make them first.

The weakness may create an opportunity if I can admit that these are not unreasonable people trying to annoy me but associates who want me to be easier to work with—and that changing the habit, uncomfortable as changing may be, will be to my advantage. That realization is easier to reach when the climate for it is ripe and others are doing the same. Also, it is easier to develop a new habit to replace the old one in such an atmosphere. When a group achieves that spirit it will have conquered, at least for a while, the too frequent process of negative reactions and looking for devils—and can concentrate for a time on thinking constructively instead. We say, "for a time," because backsliding is inevitable. Every time a group meets, the conditions influencing the session differ from those of prior ones. The groups we are thinking about have their peaks and slumps, like athletic teams, though, unlike those teams, they seldom practice daily and rarely have a coach or manager to keep pushing them.

These groups must rely instead on the members' eagerness to do their job as quickly, easily and pleasantly as possible and, in the beginning, on practice at every opportunity. It is usually wise to continue using post-meeting evaluation sheets for several sessions, analyzing them at the beginning of the next meeting. However, on that happy day when an atmosphere of using the comments constructively becomes apparent, the members may want to shift to making verbal comments and analyses at the end of sessions instead of at the beginning of the subsequent ones. Being immediate and fresh, this prompt evaluation may have more weight than the postponed one, but if the elapsed time between meetings is long, members' agreements may lose valuable momentum. Other advantages of delayed evaluation are the opportunity to reflect on the comments and the use of that discussion as a warm-up at the subsequent session. A group can try both ways and take its pick, shift from one to the other—or skip evaluation for a few sessions if it seems to be getting unnecessary, routine or boring.

When a group resumes evaluating itself, or if it never stops, there are alternatives to the wide-open evaluation sheet. In one the members use a form like our Form 9, "Suggested Questions for Observers" (see Appendix, Chapter 14), as a guide to making more specific comments. This method, if used frequently, will probably lead to their changing the form's questions to fit their situation more usefully. Another alternative requires that one member serve as an observer, staying out of the discussion and using Form 9 or its modification to facilitate evaluation in much the same manner as discussed in Chapter 14.

Three still different methods requiring an observer use the form "How Good a Discussant Are You?" (See Chapter 14.) In the first of these, very useful for either a new group or one that has gone stale, the observer classifies each discussant's remark by item on the form and makes a mark in a right-hand column. At evaluation time, a quick total of the number of marks on each line gives a summary of the group's activities as the observer saw them. The chief value of this summary is that it brings out not only the frequency of negative activities but the inadequacy of constructive ones as well. For example, few marks on one or more of items 1, 6, 8 or 9 may give a clue as to why a discussion never really came to grips with the problem. Limited activity on 2, 12, 13 or 15 can highlight lack of progress because of members giving their own concerns a higher priority than needed teamwork, including poor listening to others' ideas.

Weakness in 7 or 20, on the other hand, may show insufficient imaginative thinking, again possibly due at times to poor listening. Items 3, 4 and 5 show attention, or lack of it, to orderly discussion. Numbers 21, 22 and 23 have a nature all their own. Too little of them can create a frigid climate in which nothing grows; too much, an atmosphere of pseudo-loving kindness that smothers all else. The other constructive points can also be performed to excess, of course, but in our experience they are less likely to be.

A variation of this method is to separate the marks for the facilitator's activities from those of the other members, thus highlighting facilitator-group interaction when the observer summarizes the various items. In a second variation the observer gives each member a column so both group and individual activity can be evaluated. Any of these three ways can, of course, be used in conjunction with one of the all-member evaluation techniques discussed previously.

Conclusion

In this chapter we have included only material from our recent experience which we feel adds to that on continuing groups in Bert and Frances Strauss's *New Ways to Better Meetings*. We suggest that anyone responsible for a continuing group who would like more information read these short chapters in that book:

1. "What It's All About"
** 2. "What's Wrong With Our Meetings"
** 3. "Once Over Lightly"
** 4. "Can the Chairman Stop Being Boss?"
** 6. "It's New to the Members, too"
** 7. "Know Where You're Going"
9. "Buzz Groups in Small Meetings"
11. "Role Playing"
**12. "Salvaging Problem Members"
14. "Don't Blame the Expert"
**15. "Stimulating Change"
18. "Misapplications and Misconceptions"

We also recommend that anyone wishing to try our techniques to improve the functioning of all or part of a continuing organization also go on to the following chapters of the 1964 or 1966 editions.

19. "New Developments in Management"
20. "Communication"
21. "Situations With Built-In Trouble"
22. "Selecting Personnel"
23. "Training Personnel"

** These chapters focus on improving the quality of discussion and related matters.

Epilogue

As John Gardner, the head of Common Cause, stated a few months ago, Americans value the dignity and worth of each person and freedom from all forms of subjugation and suppression. We have a special feeling about opportunity and the release of human potential. We want to live in a meaningful world, but there is a great gap between our ideals and reality. "The tough step is to make our values live in our institutions. . . . If we can perceive the challenge and forge instruments of social action that will enable individuals to regain a sense of their own role in tackling the great problems [we face], we just might succeed in striking a spark that would move a civilization."

We submit our discussion process as one of those instruments.

Part Four

APPENDIX

Chapter 1   THE ORGANIZATION EVERY COMMUNITY NEEDS

Committee of 55

"10 P.M. Thoughts"

Tonight's meeting (check one):
    I enjoyed it very much.
    I was mildly interested.
    Frankly, I was bored.

The chosen subject was (check one):
    Significant and well-handled.
    Handled well, but not of enough importance.
    Significant but poorly handled. (Please explain briefly.)
    Unimportant and poorly handled. (Please explain briefly.)

The moderator (check one):
    Handled the question and answer period very well.
    Let a few people dominate the questioning.
    Let the questions go on too long.
    Stopped the questions too soon.

The discussion period at the table (check one):
    Lasted about the right length of time.
    Lasted too long.
    Should have been longer.

Suggested subject (or subjects) for future meetings:

Suggested improvements for future meetings:

I am a member ( ) / guest ( ).

Chapter 2 APPROACHES TO PROBLEMS OF YOUTH

Bailey's Cross Roads Community Group, 1966

Flip Chart Records

What is it that we want leaders who live or work in the Bailey's Cross Roads area to accomplish?

1. Help the people define the problems in the community.
2. Help the people find practical solutions to the problems.
3. Earn the respect of the people for their leadership and help the people increase their respect for themselves.
4. Acquaint community with available agencies and facilities.
5. Work for unity within the community (church-school-recreation, etc.).
6. Develop self-confidence in the people of the community.
7. Improve communications within the community.
8. Work to improve community pride.
9. Develop an awareness of existing programs and activities in the community.
10. Encourage maximum participation in community activities.
11. Help the people identify community interest with their self-interest.
12. Provide informal groups or occasions in which adults can do things together and express common problems.
13. Be able to provide an atmosphere of trust in the group which will enable the members to participate fully in expressing themselves and working to solve group problems.
14. Discover the goals of the group.
15. Help in goal setting.
16. Help people make progress in changing community attitudes and behaviors.
17. Encourage group participation.
18. Uncover real leadership in group: help develop leadership quality in group members.
19. Expect slow growth.

Suggestions for Interviewers

1. Matters of attitude:
   a. Know his name and give yours.
   b. Be polite.
2. Technique for entrance: meet the prospect on common ground (of one or more of his interests).
3. Give information about the Association:
   a. Time and place of meeting.
   b. Accomplishments.
   c. Projects under way.
   d. Background of Association.
4. Arouse interest:*
   a. Get background of person.
   b. Find out what problems he is interested in and how Association can help.
   c. Discover usable talents.†
   d. Offer suggestions.
5. Ability to listen: be alert and capitalize on any opening or lead given (sign of interest or weakness) on part of prospect.
6. Timing: judge period when he is ready to listen about the Association.
7. Show prospect the advantages or benefits the Association might give him.
8. Show willingness to accept suggestions which might come from person being interviewed. Respect his ego.

* The program team suggests that no more than two or three sentences about the Association precede the interest arousers. Meeting the prospect on common ground is so important that it should come first and information about the Association be fed into the conversation piecemeal or, as suggested above, when the prospect is ready to listen.

† The interviewer at his best is not primarily a persuader of people to attend meetings. The best interviewer is a sort of talent scout looking for talents that can be put to work in the service of the community, persuading new people to join the team and doing what he can to see that the discovered talent is put to worthwhile work.

People should beware of overemphasizing the meeting aspect of the Civic Association, of judging the Association by the number who turn out to meetings. The Civic Association is most properly thought of as a group of people working together to identify and solve their common problems. The general meeting is but one aspect of what a good association does, not necessarily the most important aspect. How good an association is depends not so much on how many people turn out to meetings but rather on the extent to which it involves the people of the neighborhood in working together to discover their common concerns and solve their common problems. Of course, as people do become involved in working together on common concerns, meetings are likely to be well attended.

Vienna Teen Center, 1967

Guidelines for Chaperones

Follow the VTC motto—try a little understanding.

1. Try to take a personal interest in the members and find out who they are.
2. Know what the rules of the house are and how to help enforce them as well as making them apply to yourself.
3. Don't stand in the corner (and be an examiner). Try and be part of the action.
4. When approaching a member or members who are starting trouble, use the group to help. Trust the group: for example, "You're making it hard for us to operate as VTC."
5. It is best to talk to a member alone if he seems about to break the rules and be honest with him about your feelings. If he doesn't respond, try to work with his friends and get them to approach the member. Ask him to leave—if there is no success, call a staff member.
6. Come when scheduled.
7. Mingle with younger members as well as older ones.
8. Friday, Saturday and Sunday nights should have two chaperones—one at the door, one mingling. Be sure to wander outside to check for drinking.
9. Don't play favorites (letting someone get away with something and not others).
10. Don't be a soft touch. Don't pass out dimes and cigarettes.
11. Say what you mean and mean what you say.

VTC Rules

1. No drinking on the grounds or in the house.
2. All members must have a membership card and only members are allowed in.
3. Eligibility to remain on the premises lies only with suitable behavior.

News Release

WHAT IS A CHAPERONE?

A chaperone to most teenagers is a necessary evil that youngsters must learn to tolerate if they are to have any social functions that are "acceptable" to the adult world.

VTC teenagers see chaperones in a kinder light—even observe many of their own chaperones as "hip" or just plain "o.k."

A VTC chaperone (and there are never enough steady ones) is a person who is honestly and openmindedly willing to work with VTC youngsters.

VTC youngsters are an assortment of young people from every walk of life:

> The poor, the not so poor
> the black, the white
> the kid with a record, the most
> who don't have a record and never will

Yet all of them look to probe counseling as the core of their program. Here by means of psychodrama role playing they work out their problems with their peers, with the school teacher, the boss, the cop, the old man—it is always interesting to watch the reverse role effect of all this.

The VTC needs chaperones who have a desire to be more than chaperones—not a person who "POLICES" nor another who sits in a corner. A VTC chaperone takes his turn at probe or pool, or even on the dance floor. He or she is a person who "mixes" in, comes up with projects, or supports projects.

Chapter 3   A MEETING ON JOBS—
AND WHERE IT LED

Advance Information for April 6, 1968, Conference

Agenda:

9:30 A.M.—Registration, coffee.	
10:00 A.M.—Keynote.	Huston A. Martin, Coordinator Human Resources Development, VEC
10:15 A.M.—Study Guideline.	Bert Strauss Community Education Program
10:30 A.M.—Each group explores the situation it is to study, determines its goals and the barriers it sees to reaching them, outlines its tentative study schedule.	Study groups
12:00 noon—Each group summarizes its explorations.	Study groups
12:15 P.M.—Luncheon.	
1:15 P.M.—Each of four groups reports in sequence. All participants question, comment on and make suggestions regarding each group's report.	Bert Strauss and all participants
3:15 P.M.—Coffee.	
3:30 P.M.—Each remaining group reports.	Same as above
5:00 P.M.—Participants set date, time and place for each subgroup to meet again.	Same as above
5:15 P.M.—Adjourn.	

Outline for participants (enclosed with the agenda and invitation):

Information for Participants

Glancing Ahead—The Present Plan

Phase I—4/6/68 Afternoon
The assemblage will:
1. Review the goals of the various groups, and suggest modifications so the goals will fit together.
2. Set the target date or dates for submission of work group action plans—when the Steering Group will be organized and begin action.

Phase II—From 4/6/68 to the target date or dates, each work group will:
1. Conduct its explorations, on a schedule it develops itself.
2. Prepare its data, action plan, proposed assignments and follow-up plan, and submit them to the Steering Group.
3. Select a tentative member and a tentative alternate for membership on the Steering Group.

Phase III—The Steering Group, initial activities:
The Steering Group will:
1. Be sure that it represents the assemblage with reasonable accuracy, requesting work groups for changes in their Steering Group members, if necessary.
2. Organize itself.
3. Review the work groups' step by step action plans and:
   a. Appraise their suitability for reaching the goals.
   b. Arrange any necessary coordination among them.
   c. Develop a statement of the responsibilities it plans to assume in order to promote progress in carrying them out.
4. Present these to the members of this assemblage for review.

Phase IV—The Steering Group, subsequent activities
The Steering Group will be responsible for carrying out the approved plans. The Planning Group believes at this point that such activities will be primarily helping coordination among the organizations represented here and with other groups.

Materials Previously Developed

The Originating and Planning Groups have covered much ground in their explorations. The material given below seems worth reporting to work group members, either for reference or as jumping off points.

1. *Some reasons why young people do not come to the Virginia Employment Commission.*

    They:

    a. Don't know it exists.
    b. Don't know where it is.
    c. Find transportation difficult.
    d. Lack day care for children.
    e. Believe past employer requirements have been unreasonable.
    f. Have inadequate English.
    g. Have insufficient faith in the Virginia Employment Commission, the Community Action Program and all other agencies related to employment.
    h. Have inadequate job motivation:
        —No motivation.
        —Negative gang motivation.
        —Want to work only when they want to.
        —Are still in a formative stage.

2. *Whenever legal factors come into play, consider persons 16 or 17 separately from those 18 through 21.*

3. *Employers' (and everyone else's) difficulties.*

    a. Governmental restrictions:
        —Minimum wage regulations.
        —Minimum wage in some areas is above the national minimum in some training programs and/or the capacity of some persons.
        —Working hours.
        —Safety regulations.
        —Complications within government programs.
    b. Union restrictions:
        —Non-integration.
        —Inadequate apprenticeship programs.
        —Antagonism to government training programs.
        —Attitude toward hard-core unemployed.

4. *Virginia Employment Commission difficulties.*

    a. Inadequate statistical data.
    b. Individuals' lack of:

    —Faith in the VEC.

    —Self-image.

    —Motivation.

  c. Individuals' desire for instant gratification.

5. *What's wrong with employers, and in some instances with the VEC.*

  a. Lack of or inadequate job training.

  b. Unrealistic entrance requirements.

  c. Lack of our inadequate transportation.

  d. Inadequate feeling of personal interest.

  e. Lack of fringe benefits in low level jobs.

  f. Feeling of inadequate recognition of the employee's worth.

  g. Inadequate wages.

  h. Discrimination: race, nationality, age, distant past difficulties.

  i. Employer who does a good job doesn't get adequate publicity.

  j. Employer feeling that the hard-core are a government problem.

  k. Too many part-time employees.

  l. Employer won't take a person unless he thinks the person is able and ready to do an adequate job.

  m. Failure to understand why people stop coming to the VEC.

  n. VEC needs to sell—people don't trust them to help or upgrade.

6. *Placement Procedures at the Seven Corners Employment Office.*

  a. Applicant comes in and registers.

    1. Ideally, if he has been referred by a school or other agency, an agency representative accompanies him so they can all talk together.

    2. Less ideally, the agency representative talks with the interviewer by phone.

  b. The applicant and interviewer discuss the situation.

    1. The interviewer, hopefully, establishes rapport.

    2. Appraises the applicant in relation to the situation.

    3. If he sees any major barriers to the applicant's getting and holding a job, refers him to the employment counselor.

  c. Employment counseling process:

    1. Recognition of the problem. Employment counseling

problems fall into three categories: vocational choice, vocational change, or job adjustment.

2. Analysis of the individual through individual appraisal. (During the interview analyze interests, work experience, education and training, leisure time activities, potential abilities, physical capacities, family background and finances. Supplement as needed by: interest inventories, employer reports, school reports, reports from other agencies, aptitude tests, doctors' reports, proficiency reports.)

   a. Self-concept—how he sees himself.

   b. Personal factors:

      —Vocational interests (what he would like to do).

      —Acquired skills (what he can do).

      —Potential abilities (what he can learn to do).

      —Personal traits (affecting job adjustment).

      —Physical capacities (what he is able to do mentally and physically).

   c. Environmental factors (family, financial, socioeconomic).

3. Giving information to the individual.

   a. Occupational and labor market.

   b. Community resources.

   c. Educational and training.

4. Developing a plan and goal:

   a. Suited to the individual and acceptable to him.

   b. Practical and feasible, whether in terms of training, employment or other action to be taken.

5. Activating the plan by referring the individual to:

   a. Training, or . . .

   b. Job, or . . .

   c. Community resource supporting services such as health and welfare agencies or clinics, vocational rehabilitation agency, family services.

6. Follow-up with the appropriate employer training or support agency and the applicant. Begins as soon as possible and continues as long as necessary.

EXAMPLES FROM THE INTERIM REPORT MAILED TO PARTICIPANTS PRIOR TO JUNE 1968 MEETING

Group #1—Reaching Hard-Core People

Short-Range Goal Adopted 4/6/68

1. Improve our understanding of barriers between youngsters and jobs. By May 1, explore the barriers with select group of youngsters.
2. Get counselor where the kids are, e.g., teen centers, neighborhood streets, bowling alleys, pool halls, shopping centers.

Findings

1. A variety of causes lie behind the hard-core attitude of disdain for the world of jobs. Some are complex, some astoundingly simple. For example, some people:
   a. Have relatives or friends who have worked for years at dead-end jobs.
   b. Are afraid to try for a job because they lack information. They don't know what it would be like, or where to go or how to get there.
   c. Feel, rightly or wrongly, that they are not wanted on jobs.
   d. Don't want to lose face with their gang.
   e. Learn from their families, friends, schools, publications, TV, and radio that the kinds of jobs usually offered them are demeaning or, at best, unimportant.
   f. Have been badly hurt emotionally or socially at home, in school or in the community.
   g. See society as geared to keep them down because of race, national origin or historic background.
2. Everyone needs a close association with someone who has a real, evident and continuing interest in him. A person who listens—and hears what he says, speaks his language, senses his feelings. If a hard-core person is to learn to relate to the job world, he needs such a person who can be a link to it—and with his built-in distrust of society and all people except his immediate cohorts, the linking relationship is difficult to establish and maintain.
3. Two ways of filling this need have been used successfully in Northern Virginia:

a. Working through teen centers run, with the cooperation and advice of the teenagers, by adults who understand their attitudes and problems. Our example is the Vienna Teen Center, which has been run in a manner that makes clear to the teenagers who come there that its staff members are intensely interested in them, talk with them in their own terms, understand their values and are able to work with them. It provides a setting for them to entertain themselves, air their grievances, explore their feelings and learn with their associates to face the adult world.

b. Working on a one-to-one basis, or something very close to it. Dropouts tend to relate to other dropouts of similar age and situation, so the person to work with one of them is one who left school some months ago but has since seen the problems he created for himself, found a place in the job world and wants to help others. The Fairfax CAP has such young men at work. When we asked two of them how they make contact with recent dropouts, one said, "I go where they are: street corners, pool halls, anywhere. I get hold of three or four, join them and stay with them until I can turn them around." The other's reply was, "I listen until I can get a handle."

c. The hard-core people who have gotten satisfying jobs (or jobs with satisfying possibilities) through these means are still too few to have a major impact on others, but if enough channels can be opened, it could be that the grapevine would carry the story and people respond to it.

4. When a hard-core person responds he usually needs further help:

a. Restoring or rebuilding his self-image.
b. Identifying his needs, interests and capabilities.
c. Facing the reality of the kinds of jobs he is qualified to do.
d. Learning to apply for a job, and to do it when he gets one.

Group #3—Job Coaching

Short-Range Goal Adopted 4/6/68
By September 1968, set up (as a pilot project) intensive job counsel-

ing of the employee in cooperation with the employer for people aged 16–21 employed by three firms in the Northern Virginia area: 1) a large firm, 2) a medium-sized firm, 3) a small firm.

Basic Difficulties

1. Many hard-core people have no understanding of even such basics of satisfactory performance as coming to work every day; coming on time; working diligently at the job; having respect for the job, for supervisors, associates and, when pertinent, customers; appearing clean and neat.

2. An employer who does not understand that these basics have not been important in these people's lives and have no meaning for them is apt to be frustrated and disgusted when their performance doesn't measure up to his standards or their attitudes are out of touch with his. If this happens the likelihood of his rejecting the concept of bringing hard-core people into the job world is high.

Findings

The most important basic finding of this group is the same need reported by Group #1 on reaching hard-core people: for job-connected persons who have a real, continuing and evident interest in them. More specific findings on job coaching and hiring practices are given below.

The following points on job coaching were made on May 2 to the Job Coach Group by the personnel manager of a large Washington metropolitan area department store chain:

1. Hard-core kids can make it in spite of all the handicaps mentioned in the 3/26/68 memorandum of the National Association of Businessmen on "Hard Core Expectations." But they can make it only with the kind of cooperation from the employer itemized below. A prospective employer needs to understand and expect this and to take steps similar to those taken by the speaker's department store.

2. Management needs to:
   a. Give the hard-core employees a month's training before using them on the sales floor as compared to two days' training for the ordinary person. This training includes two hours a day at the Washington Concentrated Employment Program Center and the rest of the day in the store.
   b. Train the people who are to work with the hard-core em-

ployees, principally the interviewers, trainers and supervisors. The supervisory training includes both acquaintance with the difficulties to expect and the need to watch each individual's habits and to record his delinquencies so these can be discussed with him later.

c. Put the hard-core employees with good supervisors who will take a personal interest in them.

d. Make this personal interest paramount for all employees. The department store has its interviewers and trainers double as counselors to handle problems not anticipated in training. In addition in each department an old pro who knows the ropes serves as sponsor to help the hard-core employees over the rough spots.

e. Use outside counselors on occasion. They can help put problems in proper perspective.

f. Periodically review performance with the employee. The department store normally has a private performance review with a new employee in 90 days. With hard-core people it can come sooner and oftener, sometimes as often as every 30 days. At these reviews what the employee is doing right is discussed as well as what he is doing wrong.

g. Expect problems with girls who have children because of their difficulty in arranging for day care. This is the department store's #1 problem with hard-core girls.

3. Dealing with hard-core applicants.

a. The key to the success of the hard-core employee is his feeling that someone has a personal interest in him and is willing to give him some real help.

b. If hard-core applicants come in a gang, their applications should be taken and all turned down, but the next day those individuals should be called back who seemed worth interviewing.

c. Much can be learned about an applicant from the parts of his application blank he fills out and by talking this over with him and having him do it over again.

d. The interviewer should consider what he can do with the applicant in four or five years. He should show the applicant profiles of people who have been successful as examples of what the applicant can do if he wants to and tries.

e. The interviewer doesn't ask, "How long have you lived

at the present address?" nor about credit. He does ask
for the last three jobs and for an account of the time spent
since the applicant left school.

f. The interviewer emphasizes the need for an employee to
start in an entry job to prove himself and to learn funda-
mentals.

g. The interviewer asks, "Would you agree to cut your hair?
stop wearing dark glasses, etc?" If the answer is no, no
job.

h. In making assignments each employee is given working
hours which fit his situation.

i. After a group has been working for about a month, a
counselor gets them together to let them air their experiences and to get advice from them.

4. Different training approaches.

The department store has used two groups of hard-core people. The first group was trained according to the plan given
above. The second were people selected from a group which
had already had two weeks' training in the Washington Concentrated Employment Program. The first approach proved the
more effective largely because the employees identified with
the company during the training and were able to orient themselves on important matters such as transportation.

Job Counselors

After the discussion led by the department store personnel manager,
a teen center worker reported on interviews he had had with fifteen
young men who had jobs in gas stations and supermarkets. These
young men had had no difficulty in getting jobs but they did not get
enough initial guidance. In spite of that feeling, however, only three
of the fifteen said they would rely on counselors if counselors were
available. They visualized the counselor as just another boss. The
subsequent discussion touched on the belief of both employers and
employees that the right kind of counseling in high school and junior
high school would be extremely helpful.

Incidental information on hiring practices

1. Many employers ask, "Have you ever been arrested?" and turn
down anyone who answers "yes" without further consideration. There are those who estimate that 50 per cent of hard-
core kids have been arrested at one time or another. This, plus

employer use of lie detectors, rules out or scares off most hard-core applicants.

2. One food store chain makes it possible for people to apply in areas where they live. They have an interviewer at the Seven Corners Virginia Employment Commission office each Tuesday and Thursday and at the Alexandria office each Wednesday. Another hires only at its Prince George County headquarters.

3. Employers tend to avoid hiring people they see as potential problems, or as simply not promotable. It is necessary to show them that it is feasible to use these people, just as it is feasible to use the physically handicapped.

Current Situation

1. The budget and program requests mentioned under Group #1 as being prepared by the Arlington CAP and jointly by the Fairfax CAP and the Virginia Employment Commission contain provision for training in the basics of satisfactory job performance and for job coaches.

2. Group #3 is exploring the possibility of obtaining volunteers who could serve effectively as job coaches. The Director of the Arlington CAP, who has had prior experience in this connection, believes that such people can be trained to be effective, and has a three- or four-session training plan in mind.

Job Coaching and Job Counseling

Training Guidelines

Basic Functions of a Job Coach:

1. To provide an empathic one-to-one relationship with the employee and serve as an intermediary between him and his employer.

Training Job Coaches and Job Counselors

a. To help the employee:
    1. Learn necessary job habits.
    2. Establish good relationships with his employer and with other employees.
    3. Solve problems related to getting to and from work.

b. To help the employer:
1. Understand the difficulties the employee has in adjusting to his new work situation.
2. Cooperate in efforts to help the employee progress as rapidly as feasible.
3. If necessary, adjust some of his attitudes regarding the situation.

2. To refer to the appropriate job counselor situations which he cannot handle and problems of the employee outside the job situation.

Basic Functions of a Job Counselor:

The plan is to have thoroughly qualified job counselors available to support the job coaches and employees by providing information and consulting service on problems which employees have outside the job, but which affect their work. Each counselor will be a specialist in one of these problem areas: marital, budget, health, welfare, legal aid.

Job Coach Contacts:

With Employee

1. During the first weeks the coach calls the employee every day and once or twice a week sees him for a Coke or entertainment they both enjoy, perhaps going bowling or to the movies. These jaunts will necessarily have to be at times convenient for both of them outside working hours. The coach relaxes this intense communication gradually, as rapidly as the employee's progress permits.

With Employer

1. The week prior to employment, the coach talks with the employer (or his appropriate subordinates—probably a personnel officer and the employee's supervisor):
a. To learn about the job, salary, working conditions, and upward possibilities (hopefully two or three steps within a year in most jobs).
b. To pass on what the CAP knows about the employee's previous record.

2. As soon as feasible, the coach learns what the employee would really like to do and what preparation is necessary, particularly remedial education.

2. Late in the day that the employee goes on the job, or early the next day, the coach asks the employer such questions as: "How's he doing?" and "What would you like me to do?"

3. The coach continues to make contacts with the employee as the developing situation requires.

3. The coach calls the employer (or employee's supervisor) in about ten days, or sooner if clues he picks up indicate a need—but does not call so often that he becomes a pest.

With Counselors
As needed.

Job Coach
Work Load: The plan is to assign one job coach to only one employee, unless a coach finds that his time and interest lead to his wanting to work with more than one, either at one time or in sequence.

Training: Coverage:
1. Attitude and understanding necessary for successful coaching.
2. How to approach the employee:
    How to listen, how to communicate, how to be non-directive..
3. How to help the employee solve his own problems (not do it for him).
    Job problems, individual problems, environmental problems.
4. Resources available to help coach and employee.
5. Follow-up techniques.

Coach's time involved:
1. Before working with employee—
    a. Initial interview—one hour.
    b. Eight evening hours (two hours a week for four weeks) in a training group.
2. While working with employee—
    Two evening hours a week for four weeks, with the same training group so all members can learn from each other's experiences.

Chapter 5 HELPING CITIZENS COMMUNICATE

School Volunteer Aide Conference

Participating Organizations

Alexandria Education Association
Alexandria League of Women Voters
Alexandria Mental Health Association
Alexandria PTA Council
Arlington Education Association
Arlington League of Women Voters
Fairfax Area League of Women Voters
Fairfax Education Association
Fairfax County PTA Council
Falls Church Education Association
Falls Church League of Women Voters
George Mason College
Northern Virginia Mental Health Association
Service League of Northern Virginia

Supporting Organizations

Arlington County Civic Federation
Fairfax County Association for Children with Learning Disabilities
Fairfax County Federation of Citizens Associations
Northern Virginia Association for Children with Learning Disabilities
Northern Virginia District, Federation of Women's Clubs
Northern Virginia Retarded Childrens Association
Northern Virginia Society for Autistic Children

Chapter 6 TACKLING PROBLEMS OF COMMUNITY GROWTH

Content and Implementation of the Fairfax Zoning Procedures Study Committee Report

The two main Fairfax Zoning Procedures Study Committee thrusts were toward:

1. A new concept of planning which emphasizes staged development—characterized not by multi-colored maps, but by explicit statements of major development policies specifying: (a) Goals to be achieved; (b) Principles to be applied in establishing land-use designations; and (c) Relationships between land-use planning and other county decisions which significantly affect land use—i.e., not only decisions on land-use regulations, but, more importantly, those on capital improvements and real estate assessment.

2. A new concept of plan implementation—which departs sharply from the familiar reliance on land-use regulations and calls instead for an approach in which land and capital improvement budgeting, real estate assessment and zoning support each other instead of continuing to work at cross purposes.*

The report envisioned attacks along three different lines: (a) statutory change; (b) reorganization of county government to bring all county activities affecting land use into a single chain of command; (c) creation of new tools, based upon a sophisticated information system, for guiding the land-development process.

Initial efforts at implementation, like the report itself, emphasized lines (a) and (b). Within six weeks after the Community Education

---

* Land and capital improvement budgeting are terms used to describe a system which would allow the county to guide real estate development and lower the cost of such tax-provided facilities as water mains and sewers, roads, schools and playgrounds. Instead of having to put them wherever private developers chose to build housing and shopping centers, or businesses to put factories, the county would develop and publish a plan showing where it would put these new facilities each year for the next five years. Each subsequent year it would update the plan, so property owners and developers would always know five years ahead in which areas publicly supplied facilities would be available and could make their building plans accordingly.

Program conference, two major developments occurred: First, almost all the statutory changes the Zoning Procedures Study Committee recommended were before the Virginia General Assembly, endorsed by the entire Fairfax County delegation. That effort, however, led nowhere—because the bulk of Virginia's legislators, being rural and small-town oriented, did not (and still do not) see any need. Second, the county's newly elected Board of Supervisors took giant steps to revamp the structure and personnel of county government along the lines recommended by the Zoning Procedures Study Committee.

Before long, however, it became apparent that much more was required to achieve the desired re-orientation of local government activities. The best hope seemed to be in the third (c) line of attack suggested by the report. That called for a unified approach to guiding the land-development process—with the real estate assessment and land and capital improvements budgeting as components and a sophisticated information system as the backbone. This concept drew heavily on the findings of an earlier conference based on experience in nearby Arlington County, in which Community Education Program's Arlington representative and an American University real estate economics professor (a resource person at our Zoning Procedures Committee Report conference) had participated.

The foundation which funded the Arlington conference also financed a Fairfax County proposal to the federal Department of Housing and Urban Development (HUD) for funding to design and install an information system to meet requirements of the unified approach envisioned by the Fairfax Zoning Procedures Study Committee. HUD funding was secured, nearly half a million dollars. So successful was the experiment that when federal funds ran out Fairfax County assumed all the costs, and now plans to expand the operation appreciably during an eighteen-month period at a cost of one and a half million dollars, all from local funds.† Among the more significant lessons being learned is that the county can probably achieve the main objectives of the statutory changes recommended by the Zoning Procedures Study Committee (and rejected by the General Assembly) without such authority, via the emerging information-budgeting-real-estate-assessment system.

† The International City Managers Association was so impressed that it distributed to all its members a fourteen-page report on the initial experiment, and the ICMA director of research and development took leave to work with a Fairfax County task force in planning the expanded operation.

Introduction to Questionnaire Used by the Loudoun County Citizens' Advisory Commission on Community Goals

This Commission, with 46 members appointed by the Loudoun County Board of Supervisors, is charged with the responsibility for recommending to the Board and the people of Loudoun such improvements in public service, efficiency of operation, methods of financing, and forms of local government as it may find to better serve the wishes and the needs of the people of Loudoun County.

Commission members, who represent all magisterial districts and diverse fields of professional occupation and interest, have been divided into six topic committees (see below). These committees are working hard without pay to make in-depth studies of their topics and to weigh carefully the effects of any recommendations they may make. However, it was the intention of the County Board and it is the urgent wish of the Commission that recommendations reflect as accurately as possible the desires and needs of the whole county. If this is to be accomplished, YOUR voice must be heard on every topic under consideration.

For the sake of the future of your county, please take a few minutes to fill out this questionnaire and return it at your earliest convenience.

(*Optional*)   Mail to:

Name _____   Citizens' Advisory Commission
Address _____   P.O. Box 466
_____   Leesburg, Virginia 22075

[*The body of the questionnaire requested answers on points related to the assignments of the six topic committees: county objectives, the county governmental structure and working relationships, county financing, county development and planning, educational and cultural services, and other public services.*]

Health Section, Fairfax Goals Report

[Example of Goals Report format]

Goal 1.

Achieve an adequate level of physical and mental well-being for the residents of Fairfax County.

> *Objective A.*
>
> Encourage more efficient use of existing health care resources.
>
>> *Target 1.*
>>
>> As part of, or adjacent to, each County hospital facility, encourage the establishment of:
>>
>> a. Ambulatory care centers for all residents, to provide service at least eighteen hours a day, seven days a week.
>> b. Extended care facilities.
>> c. Office space for doctors.
>>
>> *Target 2.*
>>
>> Clarify the organizational structure of health services and the role of the various components, both public and private.
>>
>> a. Define where authority rests for planning, administration, and delivery of specific health services.
>> b. Improve coordination among state, regional and county agencies, and eliminate duplication.
>> c. Disseminate this information.
>>
>> *Target 3.*
>>
>> Establish an information/complaint/referral center in order to respond to citizen needs and to advise the public about the sources of both public and private health services.
>>
>> *Target 4.*
>>
>> Establish a clearinghouse for ideas and information among local volunteer and public-supported groups.
>>
>> *Target 5.*
>>
>> Assure that agencies receiving public support are responsive to public needs.
>>
>> *Target 6.*
>>
>> Require that approval of location and construction of private nursing homes, hospitals and clinics be based on need and functional design.
>
> *Objective B.*
>
> Extend availability of health care.

Target 1.

Establish a program, with the help of the medical community and State Department of Public Health, which will provide free, or partial fee, health care (including prescriptions and laboratory work) for citizens who are "medically indigent," and not on welfare/Medicaid but who do not have sufficient income to pay for necessary medical services.

Target 2.

Encourage greater use of existing County facilities in various neighborhoods by the Public Health Department for clinic services.

Objective C.

Improve quality of health care.

Target 1.

See enabling legislation which would permit the County to:

a. Set standards, license and regulate:
    1. Training and examination of paramedical personnel, including "paramedics."
    2. The operation of private nursing homes, hospitals and clinics.
    3. The practice of marriage counselors and drug counselors.
b. Permit treatment of minors without parental consent for cases of drug abuse and venereal disease.

Target 2.

Seek new and imaginative ways to confront:

a. The rising cost of medical care, including alternative methods for financing and delivering care.
b. The problem of post-institutional mental care.
c. Problems of drug abuse, alcoholism, acute psychoses, geriatrics, birth control and abortions.

Chapter 8   MAKING USE OF EDUCATIONAL TV
TO REACH MORE PEOPLE

List of Invitees to Health Care Conference

Providers of health care
Medical Societies (presidents and chairmen of legislative
committees)
Nurses Organizations
Practical Nurses Organizations
Visiting Nurses Association
Mental Health Directors and Service Boards
Public Health Departments
Health Maintenance Organizations
Hospital and Health Center Commission
Hospital Associations Boards and Administrators
Osteopathic Organizations
Rescue Squads
Blue Cross/Blue Shield
Red Cross
Medical Schools (including Washington and Maryland)
Institute for Health Care Research
Departments of Community Medicine
State Health Department
State Mental Health and Hygiene Department
State Health and Welfare Institutions
Department of Health, Education and Welfare

Officials
Members of:
The Congress
The General Assembly
Local Governing Boards and Councils
The Planning District Commission
The Comprehensive Health Planning Council
The George Mason University Board of Visitors and
Administration
Anti-Poverty Agencies
Executive Officers of Local Governments

Staff Members Active in the Health Field, from:
 Washington Metropolitan Council of Governments
 Planning District Commission
 George Mason University

Citizens Active in the Health Field, representing:
 Health and Welfare Councils
 Civic Federations
 Leagues of Women Voters
 Mental Health Associations
 Cancer Society Local Chapters
 TB Association
 Lions Clubs
 Health Committees of Business Organizations

Chapter 9   FOR BETTER LOCAL GOVERNMENT

Workshop in Applying Principles of Supervision

1. THE INFORMAL ORGANIZATION

Whenever more than two people are closely associated for some time they create special relationships among themselves. In families and schools, jobs and car pools, community activities and labor unions, clubs and athletic teams some members relate to each other more closely than to others. Football fans get together and look down their noses at those crazy soccer addicts. Rock aficionados can't stand lovers of classical music, and vice versa. The paths of gardeners and golfers seldom cross. Some people love any kind of animal, others only dogs or cats and still others only one breed. And so on for pages and pages. The one thing they have in common is that each type of fancier delights in getting together with others who speak the same language.

Hopefully, all of us find friends we like and associates we can count on, people with similar interests and attitudes. When we talk together we pass along the rumors of our community, be it neighborhood, office, sport, animal or what have you. These people make up our informal organizations, our grapevines, the channels through which information flows.

Every organization, informal or otherwise, has leaders who influence other members. They are the ones whose advice or help the others seek. They act on the information the informal organization produces and their opinions or decisions, flowing back through the grapevine, cause changes to happen or be defeated, as the leaders recommend. When knowledgeable outsiders want the assistance of a group to help make (or prevent) changes in a larger community to which the group belongs, they seek it through those leaders. So the informal organization is important in the functioning of our culture.

If you are curious about your own informal organization, sit down in a quiet spot with paper and pencil, ask yourself the questions below and list the answers:

a.   To whom do I go for information? Advice? Opinions? Help?
b.   With whom do I talk most about whatever it is I most like to talk about?

c. With whom do I most enjoy doing whatever it is I most enjoy doing?

d. Who give(s) me orders?

e. To whom do I give orders? Information? Advice? Opinions? Help?

Try it some day—you'll be surprised at how fast the list grows and how long it gets. Then, if you want to add a dimension, ask yourself, "Among these people, whose information do I value most? Whose advice? Whose help? Whose opinions? Whose conversation?"

If you repeat the process a year later you may be surprised at how much your list has changed, unless you have changed jobs, moved to another city or made some other major shift in your situation. In that case, the surprise may be at how many old associates you have retained. And, of course, you can do the same thing about anyone else, though not with the same efficiency, because you'll only be guessing about that other person's contacts—unless you can interest him in doing it for you.

2. WHAT MOTIVATES PEOPLE

(Developed by a recent training group)

1. Fear
2. Security
3. Challenge
4. Encouragement
5. Monetary gain
6. Recognition
7. Status
8. Growth
9. Respect
10. Curiosity
11. Freedom
12. Understanding
13. Desire to contribute
14. Desire for:
    —Personal satisfaction
    —Self-development
15. Love
16. Ambition
17. Pressures:
    —Family
    —Environmental
18. Feeling of belonging
19. Duty
20. Interest in job
21. Advice
22. Being needed
23. Others' approval
24. Pleasure principle
25. Tragedy
26. Survival
27. Involvement
28. Self-confidence
29. Supervisor's trust
30. Performance review
31. Excessive work load
32. Deadlines
33. Need to run the whole show

3. APPLICATION OF FACTORS WHICH MAKE A GROUP

What Can You Do:
1. To improve COMMUNICATION in your shop?
2. To help each of your subordinates find ways in which his (her) GOALS relate to those of the shop (division, whole organization)?
3. To help each of your subordinates agree on his RESPONSIBILITIES?
4. To keep in touch informally with the key people in the INFORMAL ORGANIZATION as an aid to getting and maintaining understanding between you and your people?
5. a. To keep in touch with what TRADITIONS, NORMS* and PRESSURES in your shop are making it more difficult for the shop to reach its goals?
   b. To bring them to light in a way which will help to change them?

What Else Can You Do:
1. To improve your LEADERSHIP of the shop?
2. To help develop LEADERSHIP in your subordinates?

4. SUGGESTIONS FOR SELF-IMPROVEMENT

• Think what's helped in the past.
• Pursue a specific interest, intensely if possible.
• Improve use of words.
• Put yourself in positions (situations) which stretch (challenge) you.
• Practice whatever you want to learn.
• Practice listening (really listening, concentrating on what is being said, trying to understand what is meant as well as what is being said).
• Practice keeping an open mind (so you can appraise situations objectively and separate what's important from what is not).
• If nothing else, do something different (practically anything).

* A psychological term for subconscious expectations.

5. SOME CRITERIA FOR NOTING IMPROVED PERSONAL ABILITY†

1. More significant *curiosity*.
2. New *knowledge*.
3. Improved capability in *ordering* and *arranging* data.
4. Improved *motivation* to comprehend and understand.
5. Improved ability to *think* deductively and creatively from data, to infer accurately, to make valid suggestions and select appropriate conclusions.
6. Better use of *reading* and *inquiry*.
7. Greater *initiative* and *responsibility* for independent study and work.
8. Greater interest in both *subject matter* and the process of understanding and absorbing it.
9. Better understanding of *principles* relevant to subjects explored.
10. More *sensitive awareness* to environment and to people's feelings, thoughts and reactions.
11. Improved ability to *express* with integrity your thoughts, feelings and ideas, with adequate use of words and arrangements of ideas, so as to catch and hold the interest of others, stimulate their comprehension and gain their clear understanding.
12. Improved use of *time*.
13. Better *effort* expended on self-improvement.
14. Greater *potential* for growth in using open-ended opportunities and developing maturity.

† Adapted from the criteria an outstanding lawyer, teacher and administrator, H. S. Hunn, Hi-Meadow, Plainfield, Vermont, uses in gauging the progress of students and encourages them to use for themselves.

Registration Form

Exploration of Problems to be Considered by the 1970 General Assembly

Name_____   Telephone_____

Preferences for afternoon discussions (please indicate *four,* in priority order).

Education
——* Schools, Distribution Formula for State Aid
——* Schools, Retirement Systems Retirement TIAA-CREF
——* Libraries, State Aid to
—— Development of Higher Education in Northern Virginia

Government Structure and Operations
——* Election Law Study Commission
——* Standards of Conduct for Public Officers and Employees
——* Legislative Processes
——* Zoning Procedures
—— Overlapping State and Local Responsibilities

Transportation
——* Dulles International Airport Commission
——* Metropolitan Transportation Commission
——* Urban Streets and Highways

Environmental Management
——* Disposal of Solid Wastes, Water and Sewage Plants
——* Potomac River Compact
—— Air Pollution
—— State, Regional and Local Parks

Social Problems
——* Social Work Services
——* Welfare and Institutions
——* Emotionally Disturbed Children
—— Housing

Please mail registration form not later than December 20th in the enclosed self-addressed envelope to: [Registrar's name, address and phone number].

* Indicates that discussion will relate to either a commission study or a study conducted by the Virginia Advisory Legislative Council.

Chapter 11 TRAINING FOR COMMUNITY ACTION AGENCIES

(Sample page from March, 1969 report on LKLP)

GROUP I
COUNTY: KNOTT

CENTER	COMPLETED	IN PROCESS	PLANNED	ASSISTANCE
Lower Mill Creek (6–67)	Bridges–3 vehicle, road repair–1 mile, rug hooking, quilting, day care (?)	Sewing project–children's clothes, bridges–2	Recreation area and equipment, pure water well	Road repairs
Beaver Creek (8–67)	Road repair, bridges, head walls, dry creek, windows in widow's home, privy for center	(Road repair, home repair, sewing club, handicraft, rug hooking, shooting match, Bible classes?) largely discussion	Boy Scouts, day care, little league, recreation area, home repair, bridges	Volunteer labor, financial assistance, materials
Jones Fork (4–66)	Garbage dump, garbage pick-up, repair center, bridges–2 to park	Park	Park-lake, community building	Financial, labor finish park and build lake
Hall (11–67)	Bridges–3, home repair–3, paint center and repair, road repairs	Sewing project–8 day care 18 children, 15 volunteers	Rug hooking, lamp-making	Jobs
Joshua (11–67)	Health clinic	Welfare assistance–2 families, wheelchair	Property for center funds for center bldg., day care	Roads, financial labor
Talcum (11–68)	Sewing project–1 per week (rugs, etc.) 35 rugs, 20 quilts, health clinic–1 per month	Sewing project, health clinic, building center	Finish center	Jobs, financial
Lotts Creek (10–67)	Rug hooking, quilts	Center improvement, rug hooking, quilting	Finish center	Financial help (?)
Sassafras (10–67)	Quilting, bake sale; paint house (invalid) by Nelson, fish fry, repair center, road repair, picnic shelter, Xmas program—distribute toys and candy, donation to Vicco rescue squad	Clean creek	Paint center bldg., make curtains, make rug, acquire own center	All we can get

Form 1

A Pattern for Problem Solving

1. Agree on the situation we want to change.
   a. Rapidly list the symptoms.
   b. *Agree on the essential problem.*
2. Agree on the long-range goal.
   a. *Agree on what we would like the situation to be.*
   b. Agree on a few evidences that will show when we have reached it.
3. *Make use of the barriers* we must reduce to reach our goal.
   a. Rapidly list the situations which make the goal difficult to reach.
   b. Separate the barriers we can reduce ourselves from those for which we need the help of others.
4. *Agree on recommendations.*
   a. List suggestions.
   b. Test them against the barriers or appropriate groups of barriers.
      1. Perhaps some barriers are people's attitudes, some may be parts of a system or an organization, some may arise from apathy, others may relate to forces actively opposed to what we want to accomplish, etc.
      2. See how we might fit together suggestions which would be useful against particular groups of barriers.
5. Agree on an action plan for reaching the long-range goal.
   a. If appropriate, take it by stages—each one with an intermediate goal.
   b. *Agree on the details of who does what, when, how and, if necessary, where.*
6. *Agree on an evaluation plan*—including:
   a. Points at which to check progress en route.
   b. Means to use at each point, and when the goal is reached.

Form 2

Guidelines for Resource People

In asking you to be the resource person for this group we have in mind using you and the discussion facilitator as a two-person team to help the other participants with specific problems and to facilitate their thinking as group members.

Basically, this means not giving lengthy talks or comments but limiting yourself to three types of activities:

1. Recognizing the facilitator as the discussion leader.
2. Answering, briefly, specific questions from the facilitator or other group members.
3. Intervening, sparingly and briefly, when you think you can give helpful information or suggestions.

Form 3

The Facilitator's Job

is to help you keep your discussion moving ahead in an orderly way by:

1. Following the discussion pattern.
2. Focusing on one point at a time.
3. Avoiding long statements, byways and repetition.
4. Encouraging the concise expression of all viewpoints.
5. Making a visible list of significant highlights regarding each point.

Please help her (or him) help you.

Form 4

Conference on School-Oriented Volunteers

George Mason University   *April 11, 1970*

CONFERENCE EVALUATION

Please give us your frank evaluation of the conference. Except as indicated below, give your name or remain anonymous, as you prefer. Please complete one or two of the following paragraphs:

1. This conference has been a waste of time because _____
2. This conference would have been better if _____
3. This conference has been valuable because _____
4. This conference will have been valuable if _____
    (*If your completion of this paragraph involves future action, please give your name and address.*)

_____

_____

_____

Please rate the conference on the scale below:

Excellent/   /   /   /   /   /Very poor

      5   4   3   2   1

Please check your classi-   ____Resource Person____Facilitator
fication(s):   ____Parent____Administrator
   Group Number____   ____Volunteer____Teacher
                              ____Interested Citizen
                              ____Other (please specify)

Form 5

George Mason University   *Northern Virginia*
Community Education Program   *Planning District Commission*
                                      Growth Conference 5/15/71

Evaluation of Conference

Please give us your evaluation of these sessions and your ideas for other conferences. Give your name or remain anonymous, as you prefer.

1. What do you think were the strong points of these sessions, if any?

2. What do you think were the weak points, if any?

3. What suggestions have you for other conferences?

(Please turn over if you need more space)

Please rate the sessions on the scale below:
Excellent/_____/_____/_____/_____/_____/Very Poor
        5   4   3   2   1
Your Morning Group_____Facilitator_____
Your Afternoon Group_____Facilitator_____

Form 6

Environment and Development Conference

George Mason University   Saturday, November 6, 1972

Conference Evaluation

Please give us your frank evaluation. Give your name or remain anonymous, as you prefer.

1. What did you hope to get from this conference?

2. Did you get what you hoped to? If not, what was lacking?

3. What do you see as the strong points of the conference?

4. What do you see as the weak points?

5. Were there items which should have been included but were not? If so, please list them.

6. Do you have any specific comments you would like to make for the benefit of the Planning District Commission or George Mason University?

7. Please indicate your overall opinion of the workshop by circling the appropriate number in the following scale—5 indicating high and 1, low:

    5   4   3   2   1

8. Other comments.

Form 7

Some Clues to Facilitating

1. Understand that the facilitator is a member of the group with
    a special responsibility to help the other members express and
    organize their thinking so the group can set and move toward
    its goals with a minimum of difficulty:
    a. Be one of the group, not its director.
    b. Use "we" rather than "you."
    c. Create an atmosphere in which everyone feels free to
        participate.
    d. Help the group bring out and organize its thinking as
        members build on each other's contributions.
    e. Help the group determine clear goals and progress toward
        them.
2. Have a clear idea of what ground should be covered in this
    meeting (but not what decisions should be reached).
3. *Bury your predetermined ideas and listen intently* for the es-
    sential point of what the speaker is saying (or trying to say).
    Don't let any of your own concerns or memories interfere. Lis-
    tening stops the instant you begin to think of one of them.
    When you write on the flip chart:
    a. Preferably, catch the essence of a thought in a three- to six-
        word phrase.
    b. If a speaker's point seems worth putting on the chart,
        when you think you understand it, ask him: "Do you
        mean . . . ?" "Let me see if I understand. Is your
        point . . . ?" "I think I'm with you but I'm not sure. Are
        you telling us . . . ?"
    c. If a speaker is brief but you feel sure that his point does not
        contribute, thank him and let it drop unless another mem-
        ber picks it up.
    d. If you're not sure of the value of a speaker's point, or you
        begin to wonder if he has a point to make, toss it to the

group: "What does someone else think of what Joe's telling us?"

e. If a contribution seems useful but you think it might be improved, ask the group, "Would what Joe's saying help us more if we put it differently?" Or write it first and then ask for improvements.

f. When discussion gets so rapid you can't keep up, you can:
   1. Intervene and have the group help you catch up (at the risk of slowing down that intense period or perhaps wrecking it).
   2. Gamble that you can successfully pick out the highlights (but when you start writing you stop listening).
   3. Put down fragments as clues and when the tempo slackens ask the group to go back and help you fill in whatever part is worth putting in the record.

g. When discussion (whether fast or slow) gets so intense that no one looks at the chart and you don't want to spoil it by breaking in, keep on writing. When the discussion reaches a point when you can intervene without harm, ask the group to review what you've written and correct or complete it.

4. *Try to intervene only when it's essential.* As you listen, moments will come when it seems useful for you to:

   a. *Question what a statement means*—when it is obscure, confused, overstated or understated. ("Do you mean . . . ?" "Are you saying . . . ?")

   b. *Ask about a viewpoint that seems overlooked*—either it has been mentioned but not picked up by the group, or hasn't been mentioned at all—it may be your viewpoint. If so, don't press it; give others a chance to pick it up. ("What do you think of this . . . ?" "No one has mentioned . . . —Should we think about it?")

   c. *Question the course of the discussion*—when it seems:
      1. Off-track, chaotic or repetitious.
      2. Blocked or on dead center.
      3. Acrimonious or dominated by one or two persons.
      4. Dominated by someone's personal needs (points 24–32 on the form, "How Good a Discussant Are You?" in Chapter 14), or by superfluous performance of points 22–23 (less rare than you may think).

5. When a point seems being overdiscussed, or is becoming a bore in some other way.

6. Strongly diverging from the ground the group has decided to cover in this meeting. ("Is this taking us where we want to go?" "Should we go back to Bill's suggestion that . . . ?" "We decided earlier that we wanted to . . . Have we changed our minds?")

d. *Ask questions which will:*

1. *Facilitate the members' progress* toward covering either:

   a. The ground determined in advance for this meeting, or

   b. The ground the members obviously prefer to cover instead. ("How will this help us work toward . . . ?")

2. *Help the group give shape and a cutting edge to the ideas it is developing.* ("How can we make this more specific?—or more tangible?" "What's our main point here? How can we state it concisely?" "Does that mean . . . ?" or "How could we do that?")

3. *Help improve member interaction.* ("What do some of the rest of us think about this?")

e. *Summarize*—when a recognizable degree of agreement seems to exist, even among a minority of members—or as an alternative to questioning the course of the discussion. ("Is this what we've been saying . . . ?" Write it on the flip chart if it's not too long.)

f. *Test for consensus*—as an alternative to summarizing when a degree of agreement seems to exist, even among a minority of members—or when the response to a summary indicates that consensus seems possible. ("Can we agree on something like this . . . ?" "I'm hearing . . . Is this right?" Again write it on the flip chart if it's not too long.)

5. Make questions as short as feasible. Try to include only essential points so the other members can easily get the whole picture of what you're asking—not get lost in details.

6. *Normally,* stick to the practice of *addressing questions to the whole group.* On the other hand, if the discussion seems emotionally out of control, grin (it can help you stay objective) and direct a question to an individual.

7. Other times to direct a question to an individual include:

a. Following up a previous remark of his which needs clarifying or seems valuable and is being lost.

b. When a quiet member seems eager to talk.

c. When a member is likely to have pertinent information on the point being discussed.

8. *Be concerned about what is coming from the group,* not what the members think of you.

9. *Don't hesitate to level with the members.* When you can't decide what is worth putting on the flip chart, or in what direction to lead, ask them. Normally that will bring on a useful review of where the discussion is heading.

10. When a near consensus seems to exist but there are a few strong objectors, ask (even push a bit if necessary) the majority to *explore those objections open-mindedly.* If they will, it is possible to get consensus (and, if so, much stronger follow-through) on a somewhat modified, and often better, plan.

Form 8

Some Suggestions for Cutting in on a Long-Winded Speaker

1. Summarize his point and:
   a. Ask the group for corrections, or
   b. Ask the group if that is the direction the members want the discussion to go.

2. As he starts on a repetition ask the group, coolly, such questions as:
   a. Did we go over this before?
   b. Do we need to repeat this?
   c. Is it time to give someone else a chance?
   d. Is this taking us where we want to go?
   e. Should we see what thoughts other members have on this?

Form 9

Suggested Questions for Observers

To be addressed to everyone unless otherwise noted. Follow-up questions in parentheses to be used if needed.

1. Were any of you aware of any weaknesses in this discussion? (What were they?)

2. Did anyone have a contribution to make but didn't make it? (Why not?)

3. Were you aware of any member who wanted to contribute but didn't?

4. What might another member (including the facilitator) have done to help the person indicated by either 2 or 3? (Why?)

5. Did the facilitator intervene too much? Or did he miss opportunities to do any of the following? (If so, at what points?)

    a. Question what a statement meant.

    b. Ask about an overlooked viewpoint.

    c. Question the course of the discussion.

    d. Summarize.

    e. Test for consensus.

    f. Ask a pertinent question.

6. Which of those activities did other members perform? (If not, why not?)

7. Which of you were aware at any time of thinking how to answer another member instead of listening to what was being said?

8. Which of you were aware at any time of wondering how you could help another member or the facilitator? (Which of you did it?) ([To the helped member] How did you feel about it?) (Why?)

9. Could any of our discussion tools have been used more effectively to sharpen our discussion?

Form 10

Hints for Reporters

Reporting a discussion adequately and succinctly means being able to pick out and organize the highlights and their supporting points into a coherent whole—a difficult job. These hints may help.

1. Listen steadily and carefully—so you can separate a speaker's points from his amplifying flow of words.*
   a. You can do this because the mind is faster than the mouth, giving you time to appraise what is being said and to select what seems important enough to record.
   b. Be objective—note what is important, not just what you want to hear or agree with.
2. Don't distract yourself by letting your mind wander. Don't let any of your own concerns or memories interfere. Listening stops the instant you begin to think of one of them.
3. Give yourself an adequate work sheet. (See next page.) This will help you identify the discussants and organize your notes.
4. However much the temptation, don't join the discussion. If you do, your value as a reporter will be lost completely until you extract yourself and can again listen objectively—and you may never make it. If you think you've missed a really essential point and the facilitator hasn't recorded it either, ask about it and return quickly to listening—but try to avoid asking; be sure it's that important.
5. In the absence of more specific guidance, review, highlight and organize your notes as soon as possible. Then put them on paper in a simple, easily understandable form and turn them in to the person designated by the conference director.

* One authority points out that amplifying remarks may contain definition, proof, comparison or contrast, cause and effect or an incident that gives conviction to the main point. Don't try to get this detailed.

George Mason University   Community Education Program

REPORTER'S NOTE SHEET

1

12   Give   2
     each
11 member a 3
     number
          —
10   —   4
     Cross out
9   numbers   5
     not
8   used   6

7

Member Identification

1	7
2	8
3	9
4	10
5	11
6	12

Member's name or number	His Points Worth Noting	*RA	Member's key words, arresting phrases, vivid gestures, etc.

*For Reporter's analysis of his notes, such as H1 (Highlight 1), S1 (Supports H1)

Form 11

Suggestions for Discussants

1. *Speak your mind freely.*
   The workshop is yours—a chance for you to say what you think. Say it. Your ideas are wanted—and they count.
2. *Listen thoughtfully to others.*
   Try hard to understand the other person's point of view—see what experience and thinking it rests on. Search for thoughts and attitudes which might mesh with yours.
3. *Keep the discussion pertinent and penetrating.*
   Remind yourself frequently of the problem and the goal. Dig for things that *matter*. Raise questions that analyze or test suggestions.
4. *Don't monopolize the discussion.*
   Don't speak for more than a minute or so at a time. Give others a chance. Make your point in a few words, then pass on the ball.
5. *Don't let the discussion get away from you.*
   If you don't understand what's being discussed, say so. Ask for examples, data, illustrations until you *do* understand. Try to tie what is being said to your own experience and understanding. Don't hesitate to ask questions.
6. *Disagree in a friendly way.*
   When you find yourself on the other side of the fence, say so and tell why—but in a friendly way. Whatever the goal, good-humored discussion helps the group get there.
7. *Strike while the idea is hot.*
   Don't wait for the facilitator to recognize you before speaking unless someone else wants to speak too. Then it's his job to grant the floor to one and see that the other gets a chance soon. The good discussion—

Goes this way: Not this way:

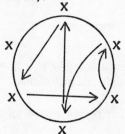   

8. *Build on what others say:*

   You can contribute to progress and also build good group feeling by saying, when you really mean it, "That's a good point, how can we fit it in?" or, "Could we fit Bill's and Mary's suggestions together [or into the picture] this way? . . ."

9. *Draw others into the discussion.*

   You can relieve your tension about a quiet member when you can honestly say:

   a. "Bill, you know a lot about this, can you help us?"

   b. "Mary, you and I were talking about this the other night. Do you have any thoughts that might help?"

   c. "Ed, you've been listening carefully for quite a while, what clues have you picked up?"

   d. (If it's true) "Jim, you look as though you want to say something."

10. *Don't let one or two people monopolize the discussion.*

    What can you do? One of several things:

    a. Summarize: "Is this what you were saying?"

    b. Open the way for others: "What do the rest of us think about this?"

    c. Ask about an overlooked angle: "What does anyone think about this aspect?"

    d. Question the meaning of a remark: "What does that statement mean to the rest of us?"

    e. Question the course of the discussion: "How is this helping us dig into our problem [or set our goal, or work out a way to reach our goal]?"

    f. Build on what's being said: "Could we tie Hazel's thought to Harry's suggestion a while back that we . . . ?"

Chapter 15 MAKING THE PLAN WORK

George Mason College
Community Education Project

Lecture Hall
George Mason College
May 15, 1971

Conference on "Growth and Its Implications"

To: Discussion Leaders & Facilitators (whichever you consider yourself)
From: Bert Strauss
Subject: Preparing for May 15, 1971

Before getting down to specifics, I'd like to thank all of you for your willingness to help with this conference. I think you'll find the job rewarding but still recognize that it will take time you could be spending in other ways.

As I promised you when we talked on the phone about May 15, here are some guidelines for conducting those discussions:

a. In both morning and afternoon sessions I suggest that you start with a quick round of introductions, perhaps having the members give their names and organizations in the morning, and names, jurisdictions and organizations in the afternoon. Then obtain a volunteer reporter who will note highlights of the discussion to supplement what you put on your flip chart sheets. These records will help in planning the later conferences and will be essential if either the college or the Planning District Commission decides to publish a report.

b. In the morning, after getting introductions and a reporter, please:

1. Quickly get from your group, and list, the forces generating growth in your jurisdiction. Make this a kind of brainstorming, taking only about ten minutes. Postpone, at this stage, all attempts to analyze the forces, group them in categories, counter them, tell personal anecdotes about them or anything except identifying and listing them.

2. Have the members determine which forces they believe are most important in the jurisdiction and then whether the group would like to examine them individually, in combinations of two or three, altogether or in some other

manner. Try to keep this to about twenty minutes, avoiding legalistic or lengthy discussions. The important thing is not the order of discussion but getting an orderly analysis started as quickly as possible rather than getting caught in some member's pet gripe or hobby.

3. Spend the rest of the discussion time having the group assess the effects the various forces are likely to have on the jurisdiction in five, ten, twenty years. Do this either roughly in the order of the group's thinking about the importance of the forces or start with an important one and if discussion of it leads into another important one, follow that path.

4. At the end of the session please pick up your reporter's notes, put your group's jurisdiction and your name on them and on your flip chart sheets and take both to Lecture Hall 2, where someone will be collecting them.

c. In the afternoon discussions, please:

1. After introductions and getting a reporter, again start with a ten-minute listing, this time of the types of decisions and activities within your subject area which can be used to influence growth. As in the morning, postpone attempts to do anything but list at this stage.

2. Have the members determine which decisions and activities they think are most important in Northern Virginia and then decide, as in the morning, whether the group would like to examine them individually, etc. Also as in the morning, try to keep the focus on getting an orderly analysis started in about twenty minutes.

3. Spend the rest of the discussion time having the group:

   a. Assess the potentialities and limitations of the various decisions and activities for influencing population growth and growth patterns.

   b. Explore what obstacles are in the way of using them, both under existing laws and under laws changed to meet the needs the group sees.

   c. Suggest what information and general procedures are needed to make these types of actions effective in influencing growth.

4. At 3:25 P.M., please have your participants and your resource person fill out evaluation sheets, and fill out one yourself.

5.   Finally, please collect the evaluation sheets and reporter's
     notes, add them to your flip chart sheets, identify all of
     them by group number and subject, and take them all to
     Lecture Hall 2.

That ends the day as far as I can see now. I hope you enjoy it and
find that it helps make you authorities on both land use and the running of meetings if you haven't reached those peaks already.

May 4, 1971

EVALUATION OF *HOW TO GET THINGS CHANGED*

We want to apply one of our evaluation techniques to this book. Please fill out this sheet, tear it out, fold, fasten and mail it.

1. Please check one item on each line. *HOW TO GET THINGS CHANGED* is ____Great ____Useful ____ Not Useful Enough _____ Fascinating ____Interesting ____Dull

2. As a result of reading it I plan to (am) _____

   _____

   _____

   _____

   _____

   _____

   _____

3. The next edition will be better if:

   _____

   _____

   _____

   Place Stamp Here

4. Your state: _____
   Kind of work, voluntary or paid, you do in your community or local government _____

   _____

   _____

Doubleday & Company, Inc.
245 Park Avenue
New York, N.Y. 10017

I suggest that you send a flyer describing *HOW TO GET THINGS CHANGED* to:

_____

_____

_____

_____

_____

_____

_____

_____

_____

BERT STRAUSS has been a management consultant to business, government, and civic groups.

MARY E. STOWE is a civic leader in the Northeastern Virginia area, a former reporter for the Kansas City *Star,* and a contributor to many newspapers and magazines.